RENDERING IN PENCIL

RENDERING IN PENCIL

BY ARTHUR L. GUPTILL
Edited by Susan E. Meyer

WATSON-GUPTILL PUBLICATIONS/NEW YORK

First published 1977 in the United States
by Watson-Guptill Publications,
a division of Billboard Publications, Inc.
1515 Broadway, New York, N.Y. 10036

Library of Congress Cataloging in Publication Data
Guptill, Arthur Leighton, 1891–1956.
Rendering in pencil.
Rev. ed. of the author's Sketching and rendering in
pencil and Pencil drawing step-by-step.
  Includes index.
  1. Pencil drawing. 2. Architectural rendering.
I. Meyer, Susan E. II. Title.
NC890.G8 1977   741.2'4   76-50547
ISBN 0-8230-4531-5

Manufactured in U.S.A.

6 7 8 9/90 89

Contents

Editor's Note

While most artist-teachers have influenced their students through the classroom, Arthur Guptill's greatest contribution as a teacher was through the printed page. As founder of the magazine, *American Artist*, and publisher of Watson-Guptill's art instruction books, as well as author of several volumes, Guptill reached thousands of art students through print. Every book by Arthur Guptill, since his first, published in 1920, has been printed and reprinted, and each is still sought by art students, architects, draftsmen, and designers throughout the country. Currently in print are his ambitious books on watercolor, oil, and pen and ink. His works on the pencil—until now—were out of print.

Guptill's writings on pencil drawing date back many years, and the early volumes are now collector's items. But no single book previously published provided the kind of exhaustive treatment that had characterized his other publications. In order to reissue his writing on pencil and to publish a single book where he was as thorough to

this medium as he was to the others, I went to two of his important publications on pencil and combined them into a single volume. *Rendering in Pencil*, therefore, is a volume that combines *Sketching and Rendering in Pencil*, originally published by Pencil Points Press in 1922 and *Pencil Drawing Step-by-Step*, published by Reinhold in 1949. The two books were sufficiently different from each other that by merging them we were able to present the most thorough treatment of pencil currently available.

As an artist and architectural renderer, as an architect, as a teacher, and as a writer, Arthur L. Guptill possessed unique talents for creating art instruction books. He was a systematic thinker, capable of isolating complex principles and investigating them practically and simply so that any art student could comprehend and execute the most difficult problems. His lucid text—as well as his illustrations—work to make his books classics in each of their fields. *Rendering in Pencil* now joins that impressive group of Guptill books.

Susan E. Meyer

*Kenneth Conant: Durham Cathedral. The virtues of the pencil are evident in this archi-
tectural drawing: it is capable of varied strokes and tones, it lends itself to accurate rendering, and it is ideal for a finished drawing as well as a preparatory sketch.*

1.

Introductory Considerations

Before plunging into our technical discussions, let's take a minute to consider some of the virtues and faults of the pencil. If you are a beginner you should pay particular attention, because you may be inclined to say, "Oh, it's only a cheap lead pencil! What can I expect from it?" Far from being trivial, the pencil is one of the most useful tools at the artist's command—a thing of amazing potential.

Merits of the Pencil

Let's enumerate a few of the pencil's outstanding virtues:

1. It is cheap to buy, as are the papers and other materials to use with it. Even the most prolific pencil artist rarely consumes more than a hundred dollars' worth of such materials yearly; the beginner can make dozens of drawings for very little money.

2. Equipment is accessible everywhere. This equipment (as well as the finished pencil drawings) can be packed away in small space, or easily carried about. It requires no lengthy or difficult preparation, being ready for instant use. It is not messy, and it seldom deteriorates with age. Finished pencil drawings need no special care; if they have been made on fine-quality paper, they will remain fresh and attractive indefinitely. If exposed to light, they may eventually yellow slightly, but they will not fade.

3. The common use of the pencil for writing and figuring has given us all some familiarity with it, so the beginning artist finds the pencil natural to hold and to manipulate properly when drawing. This comfort leaves him free to concentrate on other problems.

4. The pencil responds readily to almost any demand. Sharply pointed, it gives a line as fine and clean-cut as that of the pen; bluntly pointed, it can be used much like the brush. It will make strokes sufficiently light and delicate, or bold and vigorous, to suit the most exacting technician, or tones so smooth that no trace of line can be found. It is responsive to the slightest variation of pressure or direction, allowing the artist to produce almost any type of individual stroke or, in the case of tone, to create uniform areas or to grade at will from light to dark or vice versa. Pencil tones may range all the way from the white of the paper to intense black—as full a gamut as any medium can promise.

5. Not the least of the virtues of the pencil is that it permits unusual freedom in correcting or erasing at any time during the progress of the work. (As we will see later, the eraser can be used as a supplementary tool for producing unique and pleasing effects.)

6. If speed is desired—as when the artist is trying to record some fleeting aspect of nature—the pencil permits amazingly rapid manipulation, yet, when time is not pressing, the same pencil proves suitable for the most painstaking study.

7. The pencil is excellent for either finished results—drawings that are ends in themselves—or preparatory sketches or studies for final interpretation in pencil or other media. Even important paintings, lithographs, etchings, and drawings in pen or brush often get their start through the aid of the pencil.

8. The pencil combines perfectly with many media, frequently playing an important part in conjunction with pen and ink, brush and ink,

wash, watercolor, etc. There is also a unique method in which a solvent, such as kerosene or turpentine, is brushed over pencil work; this partially dissolves the graphite and spreads it in a washlike manner to bring about agreeable results.

9. When it comes to color, the pencil admittedly is not at its best. Yet there are many satisfactory colored pencils available, including the so-called "watercolor pencils." In using these, the penciling, once in place, is brushed over with water, the action creating something of a watercolor effect.

10. Practice with the pencil is ideal training for work in other media: drawing in fine line prepares you for pen and ink and etching; broad line shading, together with shading in mass—"pencil painting," as it is sometimes called—helps you greatly with crayon, charcoal, and other chalky media. Pencil also provides an excellent approach to lithography, along with at least a limited background for painting in wash, watercolor, and oil.

Limitations of the Pencil

Regarding the pencil's limitations: this simple instrument quite naturally cannot approach oil paint, watercolor, or pastel in an ability to provide richness and depth of hue. Nor can it yield their types of tone or texture. The pencil is not a logical tool for covering large surfaces; it is far better adapted to relatively small drawings. In fact, there is sometimes a danger that—because of the fineness of the pencil's point—the student may fall into finicky ways, losing all breadth of effect in the struggle to cover large surfaces or to interpret a maze of detail.

When we check such faults against the virtues, it becomes evident—if proof be needed—that within certain natural limits, the pencil can be the artist's real friend.

The Architect and Draftsman

It is not difficult to see that the pencil is an instrument that no artist or art student can afford to ignore. But if the pencil is valuable to the artist or art student, it is absolutely indispensable to the architect and his assistants. Although the artist has numerous media from which to choose, the architect has nothing that can take the place of the graphite point for a major portion of his work. What other medium can he use for laying out his accurate plans and elevations and sections, and what else would do for all the various detail drawings which must be carefully made to scale?

Aside from instrumental work, there are other ways the architect uses the pencil as well. Many drawings of a freehand nature are required, such as details of carved stone and wood, ornamental iron, lettered inscriptions, and the like. The pencil is particularly valuable for making rendered presentation sketches for submission to a prospective client to show how a proposed structure will appear when completed. Then, too, free-hand perspective sketching also aids the architect. In other ways, with a few strokes of his pencil he can make some point clear to his client or express his ideas satisfactorily to his draftsmen, or help his contractors to visualize some matter not readily understood from the working drawings.

The architect's indebtedness to this little instrument helps him to get work and to execute it. But if he feels a debt to this constant friend, so indeed should the architectural draftsman or student, for the pencil offers more assistance in learning architecture and in advancing in this profession than does any other single material.

For a student of architecture, drawing from photographs or buildings increases your knowledge of architecture; but it does far more than this. It improves your powers of observation and retention, for you are forced to observe in order to draw at all and in drawing you unconsciously assimilate knowledge of the buildings drawn, as well as a sense of relative proportions and shapes applicable to original problems in design. The more drawings you make, the greater the power to visualize the appearance of a proposed building long before a single study on paper has been made. The ability to form an image of the completed structure is most desirable. The average draftsman gives so much time to working in elevation or plan that he's likely to forget that the building will be finally judged by its appearance in three dimensions and not by the drawings from which it is built. The draftsman who has the power to visualize does not forget this, and so makes all his drawings with greater intelligence.

Other Professional Uses of the Pencil

There are others connected with the architectural profession besides the architect and his draftsmen and designers who find sketching of value. Engineers and construction superintendents can often explain to others or make clear in their own minds certain obscure points in construction by means of quick sketches.

Just as the architect and his assistants find skill in pencil handling advantageous, so do those connected with such professions as interior decoration and landscape architecture. This should be obvious. What is not so commonly understood, however, is that skill in pencil sketching often proves of practical value to the layman. There are problems that sometimes come up in the daily life of any person difficult to express or explain by oral or written word but which can be easily made clear by even the crudest sketch.

Learning to Use the Pencil

Granting, then, that the pencil is a mighty useful medium, well-worth studying, what is the best way to master it? Probably no two authorities would give an identical answer, though fortunately the days of the dogmatic, "Do it my way; there is no other right way!" seem to have vanished. In this book we shall stick to teaching the time-tested fundamentals, endeavoring to lead you along a logical and, we hope, enjoyable path, all the while stressing the need to develop your own judgment as to what suits your particular requirements.

We are assuming that you already possess a passable knowledge of the principles of freehand drawing. Until you can portray things correctly in proportion—including perspective—and have some knowledge of light and shade, whatever technical facility with the pencil you may gain will be of little use. For the occasional reader who is not so qualified, however, we offer a reasonably adequate course in the methods of constructing a freehand drawing, while in other pages we include basic suggestions on light and shade.

To the student somewhat versed in these principles, the logical start with the pencil is to experiment thoughtfully for at least a few hours with all sorts of graphite points on different kinds of paper, performing exercises such as we shall soon offer. Then, one at a time, explore contrasting types of subject matter: still life, flowers, landscape, animals and birds, figures, and faces. Simultaneously learn to vary your handling. You can best accomplish this by concentrating in a natural order on the several techniques typical of the pencil—fine line, broad line, mass shading, etc.—acquiring reasonable facility in each before going on to the next. Also, you would be wise to try quick sketching, perhaps alternating it with more painstaking study. Memory sketching will provide salutary practice, too. We will refer to all of this again and again as we go along, leaving you to select those of our suggestions that you think will prove beneficial if you are eventually to gain the all-around versatility rightly expected of the true pencil master. There's one encouraging thing: every step you take will prepare you for the next and more difficult step; every bit of skill you acquire will apply forevermore.

Fig. 1. Here is a checklist of materials: 1. A dozen or so assorted graphite drawing pencils; 2. A few pencil holders; 3. Block of pencil drawing paper, or several sheets of different kinds; 4. Drawing board, perhaps 16 x 20″/47 x 21 cm; 5. A kneaded eraser, and a medium red or green eraser; 6. Thumbtacks; 7. Draftsman's erasing shield; 8. Sharp knife or razor blade; 9. Sandpaper pad; 10. Bottle of fixative and atomizer. Gradually, as we proceed, other items will be added to this list.

2.
Equipment and Studio

There is perhaps nothing that kindles the interest and enthusiasm of the student as much as surrounding himself with the required drawing materials. Even the experienced artist, accustomed to the everyday use of these accessories, can hardly gaze upon a new clean sheet of paper and pencils pointed ready for use without itching to begin, a desire to seize a pencil and be at it. There is something about such materials that lures you on and urges you to do your best.

In fact, the appeal is so strong that the beginner is almost sure, without guidance, to buy too great a variety and quantity of materials and is inclined to attach too much importance to them. Important as they are (and no one can do good work with poor tools), the truth is that few and comparatively inexpensive materials are needed for such work, and especially for the earlier problems. But these should be the best of their kind, for the difficulties in the beginning are so many and great that it would be a grave mistake to use anything of an inferior nature. Even the best materials are none too easily mastered.

If you have no teacher to aid you in your selection, you are usually safe in securing the standard drawing pencils and papers carried in stock by reliable art supply dealers.

Pencils

While it is sometimes possible to do a good drawing with a cheap pencil—the kind used in schools and offices—the standard drawing pencils made especially for the artist and draftsman cost only a little extra and are vastly superior. Their lead is more highly refined, comparatively free of gritty particles that—in cheaper pencils—often cause defective strokes or even scratches or tears in the paper. Also, the wood of drawing pencils is of uniform grain (making them easier to sharpen) and better seasoned (which means that they are less likely to warp, breaking the leads within). Still more important, these higher-priced pencils come in many accurately graded degrees of lead, so that by referring to the letters or figures prominently displayed at the end of each pencil, the artist can tell exactly how soft or hard the lead is and can judge instantly whether or not it is suitable.

Grading

Most manufacturers offer their pencils in 17 degrees, graduated from 6B, the softest and blackest, to 9H, the hardest and least black, in this order: 6B, 5B, 4B, 3B, 2B, B, HB, F, H, 2H, 3H, 4H, 5H, 6H, 7H, 8H, 9H. Of these, artists generally prefer the softer points, particularly the 3B and 2B. The 6B and 5B are also well liked but, due to their extreme softness, they wear down quickly, requiring almost constant resharpening. They are also inclined to break, and drawings made with them smudge badly if rubbed.

For many purposes, you may prefer the medium pencils, such as the HB, F, and H, and occasionally even as hard a lead as a 3H or 4H. On the whole, however, pencils harder than H are used almost entirely for instrumental drafting or for ultra-precise types of freehand work.

The choice of pencils depends largely on the character of paper to be used, a smooth, glossy paper demanding a much softer pencil than for work on rough paper which has considerable "tooth." For quick sketches, a soft pencil—perhaps a 2B or B or HB—will sometimes do for the whole drawing, but a carefully finished sketch, showing considerable detail, may require as many as seven or eight pencils, grading all the way from 3B, 2B to 4H or 5H. In such a drawing, most of the work would be done with the softer pencils, the harder ones being used for the light, transparent tones and fine detail. A little experimenting will usually show what pencils are best suited to the paper to be used and to the subject to be drawn. The fact that the weather makes a great difference in the pencils required is not usually recognized, but it is true that pencils that are just right on a dry day will prove too hard when the air is damp and the paper filled with moisture.

By performing the exercises that follow, you will soon learn exactly what kinds of line and tone you can make with each grade. You will probably narrow the choice to six or eight pencils and, of these, most of your work will be accomplished with two or three.

As the products of different manufacturers vary somewhat, particularly in the composition of their lead and their standards of grading (neither of which is exactly uniform throughout the trade), it is probably just as well for you to become fully familiar with one good brand and then stick to it. (Some artists prefer one brand and some another, though artists as a general rule have less definite predilections than do draftsmen.) Experimentation with the various brands of pencils will determine your personal preference.

Mechanical or Refill Pencils

One of the great annoyances of the wood-cased lead pencil is that it demands constant sharpening. Many pencil users therefore prefer mechanical pencils. These should be of the kind made especially for the artist or draftsman. (You will need a separate pencil for each degree of lead.) Try them if you wish; you will discover that they have both advantages and disadvantages.

Pencil Holders

It's hard to work with stubby pencils and rather expensive to throw them away, so most artists (unless they choose mechanical pencils) like to keep on hand a half dozen or so holders (Fig. 1), one for each frequently used grade. Then, as a pencil gets shorter than half length, it can be inserted in a holder and utilized to the very end.

Paper

There are numerous papers on the market and, as artists seldom agree as to which kinds are best, it is impossible to give specific recommendations here. Your dealer can probably advise you as to the relative merits of the types he carries.

Almost any drawing paper will do, but the choice depends mainly on the size and character of the drawing to be made. For small sketches it is best, as a rule, to use smoother paper than for large work. In fact, it is almost impossible to draw fine detail on extremely rough paper. A glazed (or glossy) paper, however, is seldom desirable, as the shiny surface is dulled in an objectionable manner if an eraser is used. Sometimes, however, very crisp, snappy sketches are made on glossy paper, but a soft pencil is required for such work. Extremely rough paper is occasionally satisfactory for a large drawing, but a medium-rough surface is best for general work because it has a "tooth" to "bite" the pencil. Without this tooth, the pencil would not give off its graphite freely, nor would the paper retain it. The slightly rough cardboard known as "kid-finished bristol" is also desirable—being the author's preference for many purposes—while some of the better grades of the still heavier "illustration" boards also have their virtues, particularly for large work.

Paper comes in loose sheets and in pads (blocks); also in sketchbook form. The common types of paper measure approximately 8.5 x 11"/ 21.5 x 28cm (standard notebook size), 9 x 12"/23 x 30cm, and 11 x 14"/28 x 35.5cm or 11 x 15"/28 x 38cm. You can also buy paper in larger sheets and by the roll. Some like to purchase drawing paper of Imperial size (22 x 30"/56 x 76cm) and then halve or quarter it when smaller proportions are desired—a good plan.

Tracing paper—long a favorite among architects—has become very popular with pencil artists. Its transparency makes it possible to rough out a subject on one sheet and then to render it on a second sheet laid over the first. Tracing paper often has an ideal surface for pencil drawing, possessing just the right amount of tooth. Such paper comes in pads, sheets, and by the roll. A pad measuring about 9 x 12"/23 x 30cm can prove useful in innumerable ways; frequently a still larger one is convenient.

Certain papers made for other purposes—bond typewriting paper, to name one—serve very well for drawing. And later we will have something to say about tinted papers; they can prove highly effective.

Drawing Board

Unless you draw in a sketchbook, on a pad, or on stiff cardboard, you will need a support for your paper. A wooden drawing board is excellent—one about 16 x 20"/47 x 51cm is large enough to accommodate most drawing paper and still leave room to support the hand. The smoother the board, the better. Even tiny irregularities like thumbtack holes or the grain of the wood may transfer through and injure the appearance of a drawing.

Thumbtacks or Tape

You will require a few thumbtacks for fastening your paper to the drawing board. If you prefer not to mutilate the paper with thumbtack holes, the tacks may be placed just outside the edges, their heads overlapping the paper, to hold it in position. Some artists substitute for tacks draftsman's tape, adhering the drawing sparingly at the corners or wherever necessary.

Unless drawing paper is unusually thick, several extra sheets (or a sheet of smooth cardboard) should be placed beneath it, before it is secured to the board, so that any defects on the drawing board will not transfer to the drawing.

Erasers

Do as little erasing as possible, not only because erasers tend to abrade the paper surface—making

it difficult to draw over it again—but also because it is hard to erase a given area without smudging the surrounding tone.

When erasing is necessary, kneaded rubber has a unique virtue: it is possible to press a clean piece of it against the offending penciling and "lift" many of the graphite particles without disturbing adjoining areas. If the tone is so firmly embedded that this pressure, several times repeated, doesn't do the trick, use the kneaded rubber like any other eraser. Even when used in this way, it is less likely than most erasers to create a messy effect. Kneaded rubber is also ideal for lightening construction lines before the final penciling is done, as it picks up its own erasings, leaving the paper relatively clean.

Occasionally it may be necessary to remove lines or tones that will not yield to even brisk applications of the kneaded eraser. Under this condition, the typical red or green eraser will usually do a satisfactory job. On glazed, or glossy paper—or other delicate surfaces—the abrasive action of kneaded rubber and most other erasers may prove too strong, marring the effect. For these, substitute artgum or some other extremely soft eraser.

Erasing Shield

A draftsman's erasing shield (see Fig. 1) is an exceptionally valuable gadget, because it enables the artist to erase a limited area of almost any shape without injuring the nearby penciling.

Dust Brush

An extremely soft brush is of great help in keeping the drawing free of erasings, dust, etc. The paper should always be dusted (or blown free of dirt) after any erasing, but with maximum care in order to avoid smudging the drawing. This dusting is a wise precaution, because even tiny specks that look harmless can cause unsightly spots or streaks to develop as the pencil passes over them.

Knife

The proper pointing of wood-cased pencils is an art. The first requisite is a sharp knife or razor blade for cutting away the wood. (The X-acto knife is good.) Few pencil sharpeners will do this without simultaneously removing too much lead. The knife will also be useful for trimming paper, lifting thumbtacks, and cutting tape.

Sandpaper Pad

A block of sandpaper such as draftsmen use—preferably the type with a handle—is convenient for pointing the lead after the wood has been cut away. (Another use for this block is demonstrated in Chapter 19.) If such a block is not obtainable, a sheet of fine sandpaper or emery cloth (or even a rough sheet of drawing paper) may be substituted.

Fixative

Work done in pencil—especially soft pencil—is so easily ruined if accidentally rubbed that it is generally sprayed on completion with a simple mouth atomizer containing a varnishlike liquid known as fixative. This produces a thin protective coating. Both fixative and atomizer can be purchased for a modest sum at any artists' materials store. (You will be shown how to use fixative later in Chapter 19.)

Planning Indoor Working Space

Pencil drawing can be done successfully practically anywhere and under almost any conditions. To work to the greatest advantage, however, you need a well-lighted spot where you will be free to draw with a minimum of interruption. A private room—a sanctum over which you have absolute control—is ideal.

Lighting

Studio lighting calls for careful planning. Not only should you have adequate light on your paper, both day and night, but it should fall in such a way that your hand and pencil will not cast disturbing shadows on your work. Nor should the light create unpleasant reflections to tire your eyes. For the right-handed person, light from the left is recommended, and vice versa.

North light is desirable, for if windows face east, south, or west, sunlight will stream in at times during the day, causing the shadows and reflected lights on the objects to shift in position and to change in value constantly. North light, on the other hand, is an indirect light; it does not come straight from the sun but is, instead, largely reflected from the sky. It is therefore more diffused and gives softer and less changeable shadows. It also remains more constant during the whole day, since it is relatively unaffected by shifting in the sun's position or by the passage of clouds. And north light is purer in hue, too, being less yellow than the direct rays of the sun; though this is of special advantage only when working in color. Light from too many sources is disturbing, as it causes complexity of shadow and reflection.

It is best to have the illumination from one window only, the shades being arranged in such a way that the light may be cut off at either the top or the bottom as desired. (See Fig. 2, which shows a room arranged practically for indoor work.) Generally, the lower half or two-thirds of the window should be shaded, as light from above gives more pleasing shadows. Many studios are, for this reason, provided with overhead light from skylights or dormers, though for our purpose, the upper half or third of the ordinary window will do very well.

The still-life objects to be drawn should not be too far from this window, or they will lack sufficient light and their shadows will be too elongated. It is best if light enters the room at an angle of about 45 degrees from the left, and the objects being placed anywhere between 3 and 10'/1 and 3m from the window.

Object Stand

There should be some sort of stand on which objects may be placed. Usually a small table of average height (about 30''/76cm) will do very well. One painted white or with a white cover is good. If a dark table is used, cover it with a white or very light cloth or paper so the objects contrast

Fig. 2. For indoor work, this is a practical working studio: notice the position of the window, chair, object stand, and drawing table.

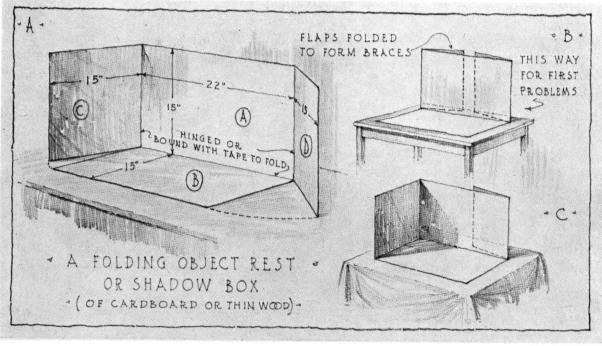

Fig. 3. Here is a method of making an object stand or shadow box from cardboard or thin wood.

Fig. 4. This is a drawing table shown in an upright position.

Fig. 5. The drawing table is shown here in a sloping position.

strongly with the table. Also provide a background of the same material to create sharp relief between object and background and to hide the surroundings.

The diagram in Fig. 3 shows a method of making a convenient folding object rest or shadow box of heavy cardboard which may be used on any table. Thin wood or wallboard may be substituted if desired. Cut two cardboards, *A* and *B*, of equal size, about 15 x 22″/38 x 56cm. Bind them together with tape in such a way that *A* can be raised to a vertical position while *B* remains horizontal to rest on the table. Flaps *C* and *D*, each 15″/38cm square, are attached to *A* in the manner shown. Fig. 3 gives at *B* and *C* two of several positions in which the box may be used, the first being the best for the early problems.

Chair or Seat

Your working position must be thoughtfully considered. To draw well, you must always be relaxed. Sit naturally in a comfortable chair, with your paper at such a height and slant that you can view it directly—i.e., it must not be viewed at such a foreshortened angle that distortions of proportion may develop as you work. A simple chair with a rather straight back and no arms is best. This type of chair, while permitting freedom, will at the same time not be so comfortable that it will invite laziness.

Drawing Table

While thousands of artists—even professionals—manage very well by leaning their board or pad against the edge of an ordinary table (or placed on the table top, its far edge propped on a few books or similar support), others think it a good investment, sooner or later, to purchase a drawing stand such as pictured in Figs. 4 and 5. This one is adjustable to many positions. It can be used like an easel, with the paper upright—the artist may either sit or stand—or the top can be slanted to an angle (perhaps 15 or 20 degrees from the horizontal) which will permit comfortable working when seated. Such stands provide ample leg room and are very steady. When not in use, they take up little space.

For object drawing, keep the table in an almost vertical position so the sketch is at right angles to the line of sight. If the board is tipped in some other manner, the paper will be foreshortened, preventing accurate work, unless you change your own position in order to view it at right angles. Place the table slightly to the right as you face the objects, just enough to one side to keep it from obstructing the view. This position and the height of your chair should make it easy to glance from the objects to the drawing and back again.

Storage

For an indoor studio, therefore, these three things—the stand on which the objects are to rest, the seat, and the drawing table—are most important and, taken together with paper and pencil, constitute the essential equipment. Cases, drawers, or folios in which new paper and finished drawings may be kept are convenient. In addition, there should be some provision made for taking care of the pencils, erasers, and knives which must be nearby. Attachments may be purchased for the type of table pictured in Figs. 4 and 5, specially designed to accommodate such accessories. As an added improvement to the studio, a shelf should be provided where the drawing may be placed from time to time for comparison with the objects drawn. A portable music rack, such as musicians use, placed near the object stand can serve this purpose.

Lamp

If you plan to work by artificial light, try to arrange it to take the place as much as possible of the natural daylight. The lamp near the window in Fig. 2 is excellent for the purpose. The kind of lamp, in fact, is probably of less importance than its placement, as great care is necessary to avoid unpleasant glare or reflection. The light should be secured against swaying or moving.

And last, but not least, a wastebasket proves a desirable adjunct to the studio.

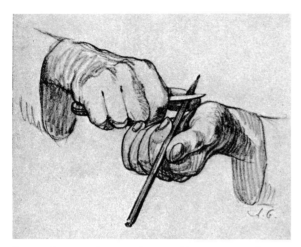

Fig. 6. Start to sharpen the pencil by removing the wood. Use a sharp knife and hold it naturally.

Fig. 7. Now point the lead. The position of the pencil on the sandpaper will depend on the type of point you want.

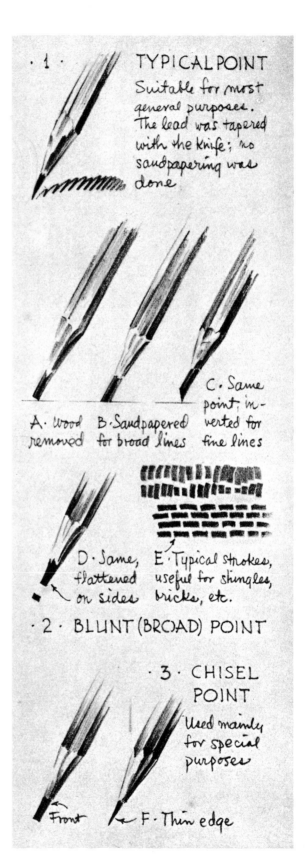

Fig. 8. Here are some of the kinds of points you can obtain with your pencil.

3.
Preliminary Exercises

Familiar as the pencil may be to you as an instrument used in daily life, you will benefit greatly by this basic introduction to its preparation and use.

Sharpening the Pencil

Before beginning the exercises, concentrate for a few minutes on different ways of pointing the pencil. It takes a quite a knack to do a good job, especially with the softer grades; their leads are forever breaking, particularly if the pencils have previously been dropped or abused.

First, a word as to tools. We have already hinted that there is little to recommend most pencil sharpeners, whether mechanical or hand. Though occasionally they may serve (when leads are fairly hard, and sharp points wanted), a keen-edged knife or a single-edged razor blade will usually do a vastly superior job.

With your knife ready, remember that each pencil has a right and a wrong end to sharpen! If you whittle off the letters or numbers, it won't be easy to identify the pencil later. Start by cutting away sufficient wood, using extreme care not to break the precious lead or reduce its size greatly. (See Fig. 6.) With the harder grades, you can safely expose half an inch of so, but when sharpening soft pencils—6B, 5B, 4B—you can't cut away much wood without risking immediate breakage.

Next, shape the exposed lead into the desired point on your sandpaper pad or a sheet of rough paper. (See Fig. 7.) Sometimes you can use both, the paper providing the means for a final slicking up after the lead has been shaped. Each time you finish with the sandpaper pad, rap it repeatedly on the rim of your wastebasket (or other suitable receptacle) to free any loose graphite. Also, wipe your pencil point with a rag or paper tissue. If graphite particles find their way to your drawing paper they can easily cause "smooches."

Types of Points

There are several rather definite types of points, your choice usually being determined by the purpose you have in mind for the job.

1. The first, and simplest to make (and very satisfactory for all-around work), is that shown at 1, Fig. 8. This, with its taper quite uniform, is not unlike the point made with a pencil sharpener, except that less lead is cut away and the tip is not quite so sharp. No sandpapering is done.

2. A second type is the blunt or broad point shown at 2, Fig. 8. In making this, the wood only is first cut away (A), a fairly long lead of full circumference being exposed (except in the brittle, softest degrees). With the pencil then held in normal drawing position (B), the point is rubbed on the sandpaper until quite blunt, after which the end of the lead is smoothed by means of a few strokes on paper. This point will make either a broad or a fine stroke, depending on whether the pencil is held in its normal drawing position as at B, or inverted as at C. Occasionally, the sides of the lead are also sandpapered to create a flat point (D) that is ideal for broad, crisp individual strokes (E), which you may need for indicating square or rectangular details such as bricks, shingles, or panes of glass.

3. Some artists like what is known as a *chisel point*—one sandpapered on two sides to produce a thin edge (F). This will draw either a fine or a broad

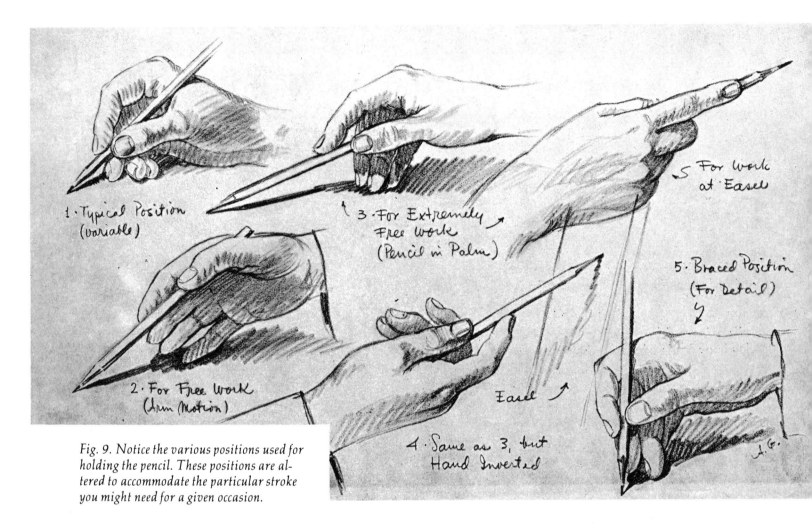

Fig. 9. Notice the various positions used for holding the pencil. These positions are altered to accommodate the particular stroke you might need for a given occasion.

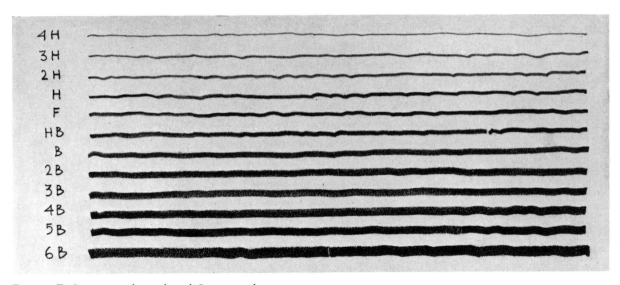

Fig. 10. Different pencils produce different results.

line, according to how it is held, or it may be manipulated to form a stroke varying in character throughout its length. It breaks rather easily.

Artists do most of their work with the medium or blunt point (1, Fig. 8), to which the pencil naturally wears, preparing a special point only for some particular purpose. The main thing is to always use the type of point—as well as the degree of lead—which you think will best serve your need at the moment. As you carry out the following exercises, try all sorts of points and you will gradually learn the possibilities of each.

Holding the Pencil

Your hand position will depend largely on the placing of your paper—whether it is vertical, steeply sloping, or nearly flat—and on the technical requirements of your drawing—whether it calls for sweeping strokes, carefully executed lines, or what. For typical work, most artists hold the pencil much as for writing, with the hand resting lightly on the table as shown in 1, Fig. 9, though they use the pencil with far greater freedom. For short strokes, and strokes demanding considerable pressure, little arm movement is needed. The hand may swing at the wrist, or the fingers alone may perform the necessary motions. For longer strokes—notably quick, dashing strokes—the pencil is more likely to be held well back from the point, and often the entire forearm and hand are swung freely from the elbow, with a minimum of wrist and finger movement as shown in 2, Fig. 9. For particularly unrestrained effort, such as that required by the quick blocking in of the construction lines of a subject (especially if you are engaged at an easel or on drawings of large size), the pencil (which should preferably be of full length) may be held with the unsharpened end in the palm (3), the hand and wrist being very boldly swung. The hand may even be inverted (4); a position that permits amazingly rapid progress.

For most shaded work, the quality of line and tone desired will determine the hand position, which will therefore change frequently. Occasionally, the pencil will be kept almost vertical (5). This position sometimes proves useful when building up tone very carefully with a sharp point.

Eventually, try all such positions.

Line Practice

Because the pencil is primarily a linear tool, a good starting point for the student is to experiment in the drawing of lines—hundreds of lines of all kinds: long and short; fine, medium, and broad; straight, crooked, curved; unbroken, broken; dots and dashes. Every grade of pencil should be employed, and on different papers. Pressure should be varied, too, as well as hand position and speed.

Figs. 10, 11, and 12 provide suggestions for practicing this linework with your pencil. Try some of these lines and invent others of your own. Your purpose is to discover every type of line your pencil is capable of making.

As the sharp point best expresses the linear character of your medium, you might begin with that, next trying broader and broader points and, finally, the full-sized lead, as shown in Fig. 10.

Although the accompanying examples were reproduced at the exact size of the originals, do at least a part of your work at larger scale and with greater boldness. Try drawing lines ranging from 1 to 6″/2.5 to 16cm long. Sweep in still longer strokes; let some of these take the natural curve which the swing of the arm tends to impart. Draw others as straight as you can.

Turn through the pages and copy a few lines here and there, remembering that most of these reproductions have been reduced considerably from the original. If you have access to any original drawings in pencil see how closely you can imitate their individual strokes.

With these exercises you will gradually come to a fuller appreciation of the pencil's possibilities, while developing your own technical repertoire. Eventually you will make, almost subconsciously, the type of stroke every purpose demands.

Tone-building Exercises

Once you have thoroughly tested all of your pencils as linear instruments, experiment to see how

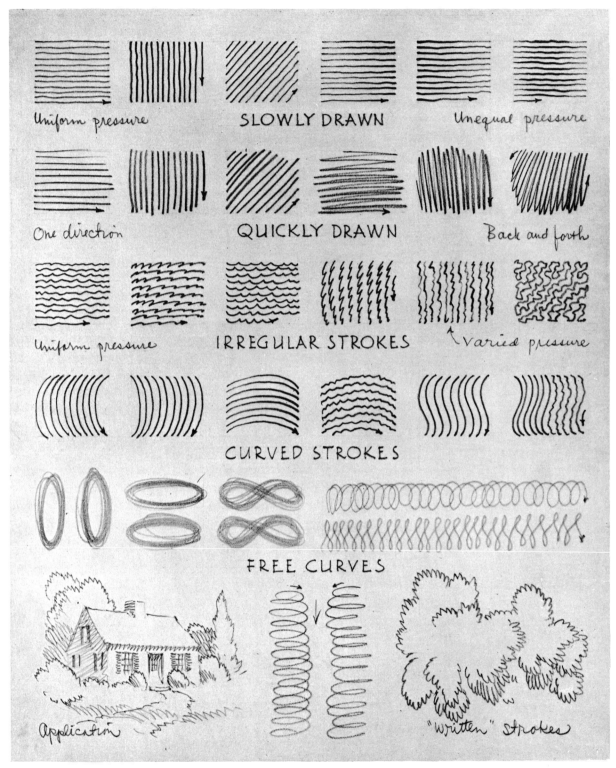

Uniform pressure   SLOWLY DRAWN   Unequal pressure

One direction   QUICKLY DRAWN   Back and forth

Uniform pressure   IRREGULAR STROKES   Varied pressure

CURVED STROKES

FREE CURVES

Application   "Written" Strokes

Fig. 11. An amazing variety of fine lines is possible. Make pages and pages of strokes, using all of your pencils.

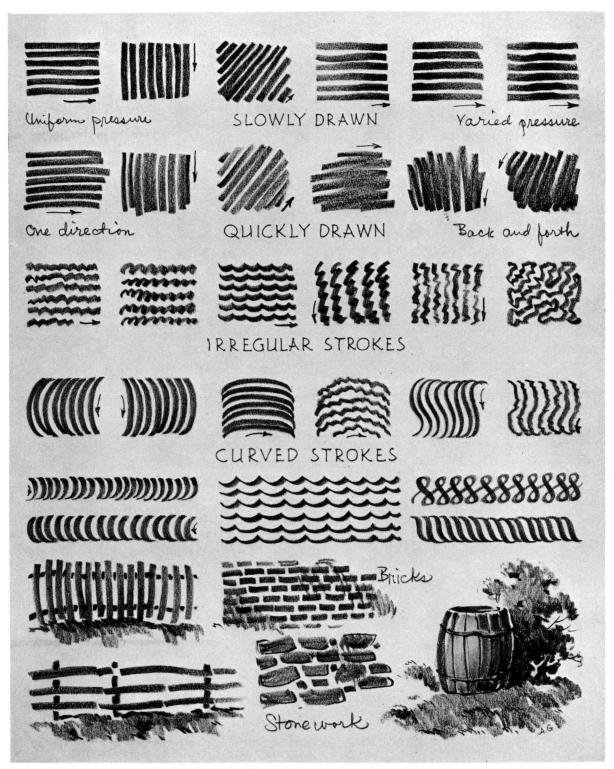

Uniform pressure SLOWLY DRAWN Varied pressure

One direction QUICKLY DRAWN Back and forth

IRREGULAR STROKES

CURVED STROKES

Bricks

Stonework

Fig. 12. The most natural strokes are usually the best. Copy these strokes freely and invent others of your own.

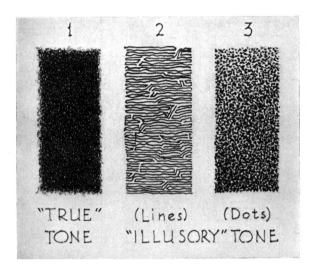

Fig. 13. Basically, there are two types of tones: the "true tones" made by strokes of the pencil, and "illusory tones" built up from pencil lines or dots.

many varieties of gray and black tones you can produce with them.

Two Types of Tones

Fundamentally, there are only two types of tones: those where the component pencil lines (or dots) are so merged that their individual identity is wholly or largely lost, and those where at least some lines (or dots) are plainly visible. Tones of the former type might be called "true" tones; an example is shown at 1, Fig. 13, where the area was repeatedly gone over in different directions with fine strokes until all traces of line disappeared.

At 2, Fig. 13, we have a typical example of the second type of tone, consisting of lines so closely grouped that we are conscious—particularly if we view the area from a little distance—of a tonal, rather than a linear, impression. Such a tone might be called "false" in that it is only an illusion of tone, the eye gaining a tonal impression by automatically blending (to some extent) the dark lines and the white spaces between.

Similarly, example 3 in Fig. 13 is another illusory tone, for here closely spaced dots are merged through the process of vision. Short dashes, if close together, would also create a tonal effect of this basic type.

In pencil drawing, all such tones—we find them in infinite variety—are utilized according to need, often in combination. You should therefore experiment with every method of creating tone that occurs to you. The examples in Fig. 13 typify both the solid and the linear (or dotted) kinds.

Flat and Graded Tones

For some purposes, tones which are uniform throughout—"flat" or "ungraded," as they are known—are preferable; other requirements may call for "graded" or "graduated" tones in which the amount of light or dark varies by degrees from part to part. More rarely, we find "hit-or-miss" tones that follow no set pattern. Note the decorative tones in Fig. 14. Much more will be said about graded tones in Chapter 11.

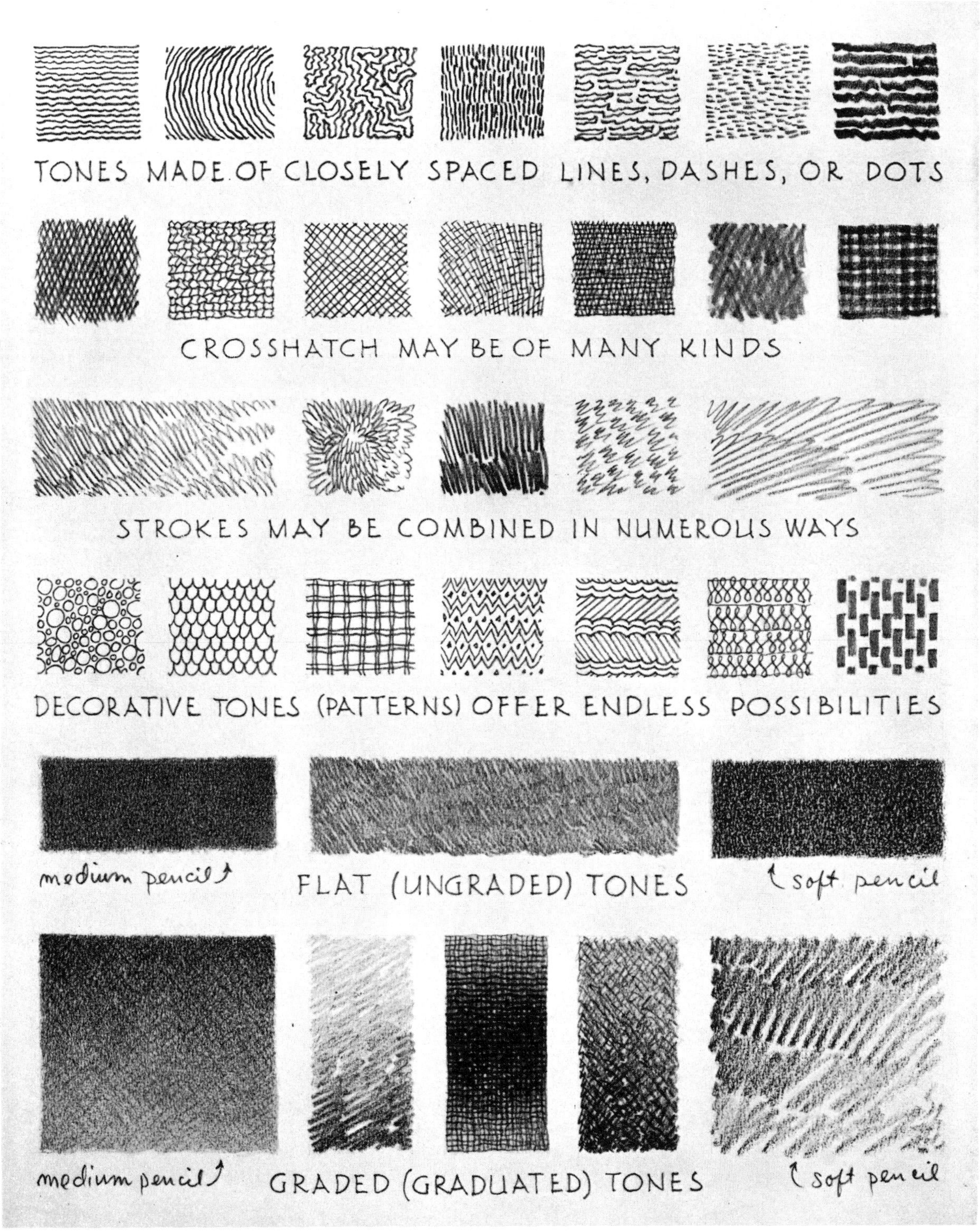

TONES MADE OF CLOSELY SPACED LINES, DASHES, OR DOTS

CROSSHATCH MAY BE OF MANY KINDS

STROKES MAY BE COMBINED IN NUMEROUS WAYS

DECORATIVE TONES (PATTERNS) OFFER ENDLESS POSSIBILITIES

medium pencil→   FLAT (UNGRADED) TONES   ←soft pencil

medium pencil→   GRADED (GRADUATED) TONES   ←soft pencil

Fig. 14. The pencil is a versatile instrument for tone building.

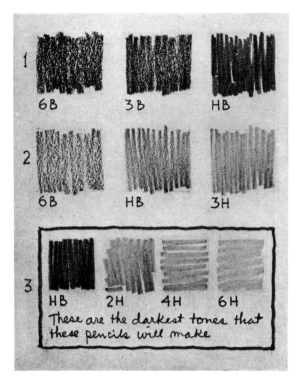

Fig. 15. Pencil grades do, of course, affect the tone quality.

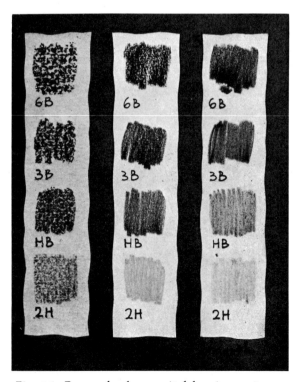

Fig. 16. Paper also has a vital bearing on tone quality.

Grade of Pencil

Obviously, your darkest tones can best be made with your softest pencils (Fig. 15). By using less and less pressure, these same leads can produce medium or light tones, but such tones may be granular in effect—perhaps unpleasantly so. Medium pencils are therefore generally better for medium tones, and hard pencils for light tones. (The latter pencils, in fact, can seldom be used for other than light tones.)

In Fig. 15, we further demonstrate how essential it is always to select the right pencil according to the tone quality you desire. In the upper row of tones (1), an attempt was made to produce the same gray by using three different pencils on a single paper. Observe that the 6B makes a more granular tone than the HB. (Sometimes one type would be preferred; sometimes the other.) At 2 you can see that while the 6B can be used for light tones, it is seldom at its best for them. At 3 we are again reminded that hard pencils will produce only light tones.

Paper Selection

Paper also has a vital bearing on tone quality. In Fig. 16 we see in what way four typical grades of pencil respond to three different kinds of paper: rough, medium, and smooth. A soft pencil on rough paper gives an extremely broken, granular tone. A hard pencil requires the bite of a somewhat rough paper; it will scarcely mark on smooth. (These basic truths, of course, apply whether you work in line or tone.)

Textures

Though textures are a matter for consideration later, we should at least point out here that in representative drawings of natural objects it is not enough to interpret the shapes correctly, along with the tones of light and dark; textures must also be indicated simultaneously.

4.
Interpreting Nature's Tones and Textures

Now that we have learned to create many sorts of tones with our pencils, it is time to start thinking about the tones we see about us in such natural objects—people, places, and things.

Local Tones

If we look analytically at these objects (let's forget colored ones for the moment), we will observe that each has its natural or innate surface tone. If, for instance, a box is made of white cardboard, white is its true or "local" tone. If a house is painted gray, gray is its local tone. Black is the local tone of a black automobile. Some objects have only one local tone, some many. In drawing, we occasionally represent an object by local tones alone, as shown in 1, Fig. 17.

Light, Shade, and Shadow

Usually, however, we can gain a far more realistic effect in our drawing if we picture each object not as we know it to *be* (with its purely local tones of white, gray, and black), but rather as it appears to the eye, with its local tones modified by the light which illuminates the object, and by the accompanying shade and shadow.

We are all aware, of course, that we can't even see an object in the darkness of night, while in sunshine (or under a brilliant lamp) it stands out very clearly. Between these extremes, its appearance varies from moment to moment according to the kind and amount of illumination reaching it, and the direction from which this falls.

In short, light not only reveals objects to us, but it so influences their appearance that *the artist nor-*

mally represents each local tone much as he sees it modified by light, shade, and shadow. (See 2, Fig. 17).

Conventionalized Treatments

It is not the artist's job, however, to imitate the camera by recording the subject matter exactly as it appears, down to the last detail. Instead, the artist is an interpreter, selecting from all the objects before him just those shapes and tones which seem essential. Each is given precisely the amount of emphasis or subordination it seems to call for. In other words, the artist filters nature's appearances through his mind before portraying them on paper. As a rule, he makes few adjustments of form—though there are plenty of exceptions—but he often takes liberties in expressing tone (and color). Not infrequently, the artist conventionalizes the subject matter, particularly in treating light, shade, and shadow. In doing this, modified tones of white, gray, or black may be used (see 3, Fig. 17), or he may rely on outline alone.

The words "shade" and "shadow," by the way, are very loosely used in the field of art. Strictly speaking, they are not synonymous. When, in nature, light falls upon an object from some source of illumination, such surfaces of the object as receive the light rays directly are said to be in light. Those surfaces from which the light is more or less excluded (because they are turned from the light source and hence do not receive direct rays) are said to be in shade. Shadow is "cast" by the object upon the background (or upon other objects) through the interception by the object of some of the light rays. Thus shadow often represents, or preserves, something of the form of the object which intercepts the light.

Fig. 17. Local tones are influenced by light and shade.

Shapes Influence Tones

While fundamentally the tonal appearance of an object depends upon (1) its local tones, and (2) the kind, intensity, and direction of light, there are several causative or modifying influences at work, of which shape is one of the most important. For instance, a flat-sided object—such as a white cube—if exposed to light from one side, will usually display (because of its shape) a very simple arrangement of flat tones. Each visible plane will quite possibly have a distinct tone of its own, limiting the effect of the entire cube to not over three well-defined tones, one for each visible plane. On the contrary, a white sphere, exposed to the very same light, may reveal an almost endless number of tones or, rather, a progressive grading of tone from that part of the sphere's surface which is turned most directly towards the source of light (and which therefore looks the lightest—pure white, if the light is bright enough) to that part which is the most turned away and so looks the darkest—perhaps almost black.

Incidentally, when the light is bright—as in the case of direct sunlight—shade and shadow areas will customarily appear clean-cut, with definite edges, while if the light is indirect or subdued, as it usually is indoors, the shade and shadow areas will blend together somewhat, and reveal soft, indefinite edges.

Light coming simultaneously from two or more sources, rather than one, will complicate matters, producing overlapping areas of tone, as well as multiple shadow edges. (Colored light still further confuses appearances, though it doesn't affect the pencil artist's work much.) Reflected light, sucn as is frequently thrown onto an object from brilliantly illuminated surfaces in the immediate vicinity—surfaces most often located beneath or behind the object—is another factor to be considered, as it modifies the effects caused by direct light.

Textures Influence Tones

Even the texture of an object—whether it is shiny or dull, smooth or rough—can greatly affect its tonal appearance. It is no news that the shiny surface of a black automobile seldom looks uniformly black. On the contrary, such a surface, though appearing intensely black in certain areas, may in others mirror the light of the sky and the tones of nearby buildings and trees, thus displaying a highly complex range of tones—some of them surprisingly light—not to mention colors. Similarly, a shiny dark vase indoors may reflect the image of a brilliant window and so exhibit an area of light which will appear extremely brilliant—far brighter than even the lightest parts of adjacent white objects that happen to be dull. Light objects (unless they are so shiny that they act as mirrors) usually appear somewhat lighter if they are smooth than they would if rough. On a rough surface, each minor surface irregularity has its own little areas of shade (and, perhaps, shadow) playing its part in darkening the whole. The artist usually tries to make some attempt to interpret these textures.

Tone Adjustments

Can the student ever come to understand the varied appearances we have just described (there are many others!) and learn to interpret them? The answer is, of course, "yes." The principles behind nature's appearances are simple, and by observation and experimentation—which you must do for yourself; we can only offer suggestions—you will soon learn how objects, whether animate or inanimate, look under different circumstances. It will then be relatively easy, through practice, to learn how to represent them.

Let us repeat that the artist does not try to be a camera to record every visible variation and intricacy of nature's effects. On the contrary, the artist has the right to exercise an amazing amount of freedom in adjusting not only forms but, more particularly, tones, arranging them almost at will. The spectator who views the finished drawing is seldom disturbed by all this adjustment even if he is aware of it. The viewer is so accustomed to nature's variety and changeableness of tone (and, so far as that goes, to the diversity of interpretation practiced by artists) that he will accept without question whatever the artist shows, provided the

effect looks convincing. That is his only criterion.

We can summarize this whole thing as follows: (1) If the artist can express his subject satisfactorily through the use of local tones only, that is his privilege. (2) The artist may render it in light and shade alone. (3) It's more than likely that the artist will combine these two procedures. (4) The artist may even forget tones and rely wholly on outline. (5) The artist may use other conventional treatments, such as a combination of outline with black or with flat tones of gray. (6) Seldom—though there may be exceptions—will the artist wholly neglect textures; if an object is rough or smooth, he will try to draw it accordingly.

Interpreting Colors

But what of color? What are you to do when you want to draw objects that, instead of appearing white, gray, or black, reveal color? How should you interpret the red of the apple, the green of the grass, the blue of the sky?

Unless you choose to use colored pencils, you must depend on artistic convention and, not unlike the sculptor working in marble, either ignore color or substitute for each important hue of nature a suitable tone of black, gray, or white. As there can be no rule about this, you must trust to your own judgment, which will, of course, improve with practice.

Values

In art, the term "value" is often used in place of "tone," whether reference is to the object itself or to a drawing. By "value" we refer to the relative degree of light or dark in any given tone. A tone may be referred to as "light in value," "medium in value," or "dark in value." In a pencil drawing, a value may stand at any point between the white of the paper and the darkest tone of which a soft pencil is capable.

Making a Scale of Values

As you will certainly be constantly representing every degree of value in nature, using all the tones

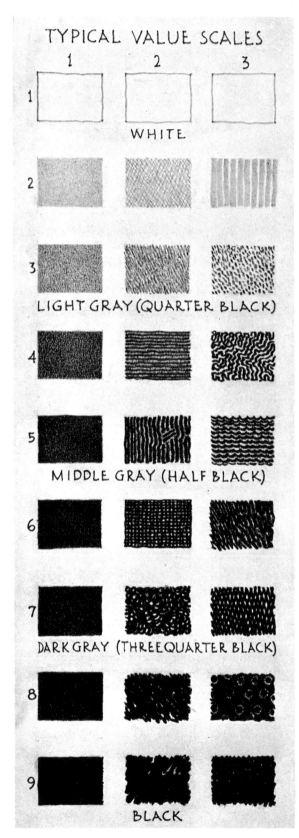

Fig. 18. Make a scale of values to increase your awareness of differences in tone.

of which pencils are capable, you will find some preliminary experimentation beneficial.

A good start is to make a scale of values like the one shown in Fig. 18. The preparation of such a scale will, in itself, increase your awareness of differences in tone, whether in the objects you see about you or in your drawing. Also, when ultimately you undertake to work from nature, you can hold up this scale as a measure for comparing every tone in the subject. In other words, by comparing a tone in nature with such a scale, you can better judge how light or dark to represent that tone in your drawing.

On a sheet of kid-finished bristol board, lay out nine squares (or other simple shapes) more or less like those at 1 in Fig. 18. (We selected nine arbitrarily, merely because this number provides a convenient sequence of graduated steps.) Leave the first of these squares (top) bare, as your white paper is the lightest value you can produce. Using a soft pencil, fill in the ninth (bottom) square with black tone—the darkest your pencil will make. Between the two, try to fill the fifth square with a gray tone exactly halfway in value between white and black; a medium pencil is best. This tone might be called "middle gray" or "half black," though its name matters little. Next, in your third square, try to create a value exactly halfway between white and middle. This might be called "light gray" or "quarter black." Similarly, in your seventh square would fall a value halfway between white and middle gray. This might be called "dark gray" or "three-quarter black." With these five stages completed, use the same means to provide the four intermediates shown at 2, 4, 6, and 8, giving you at last a scale with uniformly graduated steps.

If artists always made their drawings with solid masses of tone, this one scale might prove sufficient, but we have seen that tones are often composed of lines or dots. It is therefore good practice to do several scales similar to those at 2 and 3, seeing how close you can come to matching the values at 1. (Don't merely copy 2 and 3, but invent scales of your own.) Use different pencils and papers, and vary your manner of building the tone. This exercise should prove the best of preparation for subsequent work from nature, where you will constantly be faced with the task of interpreting values through the use of all sorts of lines and tones.

Some pencil drawings utilize many values, others but few. As we shall see later, a simple value scheme is usually preferable. Too many values, or complicated arrangements of values, can prove confusing.

Learning from Simple Objects

We have pointed out that, complex as natural lighting effects are, they follow definite principles. These are not, however, principles easily stated in words. Only through concentrated observation of objects in nature can you learn to grasp them fully. Perhaps these principles can best be comprehended by firsthand study of the simple geometric solids we have already mentioned—cubes, spheres, and the like. Often dishes or other objects found around the house serve just as well. Some of these objects should be dull, some shiny, some light, and some dark.

The lessons learned from simple objects will apply later to the handling of every type of subject matter, regardless of its size or complexity, as is suggested by Fig. 19, in which buildings are thought of as combinations of spheres, cylinders, cones, prisms, and pyramids. The dome of a building is basically hemispherical. Gas and water tanks are in many cases cylinders, with conical or domed tops. Room interiors and numerous items of furniture are geometrically proportioned, too, as are dozens of household utensils. Many trees are more or less spherical or ovoid in their leafy masses, while their trunks can be considered cylindrical. Even people and animals—their larger basic forms, that is—can be fairly well interpreted geometrically.

Rounded Forms: The Sphere

At 1, Fig. 20, we have drawn a white sphere having a relatively smooth surface. This sphere was placed on the object stand, indoors (*A*), and rendered in mass shading as fully and accurately as possible. (Some of the background tone was omitted, however.) The light was coming downward from the left, the lightest spot on the sphere being at *a* where the rays hit most directly. From this point, the tone darkened very gradually in every direction as the surface curved away, forming graded shade tones on those areas turned somewhat from the light. Because the sphere intercepted light rays which otherwise would have reached the supporting table, the sphere cast a definite shadow upon the table.

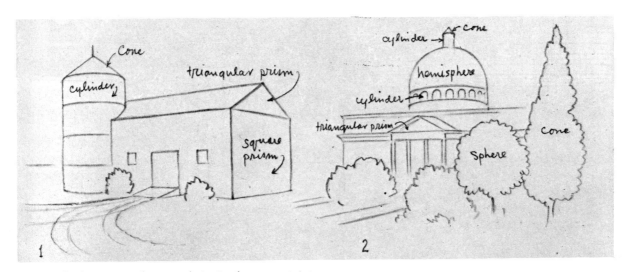

Fig. 19. *Reduce your subjects to their simplest geometric terms.*

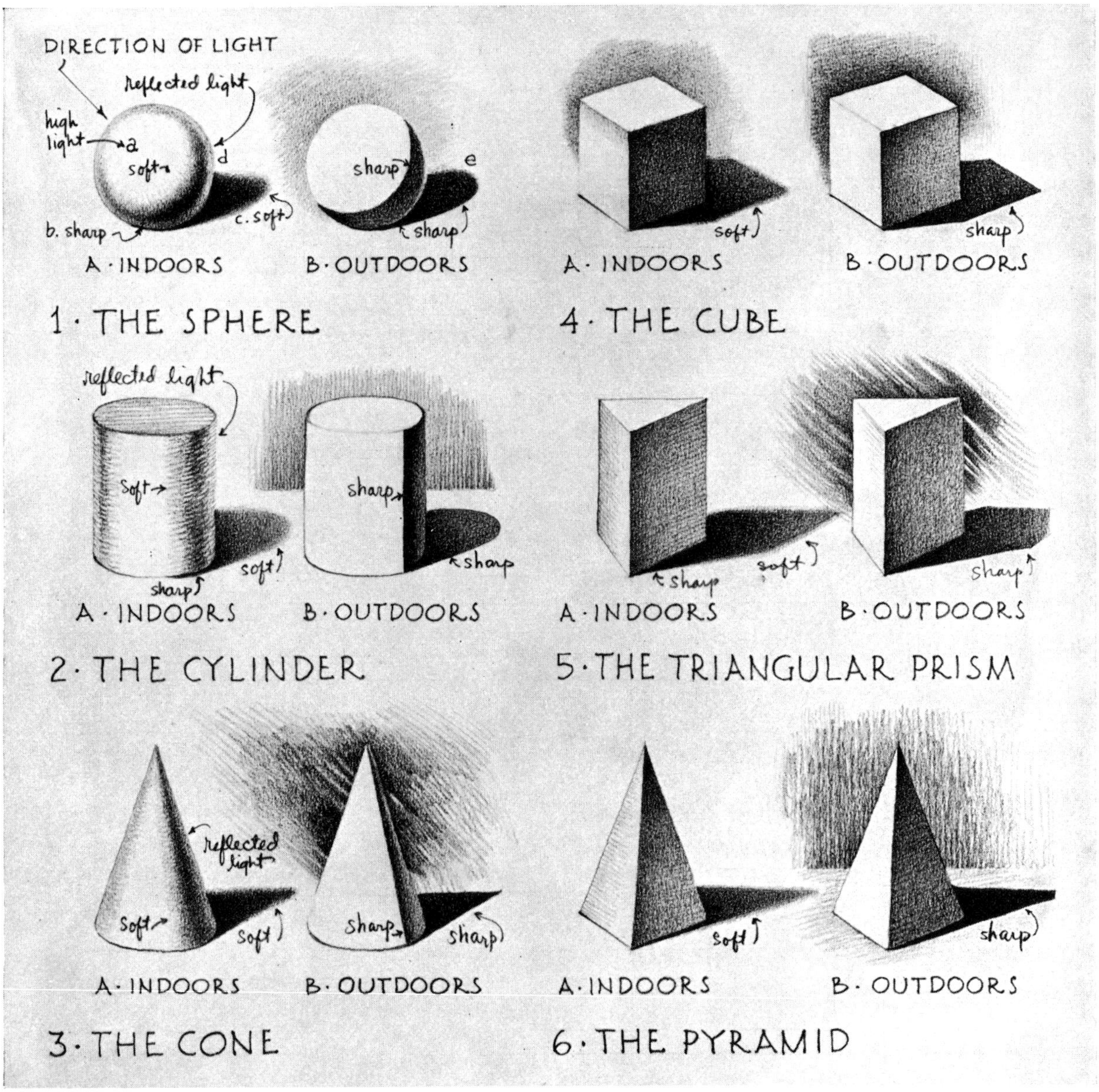

DIRECTION OF LIGHT
reflected light
high light
a
soft
d
b. sharp
c. soft

A · INDOORS   B · OUTDOORS
sharp
e
sharp

1 · THE SPHERE

reflected light
soft
sharp
soft
sharp

A · INDOORS   B · OUTDOORS

2 · THE CYLINDER

A · INDOORS   B · OUTDOORS
soft
sharp

4 · THE CUBE

sharp
soft
sharp

A · INDOORS   B · OUTDOORS

5 · THE TRIANGULAR PRISM

reflected light
soft
soft
sharp
sharp

A · INDOORS   B · OUTDOORS

3 · THE CONE

soft
sharp

A · INDOORS   B · OUTDOORS

6 · THE PYRAMID

Fig. 20. First master the simple forms. After this, other shapes will be easy.

At B we have a drawing of the same sphere placed in bright sunlight outdoors. The subtleties of surface shading are now lost. Note the distinct division between light and shade areas.

Shadow Edges

Note in 1, Fig. 20, in the drawing of the sphere at A, that when it is placed indoors, the shadow edges are sharp at b, where they are near the object, and softer at c, where the increased distance has allowed the light to become somewhat diffused. Now compare the sphere at B, placed in strong outdoor light. Here all shadow edges are relatively sharp (though diffraction has caused a slight softening at the most distant point e). This comparison reinforces a previous statement that, whether the object is indoors or out, the effect of light on its edges will vary according to the amount, intensity, and direction of the light.

Reflected Light

In the drawing at A, observe at d that light from the supporting surface is thrown back (reflected) onto the underside of the sphere. This reflection modifies the shade tone in a graded manner, which increases the effect of surface curvature. We have already seen that such reflections of light from one surface to another are common in nature. The apple at 1, Fig. 36, has a similar reflection. In fact, the apple is quite like the sphere except for the addition of its local color. The bottle at 1, Fig. 21, also exhibits reflected light, as do many of the other objects throughout the book.

To dramatize for yourself the influence of reflected light, take a large sheet of white paper or cardboard and, turning it toward a bright window, walk about your room, reflecting light into the dark corners from the paper. Or, if you wish, substitute a mirror. The effect may be even more dramatic. You can actually obliterate shadow tones if you reflect sufficient light into them; normally, you can only soften them.

Try, also, to prove to yourself that highly polished surfaces—such as those of shiny metal—act like mirrors to catch images (often distorted) of surrounding objects. When you render these pol-

ished surfaces, you will commonly picture (or indicate) at least the most prominent of their reflections. We shall say more about this in Chapter 17.

The Cylinder and Sphere

At 2, Fig. 20, we have substituted a cylinder for the sphere, while at 3, a cone serves as model. Note in these the shadow edges, the gradation of surface tone, the reflected light.

Squared Forms

At 4, 5, and 6, in Fig. 20, we see the cube, triangular prism, and pyramid. These drawings strengthen an earlier point: that tone relationships are more simple in flat-sided objects than in curved. Many tones are uniform throughout, or nearly so, rather than graded.

Draw These Objects

All the words in the world are of less value in this connection than a few hours of practice in drawing from actual objects with your own pencils. You may now like to try drawing some simple geometric solids. (Perhaps you would prefer to wait until you have read the next few chapters.)

In your selection of objects, an egg or a white rubber ball can be your model for rounded forms; a cardboard box can serve as a squared form. Pyramids, cones, and prisms can easily be made from white cardboard. But don't limit yourself to models that are white. As we advised in opening the chapter, try light and dark, dull and shiny things too.

Controlled Lighting

Inasmuch as light, shade, and shadow play so large a part in the appearance of objects, the artist, in posing the living model, or in "setting up" the still life, experiments with all sorts of lighting arrangements. Light, in other words, can be considered as an element of design. You use it consciously for creating the finest possible arrangement of tonal areas.

1. Quick, crisp strokes for shiny objects, with strong contrasts and sudden changes of tone

2. Quick strokes for smooth water. Slowly drawn strokes for stones (soft pencil)

3. Stonework should usually look rough, with many stones casting shadows into joints

4. Several pencils were here used

5. Basketry calls for special handling

6. Trees demand great variety of technique

Fig. 21. In nature you will find the key to texture treatment.

Therefore, even if your task is as simple as the rendering of a cube or a cylinder, once your object is in place, you should experiment by lighting it from different angles and with lights of diversified intensities. Try lighting it from two sides, or from two or more sources of illumination on the one side. Your task is much like that of the photographer who often takes great pains in order to create exactly the lighting effect he desires.

When working outdoors, of course, you can't arrange the lighting to your will, so, if your task is important, you must have the patience to wait until the subject is lit to full advantage. Most outdoor subjects are more attractively illuminated in early morning or late afternoon than when the sun is directly overhead.

The contrast of light against dark or dark against light gives subjects much of their appeal. No subject shows to best advantage in the full glare of light from several directions; the objects look flat and lifeless, wholly uninspiring to draw.

Texture Representation

We have repeatedly seen that the artist has to reckon with the textures of objects. If you want your work to be convincing, you must not only correctly picture forms and local values (the latter as influenced by light and shade), but you must make plain whether the objects are smooth or rough, dull or shiny. It will be a part of your job to learn to represent the textures of things as diversified as glass, wood, fur, stone, water, cloth, leather, foliage, feathers, clouds, and human flesh. When you draw a stone wall it must seem heavy and solid; foliage must appear yielding; water must give an impression of wetness and, as a rule, of mobility; clouds must look soft and ethereal. A part of your success in all of this will depend on how well you handle your textures. Try to become texture-conscious even before undertaking your first serious drawings.

Realistic Textures

There can be no definite rules for texture representation. As in so many other things, you must learn almost wholly through your own observation and experimentation. We can, however, toss out a few hints. For instance, if everything in your subject is rough, you may decide to work on rough paper; or you may use soft pencils, knowing their tendency to form granular tone. If, on the other hand, the surfaces to be represented are smooth and glassy, smoother paper or harder pencils may be in order. For mirrorlike surfaces, quickly drawn strokes such as those used for the glass at 1 and in the water at 2, Fig. 21, have merit. Hesitant, slowly drawn strokes, on the contrary, are better for portraying rough surfaces, as in the stonework at 3 and the old felt hat at 4.

Often several quite different surfaces in the same subject call for correspondingly diversified handlings. In 2, for example, see what a different treatment was used for rendering the rough stone from that selected for the calm, smooth water. Occasionally a special point on your pencil proves of help. For the basket at 5, clean-cut strokes made with a squared point quite satisfactorily suggest the woven texture of the basketry. The tree at 6, on the other hand, exhibited such differences of effect in its fine twigs, larger branches, and the rough bark of its trunk, that it called for a variety of points.

Later, when we deal with representative drawing at greater length, we shall see additional ways of indicating textures, but before we reach that discussion, you can profit from studying all sorts of surfaces in nature, trying to imagine how you would represent them with your pencil.

Decorative Textures

The use of textured tone is not limited to realistic representations. The artist sometimes imparts to a given area a certain amount of texture merely because it is pleasing to make that area more decorative or otherwise more interesting. Tones such as those used in our drawings of geometric solids (Fig. 20), for instance, are far less exciting to view (or to do) than are many others found scattered throughout the book. Turn the pages with this in mind.

Fig. 22. First locate the main points in your drawing.

Fig. 23. The second sheet of paper should be laid over the first for retracing.

Fig. 24. Correct, refine, and add more detail to your drawing.

Fig. 25. Now you are ready for the final rendering.

5.
Methods of Construction

Progression with your work, from initial drawing to finished rendering, is accomplished in a variety of ways. This chapter will explore these possible methods.

Tracing Paper Method

More and more teachers of freehand drawing have turned to tracing paper as an aid in constructing proportions. For this purpose, the paper should be quite transparent; it is most convenient in pad form—9x12"/23x30 cm is a handy size. Select a surface that takes the pencil well.

As soon as you are seated, open the pad near the center and snap on a clothespin or rubberband (see Fig. 22) to hold the paper in place. On the exposed sheet, sketch the main construction lines. Inasmuch as moisture—such as perspiration from the hand—sometimes buckles tracing paper badly (because of its extreme thinness), always keep extra paper under your hand.

Now comes the first difference between this and the other methods described. When you are ready to go to the second stage, instead of erasing as a preliminary to later drawing, merely lower a fresh sheet of tracing paper over the first (Fig. 23). (That, of course, is the reason for working near the center of the pad.) Begin tracing the main lines, improving them as you trace.

When you have transferred to your second sheet all that is needed from the first, tear out the first, or shove a sheet of bristol board or heavy paper between the two to prevent incorrect or superfluous lines from showing through to confuse you.

Now carry the second study as far as you like, next lowering a third sheet into position and repeating the process of correcting, refining, and adding more detail (Fig. 24). Make as many studies as required—normally three or four—until at last, after little if any erasure, and with a minimum of effort, you arrive at as perfect a layout as you are capable of making.

Studies for Values

If the final drawing is to be in line only, you are now ready to go ahead with it, as described in Chapter 7. Most pencil drawings, however, are in tone. For these, studies of the values of light and dark are usually made before the actual rendering is started on the final paper. Tracing paper is perfect for such studies. It is easy to make several, one over the other, comparing the results to learn how next to proceed.

Other Uses of the Tracing Paper Method

Even the final drawing, whether in outline or light and shade, can be made on tracing paper, providing it has a suitable surface (Fig. 25). When completed, such a drawing may be attached to heavier paper or cardboard by means of tape.

One unique advantage of tracing paper—especially in making studies—is that you can look through it from the back, defects becoming particularly evident when seen in reverse. (A similar effect can be obtained by reflecting any drawing—and the subject, too—in a mirror, a fault-revealing practice often utilized by professionals and described earlier.)

Another use of tracing paper (for application in more advanced work) is this: You can recompose your subject matter by tracing one portion from

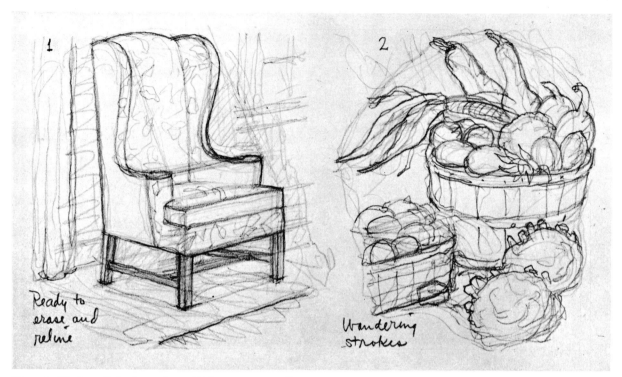

Fig. 26. "Feel out" the forms by scribbling very casually on your paper.

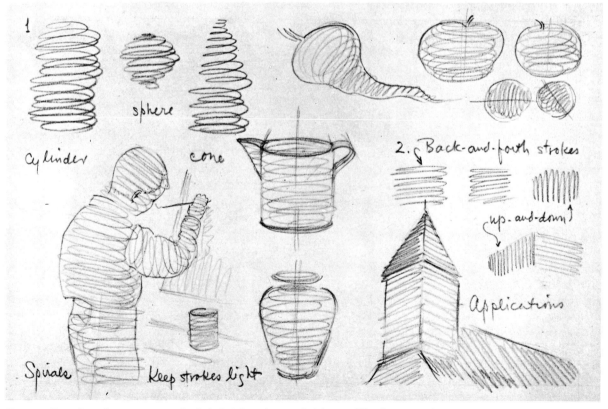

Fig. 27. Spiral strokes are particularly helpful with rounded forms. The drawings here could be developed further on tracing paper.

an original sketch, next sliding the tracing paper along and tracing another portion, and so on. Or you may trace from several sketches. For example, you may trace a tree from one sketch, a house from a second, and a roadway from a third. You must make allowances, of course, for any errors of perspective or scale which may develop. In fact, considerable skill may be required to bring such elements from different sources into close harmony.

The Scribble Method

While there is much to recommend the orderly step-by-step method of laying out the proportions of the subject, you will find that as you gain increased facility, you can quickly and accurately make your layout directly upon the final paper merely by utilizing a few light dots and dashes—or extremely delicate lines—carefully placed to locate the essential proportions.

In one approach (sometimes substituted for those already presented), the artist "feels out" the subject by scribbling away on the paper somewhat casually until, through the use of wandering strokes, he obtains at least a rough semblance of the subject. (See Fig. 26.) In this process, you keep your eye on the subject much of the time, shooting an occasional quick glance at the drawing. With the proportions reasonably well located, your next move is to darken lines here and there to define the forms with greater accuracy, after which you resort to the eraser—kneaded rubber is good—in order to obliterate the incorrect and superfluous lines. (Occasionally, these first free lines are left to show faintly in the final result.) Unless you can now discover errors in proportion that need attention, you are ready to render. This you can do on your original paper (unless it has been damaged by too much pressure), or you may transfer the proportions to a fresh sheet as described later in this chapter.

The Spiral Method

One objection made to all of the foregoing methods of constructing drawings in outline alone is that the forms may have a tendency to look flat,

lacking a sense of bulk or solidity. For this reason, some artists prefer to construct their proportions through the aid of quickly formed spiral strokes like those in Fig. 27. Strokes such as these are especially helpful when rounded forms are involved—fruit and vegetables, animals and people. Where they are not adaptable, quick back-and-forth strokes (see 2, Fig. 27) can often take their place, though these are less expressive of bulk.

No instruction seems necessary beyond stressing the obvious: layouts utilizing this method are usually made very quickly, the spirals (or the back-and-forth strokes) drawn with extreme freedom. If the first layout is not entirely satisfactory, tracing paper overlays permit you to make as many more as may be needed, one on top of the other. With the basic forms satisfactory, still another overlay sketch can be done, omitting all but the essential lines. After this, shading proceeds in the usual way; the best direction of stroke to express the form can often be determined by referring to the preliminary sketches with their spirals and back-and-forth strokes.

Tone Method

A final method of constructing the subject—the tone method—is by no means common, but one of occasional value.

Now and then there are students who have difficulty seeing form as surrounded by outline. Instead, they see each area of the subject as a tone of a certain shape. It is natural for them to try to interpret each such tonal shape by means of a pencil area of like shape. Outline to them is confusing and unnatural.

A soft pencil, especially if bluntly pointed, will serve fairly well for creating these areas. Pencils with oversize leads are still better, while another excellent instrument is the square crayon, pictured in Fig. 223. Crayons of this type come in graphite, carbon, wax, etc. Held on the side, they can cover ground amazingly fast. (See Fig. 28.) The end of the crayon can be used for finer detail.

With the proportions blocked out, a sheet of tracing paper lowered over the rough layout will permit corrections either in tone or line.

Fig. 28. Side strokes produce effects such as these very rapidly.

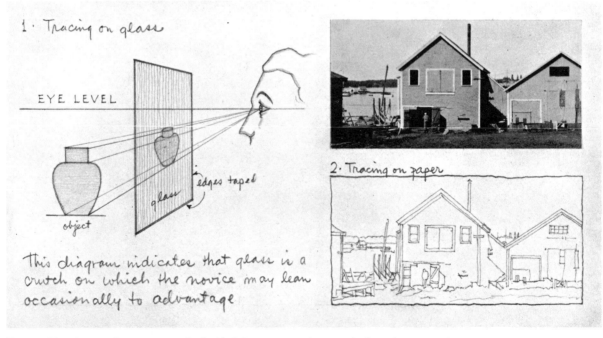

Fig. 29. Tracing on glass is one method of helping you perceive certain facts in perspective.

In addition to helping you construct forms, these tonal studies will aid you in planning value schemes for finished work. Even if you prefer to construct your subject matter in outline, it will still pay you (as earlier mentioned) to make trial value studies as an approach to rendering. And for this, the square stick has real advantages.

Tracing on Glass

For the student who has unusual difficulty in proportions, a few hours' practice in making tracings on glass may help in clarifying the relationship between natural appearances and methods of pictorial representation.

If you stand facing a china closet or dish cupboard that has glass doors, and close one eye, and then take a lithographic pencil or marking pencil, you can trace on the glass the form of some dish inside. This tracing will be a correct drawing of the dish as it appears from that particular point. Of course, it is rather difficult to draw comfortably in this way, for it is not easy to maintain the same position throughout the work. Nor is it easy, unless your hand is well trained, to follow the outline with sufficient accuracy to produce a perfect drawing. (Not that there would be any particular advantage in being able to do so!) But students who have difficulty perceiving or understanding certain facts in perspective can sometimes find help by using glass, making sure that it is at right angles to the line of sight from the eye to the object. You can also sketch on a windowpane, drawing buildings, trees or any other stationary objects visible through the glass.

Occasional use of this method (shown in Fig. 29) may help the beginner, but there is another far more valuable use to which glass may be put as a drawing surface. Place a sheet of glass on the easel or drawing table as a substitute for the usual paper, with a sheet of paper or white cloth beneath so the glass lines will be plainly visible when they are drawn. Then sketch the objects on the glass with the marking or lithographic pencil just as you would block them in with pencil on paper. When the main proportions are drawn as accurately as possible, raise the glass to such a position

that the drawing comes between the eye and the objects drawn, using one eye only. When the glass has been shifted to just the proper position, the lines of the drawing should coincide with those of the object. This method is therefore an excellent test for accuracy. If errors are noted, return the glass to the table and erase the incorrect lines with a damp cloth. Make the necessary corrections and test again in the same way as before. Repeat the process as often as necessary. When the proportions are right, wash off the drawing and try a new one of a different subject.

There is perhaps no way the beginner can better learn to see mistakes and acquire a knowledge of foreshortening than this. Glass is especially recommended to those who are unable to work with a teacher.

Testing Your Construction

Constructing the subject is usually the student's toughest problem. But there are no shortcuts to success; progress comes only through hard practice. As you gradually learn to observe what you see correctly, you simultaneously develop the skill to record it faithfully.

While in the long run you must depend on your own eye for judging the accuracy of your construction—it is by far your most reliable guide— here are a few simple aids that may sometimes help. First, if you are troubled about how nearly vertical a certain line in a subject may be, the carpenter's plumbline (1, Fig. 30) can prove of value. Similarly, if you want to judge how nearly horizontal some line in the subject is, you can sight across the top of a carpenter's level (2) at the line in question. A common way to estimate the slant of a line is to hold a pencil to the same slant (3), preferably keeping one eye closed.

Thumb Measurement

Sometimes your pencil is used as a measuring stick (4). It is held vertically (point down) at arm's length between eye and object. With one eye closed, the top of the pencil is brought to coincide with a salient upper point of the object. Then,

Fig. 30. There are several methods by which you can check your construction for accuracy.

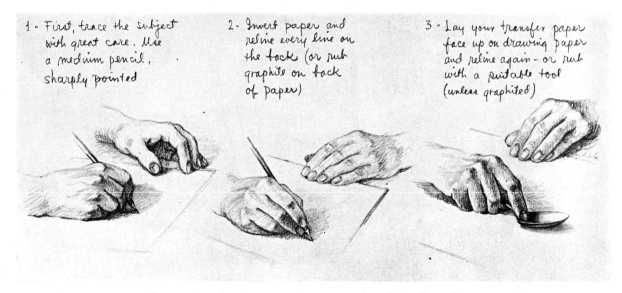

Fig. 31. Proportions may be transferred to fresh paper. First trace the subject, then reline, and then transfer.

with the pencil kept in this position, the thumb is slid down until the nail marks some other vital point. With the pencil now measuring an important vertical dimension, the arm is rotated, pencil and all, to permit a comparison of the measurement just taken with some horizontal or slanting dimension. Similarly, any other dimensions of the object may be compared. Corresponding comparisons on the drawing are then made by eye.

Making a Transfer

When you construct your work directly upon bristol board or drawing paper, you sometimes make so many necessary erasures (or damage the surface in other ways) that it becomes next to impossible to do a really good final rendering upon it. In this circumstance, the correct proportions can easily be transferred to a fresh sheet. (Such a transfer may also be in order if you use the tracing paper method of construction and decide not to make the final rendering on tracing paper.)

Here is the common method:

1. Trace the subject: Hold a sheet of tracing paper firmly over the work to be transferred. With a sharply pointed medium pencil—HB, perhaps—trace every detail with the utmost care. (See 1, Fig. 31.) (If your final construction drawing is already on tracing paper, this initial move is obviously unnecessary and you may start directly with Step 2.)

2. Reline: Turn your tracing paper over (face down) and, with a medium or soft pencil, sharply pointed, reline each line (2)—or, rub graphite on your paper wherever any lines show through.

3. Transfer: Place your tracing paper, prepared as described, right side up on your selected drawing paper and, holding it firmly, reline each line with a well sharpened medium-hard pencil. This will make a perfect transfer. (Unless you have chosen to place graphite on the back of your transfer paper, you may merely rub its face with a knife handle, spoon or other suitable instrument—the lines on the back will make a reasonably perfect imprint on the drawing paper.) You are now ready to render.

(Don't use ordinary carbon typing paper for transfers. It will ruin your work.)

Fig. 32. *The simplest outline is one of uniform weight.*

Fig. 33. *Notice the graded strokes in this varied outline.*

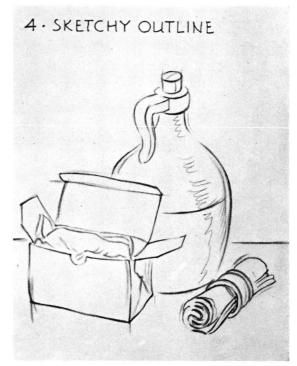

Fig. 34. *Notice the hint of shading in the accented outline.*

Fig. 35. *A sketchy outline, very quickly drawn.*

6.
Rendering Techniques

Whatever method you may follow in constructing your subject, you will soon be ready to "render" it—to make the final lines or tones on which the ultimate effect will depend. In the following chapters we will proceed to actual problems in drawing, but this chapter is a good place to review the various methods of rendering.

Outline Technique

The simplest and most direct type of rendering—and one for which the pencil is ideal—is outline. In nature there is no outline. One object is distinguished from another only because of contrasts of color or tone. (Some narrow bands of tone—shadows in cracks, for instance—may appear as lines, but obviously they are not true outlines.) When the artist uses outline to interpret the various elements of subjects he is therefore resorting to a man-made convention. It is a very natural convention, however—primitive people relied on it, apparently instinctively, as do children today. And outline is as expressive and as easy to use as it is natural.

Uniform Outline

Of the several kinds of outlines, the simplest is shown in Fig. 32, where all objects and their main subdivisions have been bounded by lines of a single width and weight. An F pencil was used.

Interesting effects may frequently be obtained by using uniform outlines of two or more weights or widths. The leading object or objects, for example, may be outlined with dark or wide lines, and less important (or more distant) objects with lighter or finer lines.

Varied Outline

Still more often, the artist varies the line from point to point in both width *and* value, making it as expressive as possible of the different parts of his subject matter. (See Fig. 33.)

Accented Outline

Whether outline is uniform or varied, added accents of solid black may prove effective, as appears in Fig. 34.

Outlines need by no means be continuous. They are often far more expressive if broken here and there, suggesting, rather than fully delineating, parts of the subject. Frequently, as in Fig. 34, whole stretches of line can be omitted without harm; the spectator's eye will supply them.

Sketchy Outline

Extremely free, sketchy outline has its virtues, too. (See Fig. 35.) Though this kind of line may give the impression of having been dashed in with great speed, this is not always the case.

Outline and Tone

Often the artist uses outline for part of the subject and tone for the rest. Combinations of this sort are endless. The tone may be in solid flat areas of gray or black; it may be uniformly graded; or it may be freely drawn. There is no rule.

Why not turn through the pages of this book, and hunt up pencil drawings elsewhere, in order to discover how many types of outlines you can find? Copy bits of drawings here and there. Your

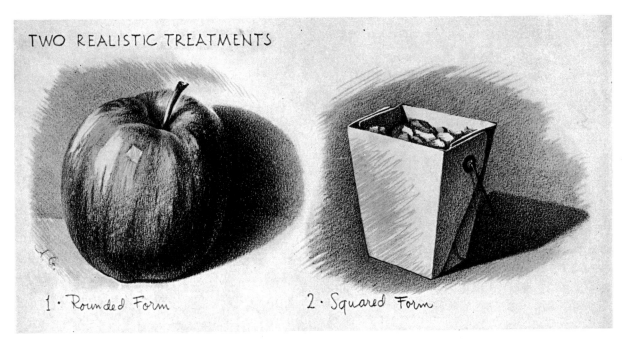

Fig. 36. In a realistic treatment the artist renders, by means of "mass" or allover shading, every visible tone in the subject.

purpose at the moment is (1) to learn of all possible types and (2) to become familiar with how artists utilize them in rendering numerous kinds of subject matter. Try a number of drawings of each of the accompanying types, varying your subject matter, grade of pencil, and kind of point. Do some on tracing paper placed over your construction layout, and others on regular drawing paper.

In all of this, remember that basic form is more important than outline.

Mass Shading Technique

Valuable though outline is, most pencil drawings are "toned" or "shaded." Of the various methods of toning or shading, perhaps the most natural for the beginner's first use is what might be called the realistic or photographic method. In this, the artist renders, by means of "mass" or all-over shading, every visible tone in the subject as literally as possible in black, gray, and white alone—i.e., without using color. The illustrations at 1 and 2, Fig. 36, fall into this category though, in these, the white paper is allowed to represent certain extremely light values in the subject—a liberty the pencil artist frequently takes.

After you have made a number of these realistic

drawings—they require painstaking handling, with considerable reliance on the sharp point— you will gradually discover that it is not only far quicker, but often more effective (and certainly more characteristic of the medium) to use your pencil with somewhat greater freedom, allowing many of the individual strokes to count strongly enough so that the drawings frankly reveal their pencil origin. (We shall deal with this kind of work later.)

Yet no matter how far you may eventually wander from the type of realistic drawings reproduced at 1 and 2 in Fig. 36, we recommend that you make some of these too, not only because it involves excellent training in learning to observe accurately the different tones and textures in nature, but for the added reason that the mere drill of attempting to fill each area with the proper tone will in itself give you a good start towards technical mastery of the pencil.

Broad Line Technique

We now come to what might be called typical pencil drawings—those done with the blunt points shown in 2 and 3, Fig. 8. In this broad line work, some of the individual strokes are often plainly visible, so that the finished drawing frankly reveals its pencil origin. Yet there is no striving for effect; you honestly attempt to represent each form and texture by using the kind and direction of stroke which seems best adapted to your purpose.

The danger of this technique is that the lines may become *too* conspicuous, detracting from the general effect. Try to avoid this.

Translating Tone into Line

If you already have some drawings utilizing mass shading, place tracing paper over each of them, and, with a blunt point try to translate your values into tones that have linear characteristics. Don't be satisfied with your first results; make a number of trial drawings for comparison.

One vital question is how to determine the most natural and pleasing direction for your lines. There are no fixed rules, but it is always logical to strive for directions that will best express the forms and textures of each object. Most objects offer hints. See how, in the drawing of the book in Fig. 37 the edges of the leaves gave the cue for stroke direction at that point, while the slant of the cover suggested correspondingly sloping lines there. Vertical surfaces can generally be well expressed with vertical strokes or, if the planes are foreshortened, by means of lines converging to the vanishing point of each plane. (We will discuss vanishing points in greater detail in Chapter 9 on freehand perspective.)

In drawing buildings, the courses of clapboards, shingles, stone, and brick, often supply the key. In outdoor work, some strokes—perhaps those in the shadows—can take the same direction as the rays of light. Therefore, before rendering each subject, determine this direction. For curved surfaces, curved strokes are recommended; straight strokes tend to make curved surfaces look flat. In rendering growing things—plants, grass, tree trunks, leaves, fruit, vegetables—the strokes may often follow the direction of growth.

By trying different treatments of the same subject on your tracing paper, you will find that most surfaces can be rendered effectively by any of several stroke arrangements. Occasionally, strokes in two directions overlap to form crosshatch.

Avoid stiff, mannered handling. Usually quite a bit of variety is desirable, not only in stroke direction, but in the length and quality of the stroke as well. You now have the quadruple task of representing simultaneously the correct value, surface form, and texture, while creating a pleasing technical result.

Another factor to keep in mind is that right-handed and left-handed people cannot easily swing the pencil in the same directions. You can generally tell whether a drawing was done by a right-handed or a left-handed artist.

Fig. 37 reproduces typical broad stroke applications. The lead for these was first pointed as at 1 or 2, Fig. 8, and then allowed to wear naturally. Occasionally, a sharper or blunter point was substituted. Note that some of the lead degrees have been indicated on the drawings. These broad leads, by the way, are especially appropriate for large areas—they cover ground quickly.

Fine Line Technique

There are certain subjects in nature so delicate in detail that they cannot always be rendered successfully with broad pencil lines. Take the bare branches of trees in winter, for example, or the masts and rigging of sailing ships. Many architectural subjects, too, and numerous forms of ornament may demand fine strokes because of their intricacy. Obviously, it would be silly to try to interpret these things with a blunt pencil when a sharp lead can perform a much better job. (Never, in fact, should an artist "force" any media to do what it cannot naturally do.)

The use of the sharp point is not confined, however, to subjects demanding fine lines. The artist often turns to it through choice, for it creates effects which are otherwise unobtainable. Without question, the fine point permits far more individuality of style than the broad. And even when used for expressing a subject which could just as well be treated in broad line or solid tone (as at 5, Fig. 38), the observer s sense of fitness is in no way disturbed.

Fine line technique does have limitations. When large areas are to be covered with tone, the

Different textures demand different treatments

Fig. 37. Here are some drawings, slightly reduced in reproduction, achieved with a broad line technique using bluntly pointed pencils.

Fig. 38. These drawings were obtained with a fine line technique using sharply pointed pencils.

Fig. 39. A variety of techniques employed in a single drawing can produce very pleasing effects.

sharp point is discouragingly slow because of the constant sharpening required and the hundreds of lines to be made. And, in any drawing, big or small, the sharp point can prove dangerous, for the artist may become so involved in the mere manual task of producing a multitude of strokes that the final result is fussy or labored, or a self-conscious display of linework. In short, never forget that it's always a question of choosing the right pencil—and method—for the task at hand.

Start your fine line practice realizing that, inasmuch as fine line shading is fundamentally linear in character, the manner of producing each individual stroke and the arrangement of these strokes to form tone are even more important than in broad linework. As soon as you have carried out a fair amount of line and tone practice such as recommended in Chapter 3, attempt some fine line experiments on tracing paper placed over drawings previously rendered in mass shading. Or, for that matter, you can put thin tracing paper over suitable photographs, seeing how well you can render, by fine line alone, the photographic tones showing through. Also scrutinize many pencil drawings by other artists to learn how they have solved similar problems. You may want to copy occasional passages from these (or portions of pen drawings, etchings, or other linear work).

Combined Techniques

Helpful as it is to concentrate on each of several techniques, eventually you will probably prefer freer approaches, perhaps combining two or more techniques in a single drawing. (See Fig. 39.)

Occasionally, the subject itself dictates how such techniques should be combined, as it has in Fig. 40. If certain areas are large and unbroken, with rather smooth textures, broad linework or mass shading may be best for them. If other areas call for fine detail or complex textures, fine line may be the thing. In the case of landscapes or marines, where certain elements are in the foreground and others more distant, broad lines can logically be used in the foreground, medium lines in the middle distance, and fine lines at the horizon. Another similar subject, on the other hand, may be treated in reverse, the distance being represented in solid tone or broad lines, and the foreground, with its greater amount of visible detail, in fine lines.

So there are no rules. When you have blocked out a subject, make studies on tracing paper, experimenting with what seem like sensible and pleasing dispositions of fine line, broad line, and tone. Then proceed with your final drawing, confident that you can develop a unified one.

Fig. 40. These sketches use a mixed technique; broad line, fine line, and tone have been employed to suit the subject.

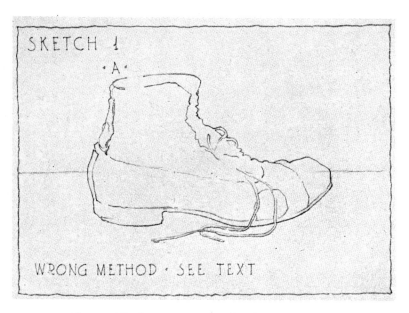

Fig. 41. The beginner often makes the mistake of beginning at one point and completing the entire outline as he proceeds.

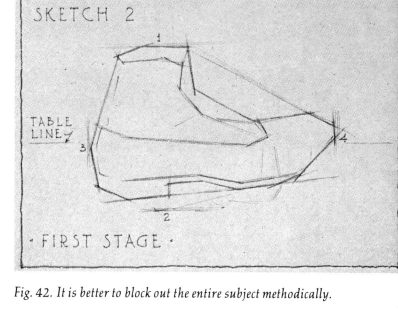

Fig. 42. It is better to block out the entire subject methodically.

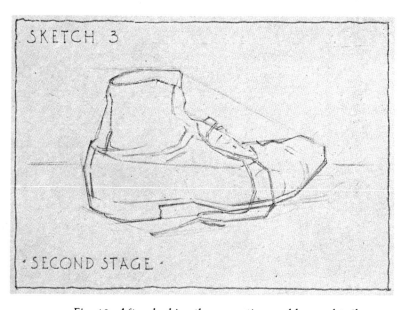

Fig. 43. After checking the proportions, add more details, retaining the larger characteristics as well.

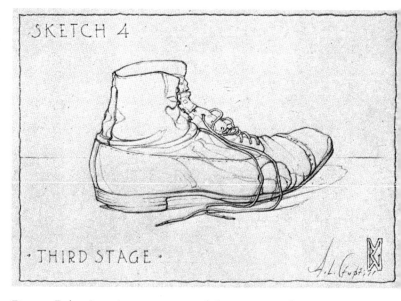

Fig. 44. Relax for a few moments, and then return to the drawing, refining the details.

7.
Object Drawing in Outline

Perhaps we have been getting ahead of our story, for until the novice has learned to lay out his subjects well, there is little point in discussions of light and shade, textures, and technique. Let's consider a specific problem—a still life—and render it in a specific way. It is advisable for the beginner to start with simple objects, drawing each one over and over again, attempting to memorize the shapes so that they may be sketched at any time without reference to the object itself. You will be helped greatly if—along with this practice—you study the principles of perspective as applied to freehand work. For this, refer to Chapter 9, which deals directly with this phase of the subject.

When you have become thoroughly acquainted with the appearance and methods of representing objects, the next step is to apply this knowledge to drawing objects with greater variety of form, surface, and color, such everyday things as books, dishes, fruit, or old shoes.

Here you may ask why it is essential to know how to draw books, for "what have books to do with sketching anything?" But, indirectly, they and similar objects have much to offer. Aside from the skill gained from their study (directly applicable to larger problems), you also quickly learn how to express all sorts of textures by trying to draw these small items, which are easily seen as complete units by the eye. Once you have learned to show the leather of shoes, the glass or porcelain of dishes, and the cloth, metal, or wood of other objects, it is not difficult to represent brick, stone, shingles, slate, and other complex subjects. Columns, balusters, and similar architectural forms also have much the same play of light and shade

and gradation of tone as is found on dishes and similar objects. It is much easier to draw from small items, near at hand, than from features like columns usually so large that a confusing amount of detail proves troublesome to the beginner.

Selecting the Subject

First set up your working space as described in Chapter 2. Once this equipment has been assembled and arranged, we can select our first subject and start to draw.

Select some simple object with which you are already quite familiar, something small enough so that it can be seen easily at a glance, and yet large enough so that little effort is required to see it. It should have a certain amount of individuality or distinctive character rather than mere prettiness. One of the first things to learn is how to analyze the subject to determine its leading characteristics, and record them on paper with a few deft strokes. It should be a simple color, too, for·you have enough to occupy your attention if the colors are few and these few not too brilliant and distracting. To meet these requirements, common, everyday objects are often best. Geometric forms may also be desirable, but because these will be especially considered in Chapter 9 on freehand perspective, we will use objects having less regularity or symmetry of form, such as old shoes or dishes. Bear in mind, however, when you read the chapter on perspective, that much here relates also to the representation of geometric forms.

So let us start with an old shoe, an object that provides both variety in shape and marked individuality.

Beginning the Work

Now that our equipment is arranged and our subject selected, we are nearly ready to begin. First place the shoe on the object stand in a natural position, with the light falling upon it in an interesting way (though the lighting is less important for outline work than for the later shaded studies). Thumbtack a sheet of paper about 11x15"/ 28x38cm or larger, to your drawing board, remembering that if several additional sheets are placed beneath the drawing, the surface will be better. Sharpen a medium soft pencil, such as an HB, to a fairly sharp point, and place your chair and easel in a comfortable position, one that provides both a clear view of the object and good light on the paper.

When you are seated, there are certain things to be decided before touching pencil to the paper. Determine what sort of a drawing you are about to make. Is it to be in outline or in black and white? Is it to be a rough sketch or a carefully finished study? Will you try to accurately represent the subject as you see it, every spot and line, every infinitesimal detail that you can discover on close search? Or are you going to work more for the general impression? As a rule, it seems best for the beginner to confine early attempts to outline, getting the main proportions as accurate as possible, seeking to bring out in his sketch the individual characteristics of the object. If the drawing is to be of a shoe, let the drawing represent that particular shoe and not some other.

I remember my own experience with my first drawing. It was in the studio of Albert E. Moore at Portland, Maine. The drawing materials had been prepared and I was eagerly waiting to see what the subject was to be. And then it was brought out— an old, ragged felt hat. And a block of wood a few inches or centimeters long, and 2 or 3"/5 to 7cm high. And that was all. The hat was raised at one side on the block and arranged to form an interesting composition. Then the work was started, the directions being to make an outline drawing of that hat, expressing its individuality, getting right at the essentials, considering the whole thing in a big way. A half hour later, the drawing was

finished, quite perfectly, I felt, an improvement on the original in every way. And then came Mr. Moore! In the light of later understanding, his patience seems truly remarkable. He pointed out how the drawing was wrong here and wrong there. In fact, though commendable for a first attempt, it was wrong in all its larger proportions, but especially how it failed to express the character of *that particular hat.* So the sheet was wiped clean and a new drawing made, and again, until the end of the morning found a somewhat discouraged youth whose pride in his newly acquired materials had received quite a setback. Finally after three or four halfdays' time, the drawing was finished (and what a feeling of satisfaction this accomplishment gave). This was simply the first of many similar studies, each of which increasingly emphasized the need for truthfully expressing the leading characteristics of the subject drawn.

Perhaps you are wondering just what is meant by "truthfully expressing the leading characteristics of the subject." Consider what a drawing is or should be. A drawing is simply an explanation. The best drawings are those that tell their story directly and simply, without confusing us with multitudinous and irrelevant details. Seldom does the artist attempt to tell in one drawing all the facts about the subject represented, but singles out the leading truths, the characteristics that appeal to him as the most valuable and interesting. Just as individuals differ from one another in their choice of clothes, so artists differ in their selection and interpretation of the characteristics of any subject.

The tiny details of nature are without number. If we study any object minutely we are almost overwhelmed with the small parts that close inspection reveals. When we glance at an object in the usual way, however, we are unaware of each tiny detail. Only when we focus our attention on one portion after another do we see the smallest of the visible parts at all. As you gradually develop your perceptions you will be able to choose what is essential according to the purpose of your drawing.

So the beginner must strive to retain in any subject the elements that have the greatest significance, in some cases even exaggerating them, and sacrificing at the same time some of the lesser truths, if this makes the drawing as a whole easier to read or understand.

The First Step

At this point you may be tempted to start your drawing at a particular point such as *A*, Fig. 4 (Sketch 1) at the top of the shoe, work down one side, completing the entire outline as you proceed, next going across the bottom and up the other side and finally back to the starting point. This method, although tempting, is a very difficult way to work. However careful you may be in drawing each small portion as you go along, the larger forms are almost sure to be wrong. Consequently, the smaller proportions are wrong, too, in relation to one another. Fig. 41 shows the result such a method is sure to bring. At first glance, this drawing may seem as correct and as interesting as the one in Fig. 44. Its chief fault, however, lies in its proportions: Fig. 44 (Sketch 4) gives the correct shape of the shoe as viewed from the one position from which it was drawn. If we start at point *A* and compare the contour of the shoe in Fig. 41, with that in Fig. 44, we find them much the same in detail, but not in proportion. That is the danger of the system; it leads us astray almost without our knowing it. When we begin to draw the sole and glance across at the heel we notice that the sole is too low, the sole and heel coming to a horizontal line. In Fig. 44, the sole is higher. Compare the height of the toe in the two sketches with the table line at the back; note that the height in Fig. 41 is too low. As we go to the top of the shoe, we find the ankle much larger in Fig. 41. Now in drawing a shoe, such inaccuracies are not entirely disastrous, but if the same method were applied to drawing a portrait, a correct likeness would surely fail to materialize.

So instead of working in the way shown in Fig. 41, attack the whole matter very methodically. As soon as the object is in place and the easel and chair in position, mark the location of the chair and the model stand on the floor in some way. A chalk mark around each leg of the easel and of the

chair will do very well. Otherwise, it is possible that some change will be made in their position. Even the slightest shift is often enough to prove very confusing and cause inaccurate results. Then when you sit on the chair, sit right in the middle and keep erect. This is most important. For if you shift a bit to one side or the other, or slump a bit, the object will present quite a different appearance (the change being particularly noticeable when drawing books, boxes, or other such shapes). So while you are working, hold the same position.

As an aid to remaining stationary, some instructors have the student sight across some mark or point along the top of the object stand to some coinciding mark on the wall. Sighting from the first point to the second point, the student thus establishes a position. If, at any time, the points are not in line, one behind the other, the student is out of position. The same marks will prove useful to the instructor when he sits to give criticism. He can view the objects from exactly the same point used by the student; in fact, if the instructor is of different height, it may be very difficult for him to assume the correct position. This system can help correct that.

Now study the object for a few minutes before starting to draw. Notice the general shape of the mass, forgetting the detail but considering the simple form. Compare the height with the width. Is the mass taller than it is wide or is the opposite true? Is the general form square, round, oval, or triangular? What are its most individual characteristics? Is it flat or rounded? Are its edges regular or irregular? Are the surfaces rough or smooth? When you have analyzed the subject with the greatest care, determine how large the drawing is to be and locate the extreme limits of the object on the paper. If the subject is higher than it is long, place the paper in a vertical position so that the picture space will be in proportion to the object (or objects). Usually the size of the drawing will be less than that of the subject itself. Place a light mark towards the top of the paper to locate the extreme limit of the drawing in that direction, next another for the same purpose at the bottom, followed by others at the sides. These marks are shown at points 1, 2, 3, and 4, Fig. 42 (Sketch 2). Next block out very lightly with a few sweeps of the pencil the larger proportions, the point barely touching the paper surface. Now set the drawing back near the objects. Compare. Is the height right in relation to the width? If it is hard to determine this, you may want to use a thumb measurement for checking (see Chapter 5).

It is not enough to compare the height of the object with its width, or the relative lengths of different lines as is done by the thumb measurement. The slant of the lines should also be studied to make sure they are pitched correctly. Hold the pencil at arm's length in such a position that it hides, or coincides with, some important line in the object. Then do the same with the same line on your drawing. Or hold the pencil vertically or horizontally and sight across it at some sloping line. Compare the angles formed by the various intersecting edges, too, and make corrections wherever necessary.

As soon as the main proportions have been properly established and the larger subdivisions blocked in and corrected, you have completed the first stage of your work, as illustrated in Fig. 42 (Sketch 2). At this time you have begun to express the larger characteristics or peculiarities of the subject.

The Second Step

In the next stage, pictured in Fig. 43 (Sketch 3), the larger parts are still further subdivided and more of the small details added. In this stage, too, place the drawing beside the subject several times for comparison. Here, as in the first stage, it is not necessary to erase all the construction lines or incorrect strokes unless they prove distracting. This second stage expresses the smaller or minor characteristics, retaining at the same time most of the larger. At this point, the drawing is really a construction diagram over which it is intended that you work.

Now, before going on to the third and last stage, illustrated in Fig. 44 (Sketch 4), get away from the work entirely for a few moments. In fact, it helps to rest your eye every fifteen minutes or half hour

by doing something else. You can even save time in the end if you go to the window and look out, or walk about a bit, forgetting the drawing completely. After a few minutes of relaxation, mistakes will usually be evident at the first glance and the brief respite will make it easier to resume and hold the correct position. This last item is important. Every time you take your seat you must be sure you are viewing the object from the right spot. The slightest difference in position will make a marked difference in its appearance.

In this last stage, remove all wrong or unnecessary lines. Then, with soft or kneaded rubber or art gum, also erase the *correct* lines until they are barely visible, showing just enough to provide a guide for the final relining. Give a great deal of thought to this last work, for the final line should not be perfect and mechanical but should express the shapes and textures represented. For some parts, the pencil will need a rather sharp point; for others, it must be quite blunt. Vary the pressure too. Certain lines should be so light and delicate that they are barely visible, while others will be bold and strong. In places, gradation will occur from light to dark or from dark to light. No rules can be given for obtaining satisfactory results; it is a matter of taste and feeling. But draw thoughtfully and observe carefully before you draw. This third stage expresses many of the smaller peculiarities of the subject, being a subdivision of the lines of the second stage, carefully refined, preserving, however, the big characteristics of the first stage.

Table Line

In order to make an object appear as if it is resting on something solid rather than merely floating in air, it is best to draw a horizontal line—often called a *table line*—which frequently represents the back of the object stand. This line gives some evidence of material support. If graded to a light value as it disappears behind the object or objects, the line will add also to the feeling of detachment and space. This line should never be just halfway between the margin lines. A second table line representing the front edge is sometimes advisable.

Margin Line

A freehand line drawn 1"/2.5cm or so from the edge of the paper all around, acts as a frame and adds to many compositions. Sometimes this line is carried only part way around, as at *A*, Fig. 51 (Sketch 7).

Study the Drawing

As soon as the sketch is completed, sign it with your name, date it, and indicate approximately the amount of time required from start to finish. Then spray the drawing with fixative, if you wish, or clip a piece of paper over it for protection and place it in your folio or some safe place for preservation. Don't make the mistake of destroying these early sketches, thinking they are of no value. Although they may not be beautiful pictures, it is often interesting and instructive to look them over later. Comparing a number of them done at different times shows just what progress has been or is being made.

When the sketch of the shoe is signed and laid to one side, select another similar subject and draw it in the same way, striving to truthfully express its individuality, as before. Proportion the object as you *see* it and not as you *think* it ought to be. There will be time enough to use your originality later on.

Marginal Notes or Sketches

When you select a subject for a drawing, it is often advisable to make a quick, tiny sketch of it on the margin of the paper before going ahead with the final drawing. A few minutes will do for such a marginal sketch or note, just enough time to allow for blocking in the larger proportions, the main lines of construction. When making this tiny sketch, observe the subject and acquaint yourself with it as preparation for the larger work. Figs. 53 to 55 show a number of these trial sketches.

Time Sketches

Time sketches are a valuable means of acquiring the skill to grasp and delineate the leading charac-

Fig. 45. A triangular composition is restful.

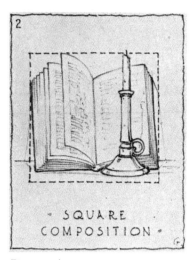

Fig. 46. A square composition is also satisfactory.

Fig. 47. With a circular composition, avoid having objects roll out of the picture.

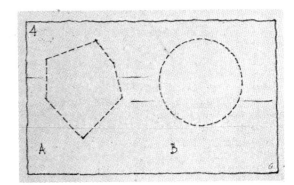

Fig. 48. Both A *and* B *have an unstable appearance.*

Fig. 49. A triangle on its apex gives the opposite effect of one on its base.

Fig. 50. The disappearing vase gives us the sense of something lacking.

teristics of an object quickly. These are drawings done in a limited time, a limit usually set in advance. For a simple subject in outline, five minutes is allowed, or fifteen, or whatever seems advisable (this depending partly on the subject and partly on the skill of the artist). Strive for the best possible drawing within the limits set. It is especially important to block out the main proportions first, adding as many of the smaller details as time permits. There is another sort of time sketch (often referred to as a "time study"), in which a drawing is pushed to completion as quickly as is possible and the required time noted afterwards. The speed and dexterity gained through all such training will prove indispensable when it comes to working from the living model or sketching moving objects. Animals, people, vehicles, boats, and clouds do not always remain still to suit the convenience of the artist.

Although all this "speed work" is essential and a pleasant change from the usual form of drawing where time is not a leading consideration, too much of it leads to carelessness and inaccuracy. Alternate your problems, then, making some quick sketches and some painstaking studies, and progress should be steady and consistent.

Memory Drawings

When you have acquired a fair amount of skill doing the types of work described above, try a few drawings of the same objects from memory. Being able to draw from memory or the imagination is a great asset to the artist. When you have finished a drawing of an old shoe, for instance, done from the object itself, leave the shoe in the same position on the object stand but hide it from view, temporarily, with a cardboard or sheet of paper and lay the study just finished to one side. Then, on a fresh piece of paper, try to draw the object from memory. When the main lines have been blocked out, look at the shoe again and compare your drawing. Hide the shoe once more, correct your drawing and push it nearer to completion, and again compare it with the object itself. Go on in this way until the drawing is completed. Then try some quick sketches of the shoe from memory, first looking at it until you get a fresh impression of it in your mind; next drawing swiftly and freely, working for only the larger proportions and individual characteristics.

This sort of work is of the greatest value in training you to observe carefully and to retain a picture of what is observed. In general, the student who looks at an object for a long time, forming sort of a photograph of it in the brain, is usually better able to memorize the form than is the student who glances back and forth constantly from the object to the drawing as he works, forgetting the impression of each line once it is represented on paper. This is only a general rule, however, and has many exceptions. Some students have the power to really observe and memorize more at a glance than do others in several minutes.

Outline Drawing of Several Objects

Drawing two or three objects instead of one is the next logical step. This step involves few new principles, though the matter of arrangement or composition now needs our attention, for it is not always easy to choose and arrange several objects to form a satisfactory whole. Refer to Chapter 10 for assistance on composition. Study what is said about unity and balance. To obtain unity, choose objects that are well related by use, objects associated together for one reason or another. Frequently things found in the cellar or attic have more character than objects that are merely pretty. Growing things are often interesting, especially if the forms are irregular.

It is not enough, however, to have related objects unless they also offer variety of form, surface, and texture (and if the drawings are to be shaded, variety in light and dark). There is little merit in a sketch of several objects of equal roundness grouped together. Instead, look for dissimilar forms. Look for dissimilar edges, too, some that are soft, broken, or indefinite, and some that are sharp and clean-cut. An enormous object fails to harmonize in size with something much smaller unless they both are arranged with the utmost care. Even then, such a composition is difficult—too much difference in form or size is as bad

Fig. 51. Margin lines (even partial ones) can act as a frame for your composition.

Fig. 52. Avoid having too many lines compete with the table line.

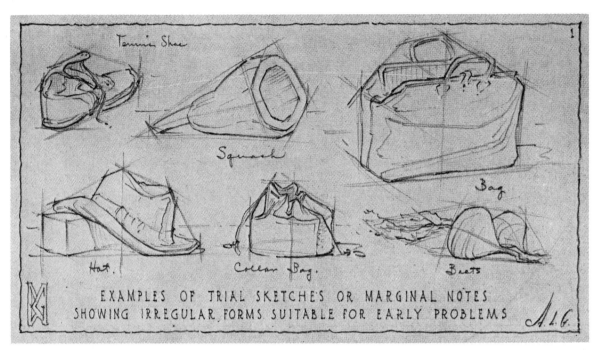

Fig. 53. Trial sketches can prove helpful in establishing your composition.

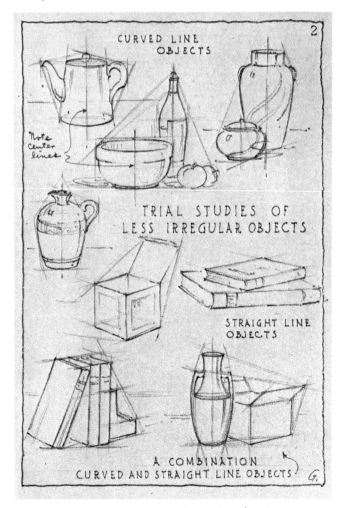

Fig. 54. Try to combine straight-lined objects with curved ones when you set up your still life.

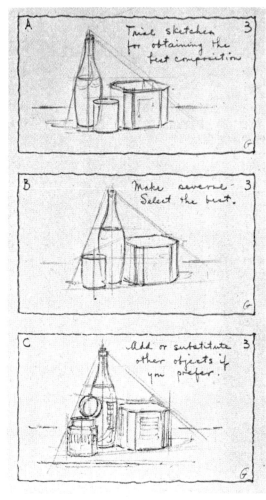

Fig. 55. Alter your arrangement until you arrive at a pleasing composition.

Fig. 56. Combine interesting objects in your selection of still-life forms.

1. FIRST STAGE

Main Proportions Located
(note use of center lines)

Fig. 57. First block in the main proportions as you did earlier.

2 · SECOND STAGE

Proportions Refined
Subdivisions Added

Fig. 58. Refine the drawing and retain the overall characteristics as well.

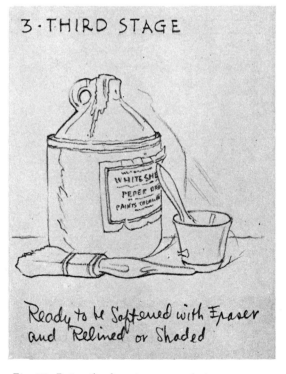

3 · THIRD STAGE

Ready to be Softened with Eraser
and Relined or Shaded

Fig. 59. Bring the drawing to completion.

as too little. Thought and care must be used, then, in both the selection *and* arrangement of objects.

When you have chosen two or three objects, place them on the stand and shift them about until they compose satisfactorily. A viewfinder such as described in Chapter 10 will be useful in this work. It helps to make a little trial marginal sketch to see how the arrangement will look on paper. Then try some different groupings of these same objects. If some object does not seem to fit, substitute another for it and make a new marginal sketch. Go through this process two or three times until you find the best arrangement. Fig. 55 shows at *A*, *B*, and *C* several such sketches blocked out as a study of grouping. Considering that still-life objects are always shown in repose, and bearing in mind that a triangle resting on its base always seems to express this feeling more strongly then some other shapes, many still-life compositions therefore conform to a triangular proportion. Fig. 45 (Sketch 1) and *A*, Fig. 55 are triangular in general mass and are, therefore, restful.

When a triangle is placed on its apex, however, or any of its vertices, the opposite is true. The two sketches of the little toy rabbit in Fig. 49 illustrate this point. At *A* the toy seems stationary; at *B* it seems to be running off the paper, showing action rather than repose, and the latter effect is obtained mainly by the position of the triangular mass. Fig. 46 (Sketch 2) shows a square composition; Fig. 47 (Sketch 3), one that is circular. Rectangular compositions frequently seem restful. When using circular or oval masses, care must be taken that the objects do not seem inclined to roll out of the picture. The more nearly horizontal the base is, the better, for if it is too round in form the objects seem unstable, threatening to rock back and forth or fall over. Both the irregular mass at *A* and the circular mass at *B*, Fig. 48 (Sketch 4) have an unstable appearance, the first seeming to rest on too sharp a point at the base. As a further illustration of the principle that objects seem more satisfactory if resting firmly on some support, notice the feeling of incompleteness and restlessness in objects which show no portion of their bases. The vase in Fig. 50 (Sketch 6), for instance, disappearing behind the book, gives us a sense of something lacking. Another point worth considering is that objects should not be placed so far below the eye that they seem to tip up, as this always seems disturbing.

The other sketches in this chapter explain themselves. Experience will soon teach you how to get a satisfactory arrangement of objects. Once they are in position, the outline drawing should be carried forward by gradual steps just as we have explained for single objects, using care that in each drawing there is relative proportion *between* all the different objects. (See Figs. 56 to 59). When it comes to the final stage, greater variety of outline may be needed to represent the larger number of surfaces and textures.

When you have learned to draw well in outline, it is time to work in light and shade.

8.
Object Drawing in Light and Shade

We now come to shaded drawings of objects in which we represent the exact amount of light and shade found in the objects themselves.

Determine the Values

In our work in this chapter, we will not be using outline. Instead, we will concentrate on making as truthful a representation of the tones seen in nature as possible. Observation will prove that we can distinguish one object from another by its light or shade or color. Most areas of light or shade have clearly defined shapes that describe the forms of the objects on which they appear. And all these shapes seem to have boundaries where one tone meets another. In elementary work, and for certain types of explanatory drawings, lines may be used to represent these contours or boundaries. Even omitting or merely suggesting light and shade satisfies the eye. But this is the result of convention, not nature. There are no outlines in nature.

We must now think in terms of tones instead of lines. We must learn to think of the exact degrees of light and shade found in the objects and represent them correctly. We must learn to translate the values of color into values of light and dark. For the value of a given color must be represented by a tone of gray which has the same degree of light and dark that the color has. These tones will vary all the way from the white of the paper to the pure black of the softest pencil. We have white tones, light tones, middle tones, dark tones, and black tones. Although there are, in reality, many more than these five groups (in fact the tones in nature are innumerable), it is best in drawing to simplify the values, not attempting to break up a

tone to express every slight difference in value that may be discerned upon close inspection.

For the first problems select some object or objects with little color, confining your choice to things that are white, gray, black, or of dull tints or shades. With these objects, relative values can be seen quite easily. It is helpful, in judging a value, to compare it with white. So take a small sheet of white paper a few inches or centimeters in size and compare it with the various objects to be drawn. Is there any tone in the objects as light as the paper? Select the lightest tone that you can find. You may discover two tones of different color but the same value. Now hold your sheet of white paper in bright light and compare its tone with that of similar paper in some darker place. Now take a piece of black paper and compare that with the objects. Is there any tone as dark as the black paper? Select the darkest tone that you can find in the objects. Now place the dark paper in brilliant light and compare its tone with that of another piece of the same paper in some darker place. Such experiments will prove that even though a surface is white it will not always appear white, and though black, its value will change in effect as it is moved from place to place. The less light a surface receives, the darker its values will seem to be.

Remember also, that if we have two objects of exactly the same form under the same lighting conditions—one light and the other dark—the darker one will have darker values all over as its local color is added to the shade.

So the lightest value on the objects will usually be found in objects having the lightest local color and in that part of it receiving the brightest light (usually that portion nearest the window). There are some exceptions to this: highly glazed dark objects, for example, will sometimes reflect a value so light that it becomes the lightest in the whole composition, being even more brilliant than the paper on which the objects are being drawn.

Procedure

In doing shaded work in full value, first of all, prepare an outline drawing as described in the preceding chapter, though the final accented outline is not needed. Instead, soften the outline with an eraser until it becomes simply an inconspicuous guide for the work in shading. Next lightly add the contours or boundaries of the most clearly defined areas of light or shade. Now determine the lightest light and the darkest dark and compare all the other values to them. Then sharpen a medium soft pencil to a fairly sharp point (a softer one may be necessary for extremely dark tones) and you are ready to begin.

At this point, there are several methods of procedure open. Some teachers feel that it is best to first draw the darkest tone, then the next lighter, and so on up through the values, leaving the lights for the last. Others start with the lightest tones, next add the grays, working down to the darkest values. Really, everything depends on the individuality of the artist and the type of drawing desired. Assuming that you are going to make as correct a representation as possible, it will probably be easiest to work over the whole drawing, not attempting to bring any one portion to the proper tone at first, but building up all the various tones gradually. In this way unity will be obtained. Set the drawing back frequently, and get away from it once in a while for a few minutes' rest.

Check Your Work

As your drawing develops, periods may come when you wonder what to do next. In this event, reflect your drawing in a mirror. Seeing your work in reverse will probably indicate the next moves. If not, place tracing paper over the drawing and experiment. Try toning together any con-

fusing values. That is, try merging two similar values only half-steps apart into a single value that represents them both and makes a stronger statement too. Define that essential object with outline or with greater contrasts of tone; see if you can bring it forward. Attempt anything, in short, that suggests itself as a possible improvement.

Changes or additions indicated by mirror reflections or tracing paper studies should now be accomplished on your drawing. Adjustments can be made: soften that obtrusive edge; subdue that complex background; lift a bit of graphite with your kneaded rubber from that too-dark tone, and clean up the soiled areas.

Shading Objects

We have already mentioned that, as a rule, the surfaces that receive the brightest light (those turned directly towards the source of light), are the brightest. If we observe an object that is rounded in form (such as a cylinder) we usually find the section lightest in value facing the window. The portions that are turned away from the light will, of course, be rather dark. There may be a gradual change of tone from the lightest parts to the darkest (see Sketch 1, Fig. 60). Or if the object has a somewhat irregular surface, such as the decagonal prism shown at Sketch 2 in the same diagram, the values may change gradually, plane by plane, from the lightest plane to a slighter darker plane, to a still darker one, and so on around to a point on the back opposite the lightest plane. It is not always true, however, that the darkest plane or portion of curved surface will be the one farthest from the source of light. Sometimes there is a certain amount of illumination from some other direction, and even if there is not, there are frequently rays of light reflected onto the parts in shade or shadow, thereby neutralizing the otherwise dark values.

Sketches 1 and 3 in Fig. 60, will serve to illustrate this point (also see Chapter II on graded tones). In Sketch 1 the brightest value is on that portion of the cylinder receiving the strongest rays of light. Then, as the surface curves more and more away from the source of illumination, the

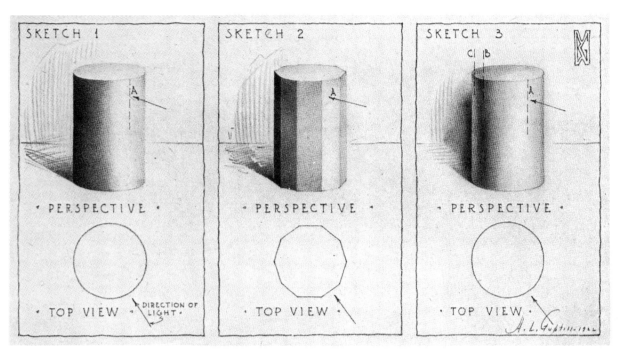

Fig. 60. Using a cylinder you can study the modeling or shading of objects.

darker it gets. In Sketch 3 a different condition exists. The brightest part of the surface is at *A* as in Sketch 1; then the tone gradually darkens until it reaches *B*, which is the darkest. Then at *C* a lighter value is found, caused by the reflection of light rays from some other object.

Planes

Few objects have surfaces curving as gradually as those of the cylinder just illustrated or planes so mechanically arranged as those of the prism. More often the objects are so irregular that the light and shade varies from part to part. There may be many portions turned towards the light and many turned more or less away. These various areas of light and shade that are seen in an object, caused by its irregular form and its position in relation to the source of light, are usually referred to as "planes," even though they do not fully meet the geometric definition of the word.

Edges of Planes

In some irregular objects, there is quite a definite line of demarcation between the various planes. In gradually curving objects, there is no such line.

The tone simply grades, as we have noted in the case of the cylinder, with no sudden, perceptible change in value. In most objects, both of these two conditions exist. In parts, the planes seem quite definite; in others, they merge together. There is nothing more important than drawing these edges correctly, sharpening them or losing them, as the case may be. In the same way, there is great difference in the edges of the objects themselves as they contrast with the background or with other objects. Some stand out in sharp relief, others are indistinct. Some dark objects become so lost in shadow that it is hard to distinguish their form. In this case, lose the form in the drawing, too.

Shadows

Shadows outdoors and shadows indoors are entirely different in their appearance. Indoors, they are softer and more indefinite; whereas some edges of shadows seem sharp, many are almost lost. Hold the end of your pencil on a sheet of paper and the shadow will seem sharpest right at the point where the objects intersect. Bear this in mind when shading. Correctly drawn shadows have much to do with the effect of modeling or projection. Needless to say, unless the objects are

THE SKETCHING
OF OBJECTS

Fig. 61. Try drawing some simple objects, representing them in light and shade.

arranged with care and the whole group well lighted, the shadows may prove very distracting. Considerable experimenting is necessary to compose a still-life grouping to best advantage. If light is coming from several sources, the shadows will create problems, because the complex forms cast in different directions will suggest restlessness and confusion.

Study the Final Drawing

When your drawing seems finished, set it next to the grouping for final comparison. Have you the same degrees of light and dark in the drawing as in the objects themselves? Have you the correct degrees of sharpness and softness in the edges? Is there too much dark on one side or at the bottom or the top, or does the whole hold together nicely? Are the tones clear and transparent, or heavy and dead? Have you succeeded in expressing space, depth, weight, and texture? Have you practiced economy of tone, or is the drawing confusing because of too many different values? Have you successfully lost the outline, remembering that the mere contrast of tones should evoke what you wish to express?

Now squint and study your drawing, reducing it to its simplest elements. Do the nearer parts seem to come forward properly and the farther parts to go back? If not, force the nearer parts a bit and sacrifice the distant portions. We must get a feeling of projection and distance. Is the highlight too complex? If so, tone down all lights a bit, leaving only the strongest of them all, for a picture is better with one lightest light and one darkest dark. Too much emphasis cannot be attached to the importance of studying the objects and the drawing through partly closed eyes, not only when it is completed but from time to time as the work progresses. For in this way you shut out all but the essentials, and are not led into seeing too many details and thus creating confusing effects.

Pencil Strokes

We have said little about the kind of stroke to be used for this work, because it is better not to have definite lines showing. The tone should be built up by going over and over it with a comparatively sharp point, merging the various lines together until they are lost. Naturally, the textures represented will affect your manner of working, but to get the most out of these studies each tone should be as nearly perfect as possible, striving for transparency and luminosity. The drawing of the apple at 1, Fig. 6, was done in this manner. Sometimes tones are rubbed smooth with the finger or with a stump, but such a procedure is not recommended for this kind of work.

There is another type of shaded still-life drawing, however, which is more sketchily done, where a few strokes of the pencil are used to express a great deal. This type of work, illustrated in Fig. 61, shows separate strokes in many places rather than continuous tone. Practice this kind of work, too, drawing the strokes in a way that best expresses the surfaces represented, using some fine and some broad lines. In linework, the strokes should normally follow the direction of the surface.

Sometimes the still life becomes a motif for a decorative scheme, or combinations of tone and outline are found, or washes of color are added to the pencil work. Student drawings, Figs. 62 and 63, illustrate some of these possibilities for decorative work and Fig. 64 is an excellent example of a drawing in which a few very dark, crisp accents are added to a clean-cut outline. Notice the direct and economical way in which the various materials are suggested, and the simplicity of the whole.

Objects for Drawing

Objects having distinct character make the best subjects for drawings. Quaint and old-fashioned things are particularly interesting, or things that are worn or broken. Rummage the attic or cellar. Look in the garage or garden. Even the kitchen will yield many simple and useful utensils excellent for our purpose. The following list may guide you in your search for objects to draw.

Objects for elementary or comparatively small compositions: garden trowel and flowerpots;

Fig. 62. A. Mershon: This student drawing illustrates a decorative use of tone and outline.

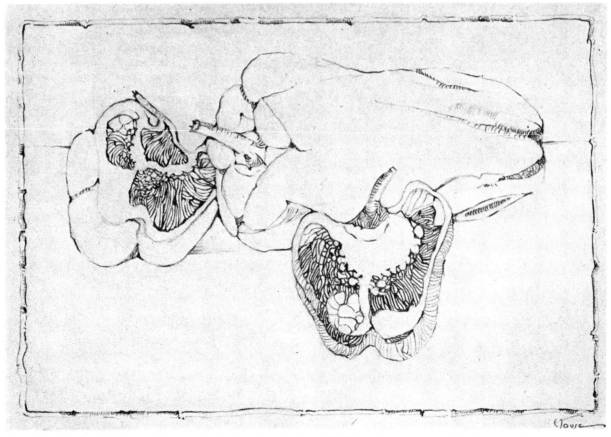

Fig. 63. Marjorie House: Here a student took a simple still life subject and used it decoratively.

Fig. 64. Ethel M. Weir: An accented object drawing was completed by this student in two hours.

hammer, box of nails; screwdriver and screws; basket of clothespins, coil of clothesline; pail with cloth hanging over side, scrub brush and scouring powder; tack hammer, box of tacks, etc.; whetstone with knife and piece of wood half whittled; sponge, soap and basin of water; dustpan and brush, featherduster; ice-cream freezer, bag of salt, etc.

Among larger objects we have: snow shovel, rubber boots, and mittens; shovel and tongs; wheelbarrow, rake, and basket; broken box with axe; watering pot, trowel, broken flowerpots; hat and coat on nail; old trunk partly opened, etc.; old hats and hatboxes; umbrellas in various positions, opened, closed, and half closed; brooms and mops with dustpans and pails; chopping block, sticks of wood, axe; basket of kindling and hatchet; baseball bat, mitt, and ball.

Books can always be arranged effectively, piled up, tumbled down, spread out, opened, or closed.

Book, candlestick, and matches; old novel partly opened, apple between leaves; half-open newspaper with books; books, paperweight, half-open letter, and envelope.

Then there are other objects found around the house, such things as are in everyday use: glove box and gloves; framed photograph and bowl of flowers; cribbage board and cards; pipe, tobacco jar, matches, etc.; opera glasses, evening bag, and program; slippers, gloves, and fan; hats or caps; basket or bag with sewing or knitting; brush, comb, and mirror; children's toys and dolls.

The following suggestions are for the uses of fruit, vegetables, etc. Such combinations are of course innumerable: paper bag with fruit, vegetables, or candy falling out and at the side; half-peeled bananas on plate with knife; lemons, squeezer, glass, sugar, and spoon; box of sardines, sliced lemons and plate of crackers; a coconut, broken open; bunches of beets or carrots or similar vegetables with tops; several apples, one cut in half, another partly pared; teapot, teacups, plate of sandwiches; fruit bowl or basket filled with fruit; pineapple with knife and plate; squash or pumpkin cut open, partly sliced; pumpkin made into jack-o-lantern; bread on plate, some sliced, with knife; salad plate with lobster and lettuce, mayonnaise bowl, spoon, and fork; roast of meat on platter with carving knife; plate of beans, bottle of ketchup, and napkin; sugar bowl, cubes of sugar, and sugar tongs; box of candy open or partly open; crackers in box or bag, bowl of milk, and spoon; strawberries or grapes in a basket; bunches of grapes with bits of vine, leaves, and tendrils; apples, pears, or peaches hanging on branches with leaves; heads of lettuce, cauliflower, and bunches of celery; sliced meat on a platter, garnished with parsley. And bowls and vases of flowers are always good, too, or branches of leaves or berries. For more elaborate studies, views of room corners or portions of a yard or street offer many possibilities.

9.
Freehand Perspective

Objects usually appear different in shape from what we know them to be. Their appearance seems contrary to the facts we know regarding these objects. We are aware, for instance, that a cube has six equal faces and that each of them is square. Yet if we draw six squares, combining them in any and every possible way, the final result will certainly not suggest a cube. We also know that the top of an upright cylinder is a circle, but we seldom see a cylinder in such a position that the top appears as a true circle. We think of it as a circle simply because we know it to be one; not because it really looks circular. Unless we look straight at the end of the cylinder, it actually appears elliptical or even as a straight line.

So when we question how something should be drawn, we not only study the things themselves, but we must also turn to the science of perspective. This science gives us principles that are helpful in drawing objects correctly—not as they actually are—but as they appear from the point from which they are viewed. Freehand perspective trains us to apply these principles to the practical problems of freehand sketching.

For the purpose of this book, we will discuss very briefly only a few of the more important principles. Nothing short of a complete volume could do justice to the entire subject, and there are already many excellent works available on the subject. In addition to your reading of these principles, you should learn to observe the perspective appearance of objects all around you. If you are studying circles and ellipses, take notice of every circular arch, or clock face, or barrel, or other similar form you see.

Two Important Principles

Fundamentally, these principles are few. Among them, the following are perhaps the most important.

1. The apparent size of an object decreases in proportion to its distance from an imaginary plane which passes through the eye at right angles to the direction in which you are looking.
2. A surface appears in its true shape only when parallel to the picture plane, or, in other words, when at right angles to the line of sight from eye to surface.

This first principle can be easily tested if you stand close to a window and look straight through it. An entire building in the distance appears only a few inches or several centimeters large on a single pane of glass. If there are several objects of equal size at varying distances from the eye, you will notice that the nearest one appears to be the largest and the others seem smaller and smaller in proportion to their distance from the viewer.

The second principle is easily demonstrated. When a surface (take a circular end of a cylinder, for example) is not placed at right angles to the line of sight, it appears smaller in the dimension that is turned away. The farther it is turned, the smaller this dimension seems; until it is turned so far that the surface coincides with the direction of sight, causing it to appear simply as a line. This apparent change of shape is called *foreshortening*.

In order to give a working knowledge of these principles in the quickest and most direct way, we will discuss the appearance and methods of repre-

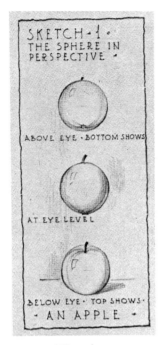

Fig. 65. *The sphere remains the same in profile, regardless of its position.*

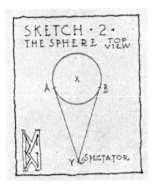

Fig. 66. *We seldom see halfway around a sphere.*

senting a few typical geometric forms. Once the simple forms are understood it will not be difficult to draw objects that are more complex, applying to them exactly the same principles.

Horizon Line or Eye Level

The horizon line is an imaginary horizontal line at eye level. In object drawing or other small work, the latter term is the more commonly used; for buildings and outdoor work in general, the former is customary.

The appearance of any object will vary according to whether it is at, above, or below eye level, and to the right, in front, or to the left of the spectator. To observe just what variation does take place in the appearance of objects as viewed from various points, take simple objects and hold them in different positions, noticing just how they look when moved from place to place, nearer or farther from the eye and higher or lower in relation to the horizon line.

The Sphere

Take, for example, a sphere, an apple, an orange, or some other object of spherical form. When held above the eye, it appears as a circle; below the eye and at eye level, its contour is practically the same. If it is a true sphere, there will not be the slightest variation no matter where you hold it. If you take an apple, however, with the stem at the top, and hold it upright, but below the eye, not only is the stem visible; but so is a portion of the surface beyond it. If we raise it until the top of the apple is at the height of the eye, still holding it upright, the stem is still seen; but none of the surface beyond is visible. A bit of the "blossom" below may now show. As we raise it above the eye, the stem will gradually disappear, as will a portion of the top surface. As this is lost to view, more of the lower part will become visible, so if it is held some distance above the eye you will see the entire "blossom" and the surface beyond. What have we learned from this simple example? Although a sphere remains the same in profile regardless of its position, we see different portions of its surface as it is moved up and down, shifted to the right or left, or spun round and round. Fig. 65 (Sketch 1) illustrates this point. Study this and then draw several objects of spherical form placed in a variety of positions.

Bear in mind that we seldom see halfway around a sphere. Fig. 66 (Sketch 2) explains this more clearly. If X represents the top view of the sphere and Y the position of the spectator, the lines drawn from Y tangent to the sphere, mark at A and B the limits of the visible portion of the sphere at the plane of its greatest circumference. The larger the sphere or the closer the spectator, the smaller this distance becomes.

The Vertical Cylinder

Now, take a cylinder—a paper tube will do—and hold it vertically and, with one eye closed, raise it until the top is level with the other eye. In this position the top circle will appear as a straight line, the circular plane being so greatly foreshortened that only its edge can be seen. Now, lower it a bit. The circular top is now visible, but is still so foreshortened that it is elliptical instead of circular in appearance. Lower it still farther and the ellipse becomes rounder. Just as this top ellipse appears more rounded as it is dropped below the eye, so if the bottom of the cylinder were fully seen, it would appear even rounder than the top, as it is still farther below the eye. Experience proves that the degree of roundness of the ellipse is in proportion to its distance below the eye.

Next raise the cylinder vertically until the lower end is at the eye level; this now appears as a straight line, just as did the top end before. Raise it still higher and the bottom comes in sight as an ellipse, the top of the cylinder being now hidden. And the higher the cylinder is raised, the rounder the ellipse of the bottom becomes, its fullness being in proportion to its distance above eye level. If the cylinder is lowered until the bottom and top are both equidistant from eye level, both will be invisible; but the visible edges of each will have a similar curvature. If the cylinder were transparent, so both the top and bottom could be seen, the ellipses representing both would be identical

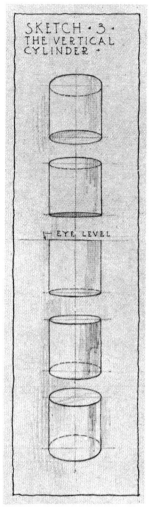

Fig. 67. Study these characteristics of the vertical cylinder.

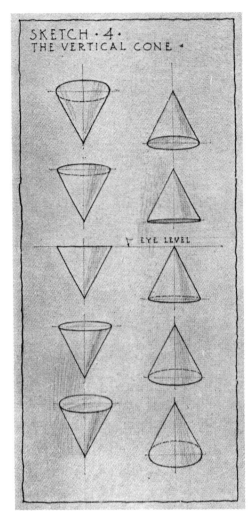

Fig. 68. Study these characteristics of the vertical cone.

in size and shape, since both circles are the same distance from the level of the eye.

Transparent glass cylinders are convenient for such experiments, or the student can make one of celluloid or some similar material.

What is true of the appearance in perspective of the top or bottom of a cylinder is true of any circle. If you would like to prove this, cut a circle from a sheet of heavy paper or cardboard and experiment with this. Hold it horizontally and level with the eye. Does it not look like a straight line? And when raised above or dropped below eye level, doesn't it appear as an ellipse? Note the apparent change in roundness and in the length of the short axis of this ellipse as the circle is raised or lowered. Only the long axis will appear of the same proportionate length, regardless of the position of the circle. Is it not true, also, that when a circle appears as an ellipse, the ellipse is always perfectly symmetrical about its long and short axis lines? And is it not divided by these axis lines into four quarters, which appear exactly equal?

Go back to the cylinder again and see if this, too, does not, when held vertically, appear symmetrical about a vertical central axis line at all times, every element of the cylindrical surface being vertical also. As in the case of the sphere we seldom see halfway around the circumference. Less than half the cylindrical surface is visible at any one time.

Now try a number of sketches of the vertical cylinder and the horizontal circle as viewed from different positions—Fig. 67 (Sketch 3) shows a few. Practice drawing ellipses, too, until you can do them well; this is no easy matter. (The tipped or horizontal cylinder will be discussed later.)

The Vertical Cone

While we still have the horizontal circle in mind, let us consider the circular cone placed vertically. Fig. 68 (Sketch 4) shows the cone in this position. Notice that the appearance of the circle is the same as in the case of the cylinder. Also, that if the apex of the cone is at the top and the cone below the eye, we can see more than halfway around the conical surface. If the cone is raised above the eye, we see less than halfway around. And if the cone is inverted, the opposite is true. Note also that a circular cone will always appear symmetrical, the long axis of the ellipse of the base being at right angles to the axis of the cone. Make several drawings of the vertical cone. (The horizontal or tipped cone will be discussed later.)

The Cube in Parallel Perspective

We now turn to the cube. Hold it with the top at the eye level and the nearer face at right angles to the line of sight so it is seen in its true shape. Only one face of the cube is visible now, and that appears as a square. Lower the cube a few inches or centimeters and the top appears, greatly foreshortened. The farther horizontal edge, being a greater distance away than the nearer one, seems shorter. The parallel receding edges of the top seem to slant. If these slanting edges were continued indefinitely, they would appear to meet at a certain point, and that point would be at eye level.

Lower the cube a few inches or centimeters farther. The top now appears wider and the two receding edges have still greater slant. If continued they would still meet at a point at eye level, the same one as before. The front face still appears square. Now raise the cube above the eye, still holding it vertically. The top goes out of sight and the bottom becomes visible. The front face looks square, as before. Now the higher the cube is raised, the more the bottom shows. The receding lines now seem to slant downward towards eye level; if continued they would meet the very same point on eye level as when the cube was below the eye.

To convince yourself that these same facts are true of other objects, take a box or any form similar to the cube, and study it in various horizontal positions above and below the eye, keeping the nearest vertical plane so turned that it is always seen in its true shape. When the object is below the eye, don't the horizontal receding lines seem to slant upward with an appearance of convergence? And when the object is above the eye, don't these horizontal receding lines seem to slope downward in the same way? And whether

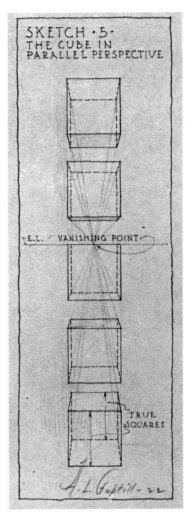

Fig. 69. Observe the cube in parallel perspective in various relations to the eye level.

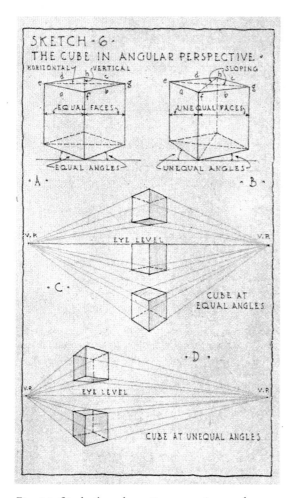

Fig. 70. Study the cube as it appears in angular perspective.

above or below the eye, isn't it true that all the horizontal surfaces appear to slope towards eye level as they recede? It is interesting to note, as mentioned above, that the receding parallel edges would, if continued far enough, appear to converge towards the same point at eye level, exactly opposite the eye itself. This point is called the vanishing point for that set of edges. The edges that do not recede have, of course, no appearance of convergence and hence no vanishing point.

All the time that you are studying the object, ask yourself such questions as the following: Is it true that every set of parallel receding horizontal lines has a common vanishing point of its own? And is it true of two parallel lines the same length that do not recede, that the one nearest the spectator appears the longer? And do parallel edges that are at right angles to the line of sight (the picture plane) actually appear parallel?

When an object like the cube or box is placed in such a way that its principal face is at right angles to the line of sight from the eye, we say that it is viewed in *parallel perspective*. Fig. 69 (Sketch 5) shows cubes in parallel perspective in various relations to the eye level.

The Cube in Angular Perspective

Now we will turn the cube into a new position, placing it in a horizontal manner below the eye and turned at an angle with all four of its top edges receding. None of the edges now appears horizontal. Notice that if the cube is turned in such a way to make equal angles with the line of sight as at *A*, Fig. 70 (Sketch 6), we will see equal portions of the lines marked *a* and *b*, and they will have equal slant. The same will be true of *c* and *d*. Now if we turn the cube so that it makes unequal angles with the line of sight, as at *B*, Fig. 70, we find that line *a* will seem shorter and line *b* longer than before.

To more firmly fix these thoughts in your mind, shift the cube from place to place and ask yourself: If two edges of the square top of the cube recede from me at unequal angles, which of the two appears the longer? Which the more nearly horizontal? And considering the complete cube, turned at an angle so that two or more of its faces are visible, can any one of these appear in its true shape? Will all parallel edges receding towards the left appear to converge or vanish to one point and those towards the right to another? And if so, will these points be on the eye level?

Continue your analysis in this thorough way and you will observe many interesting things. You will see that the edges of the cube that are truly vertical appear so, and therefore should be drawn so. You will notice that the nearest vertical edge will be the longest and that the others will decrease in length as they get farther away.

When a cube or other object is placed in such a way that no surface is seen in its true shape, or that its principal planes are at other than a right angle with the line of sight, it is said to be in *angular perspective*. Because it is rather difficult for the beginner to draw angular perspective well, it is better to work for some time from a cube itself, placing it in different positions above and below the eye. In drawing such an object, it is usually advisable to actually locate and draw a line representing eye level on paper, making sure that the various receding lines are converging to the proper vanishing points on this eye level. It is sometimes wise in these early problems to actually continue such receding lines indefinitely, allowing them to meet at the proper points, as at C and D, Fig. 70 (Sketch 6). As an aid in testing for correct drawing of a cube in angular perspective, it may help to draw diagonal lines on the top foreshortened square as we have done with the dotted lines at A and B, Fig. 70. At A with the cube turned at equal angles, the long diagonal is horizontal, the short perpendicular. Let the cube be swung around as at B, however, and the diagonals immediately tip. Point g drops lower than e, and h moves to the right of f instead of remaining above it. If the vertical faces are turned at unequal angles, then we not only see more of one than of the other, but the diagonals of the top plane will always be tipped, never vertical or horizontal. Rules of this sort are of comparatively little help, however. What counts in drawing all these objects is

the observation and practice from observing the things themselves.

The Horizontal Cylinder

Now that the drawing of the cube has given you a little knowledge of receding lines, go back to the cylinder. Only this time do not place it vertically. Hold it, instead, in a horizontal position at the level of one eye (closing the other) and turn it so that the circular end appears in its true shape. In this position, nothing is seen but the end. If you then swing it or tip it so that the end and some of the curved surface are both visible, the end will appear as an ellipse. The less curved surface that shows, the rounder this ellipse will be. Then swing the cylinder until one end appears a straight line. In this position the other end is invisible, but if the cylinder were transparent, this end would appear as an ellipse.

Study the cylinder in all sorts of positions above and below the eye, making observations of this sort. Such study and comparison will prove that the cylinder, regardless of position, will always appear symmetrical about its long axis line; that the long diameters of the ellipses forming the ends will be at right angles to the axis of the cylinder. You will find, too, that it is never possible to see quite halfway around the cylindrical surface. And when the farther end of the horizontal or tipped cylinder is a greater distance from the eye than the nearer end, it will appear smaller. This means, in turn, that the elements of the cylindrical surface will appear to converge, and these elements—being all parallel lines—they will seem to vanish towards a point. If the cylinder is placed horizontally, this point will be at eye level; if tipped in some other position, the point will be above or below the eye. To this same vanishing point, the axis of the cylinder, if drawn, will also recede. And you will also find, that regardless of where the cylinder is placed, those elements of the surface which form the straight boundaries will appear tangent to the curves of the bases. At A, Fig. 71 (Sketch 7), the cylinder has been drawn

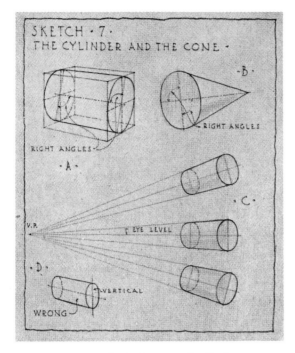

Fig. 71. *Next, study the horizontal cylinder.*

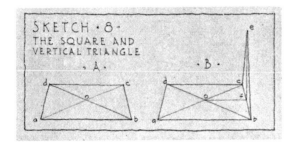

Fig. 72. *Then study other geometric forms.*

within a square prism to show the relationship between objects based on the square and the circle.

The Tipped Cone

Turning to the cone for further consideration, look directly at its apex and you will find that it appears as a true circle. And when held in such a way that its base becomes a straight line, it has the contour of a triangle. The visible curved surface of a cone may range from all to none of it. The boundaries of the cone are always represented by straight lines tangent to the ellipse, which represents the base. And the cone, like the cylinder, will always appear symmetrical, being divided by its long axis into two equal parts.

Study the little sketches of cylinders and cones in Fig. 71. Then make many of your own.

Other Geometric Forms

In just the same way, consider other geometric forms, such as the triangular prism placed vertically and horizontally, and the pyramid and hexagonal prism placed in various positions. Though space does not permit full discussion of these here, a few facts regarding the appearance of the triangle, the hexagon, etc., are worth noting. But first, let us say another word or two about the square.

We have drawn a square at Fig. 72 (Sketch 8), and have crossed its diagonals. Doing this locates the true center of the square *o* as it appears in perspective. It seems more than halfway back, for the farther half of the square, being a greater distance from the eye than the first half, seems smaller. For the same reason, line *bo* seems longer than *od*, though in top view we know they would be equal. This will perhaps clarify the fact that equal distances on any receding line seem unequal, the farther one seeming the shorter. Now suppose that at the end of this square we draw a triangle, as at *B*, Fig. 72. We locate its apex by drawing a line horizontally from center *o* to line *bc*, erect a vertical altitude at the point of intersection *f*, choose point *e* arbitrarily on the altitude, and then draw *ec* and *eb*. This triangle illustrates the truth that the apex of a vertical isosceles or equilateral triangle having a horizontal base appears in a vertical line erected in the perspective center of the base. As it is easier to judge the correct proportion of a square in perspective than of a triangle, a square is sometimes drawn first as a guide, as in Fig. 73 (Sketch 9).

In Fig. 74 (Sketch 10) we show a hexagon. Notice at *A* that the two short diagonals *bf* and *ce* and the long diagonals *be* and *cf* divide long diagonal *ad* into four equal parts. In a correct drawing of a hexagon, it is always true that any long diagonal, when intersected by two short and one long diagonals, will be divided into four equal parts. When a hexagon is sketched in parallel perspective, as at *B*, all sides appear equal. In drawing polygons, especially regular ones such as the hexagon just mentioned, it is often easiest to first draw an ellipse representing a circumscribed circle. In drawing the decagonal prism in Fig. 60, for instance, an ellipse was first drawn just as for the cylinders, then the decagon was drawn within it. So try a number of polygons, and later prisms and pyramids built upon polygonal bases.

Concentric Circles

Even in so brief a treatise on perspective, it is necessary to make some reference to concentric circles, because they are frequently drawn and often cause trouble. Students sometimes are under the mistaken impression that circles in perspective do not appear as true ellipses. They argue that, since the nearer half of the ellipse is not as far from the spectator as the other half, it appears larger, and hence must be drawn so. Although this may sound logical on the surface, it is not true. If you test actual objects, you will find that circles always appear in perspective as true ellipses.

We can make this more clear by referring to Fig. 75. We have already mentioned that you cannot see halfway around a cylinder. At *A*, we have drawn the top view of a cylinder. The spectator is standing at *s*. Lines of tangency from *s* to the cylinder give us at 1 and 2 the points representing the extreme limits of the cylindrical surface visible from *s*. If we draw a straight line across the top of the cylinder from 1 to 2, it marks the greatest

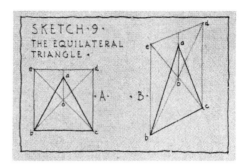

Fig. 73. *Use a triangle to judge the correct proportion of a square in perspective.*

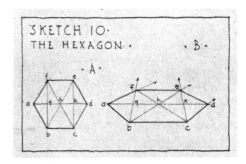

Fig. 74. *Study the perspective of a hexagon.*

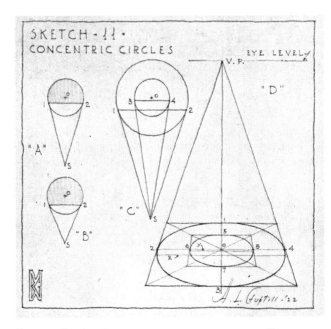

Fig. 75. *Circles always appear in perspective as ellipses.*

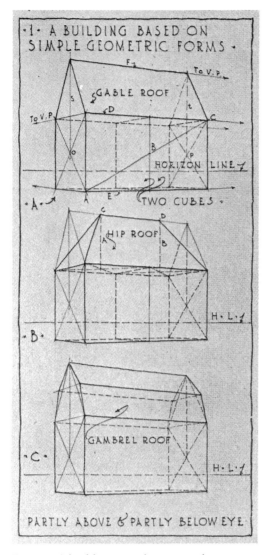

Fig. 76. A building is nothing more than simple geometric forms to which the same principles apply.

width of the cylinder as it appears from point *s*. This line really does not pass through the true center of the circle, represented by *o*, but is between this center and the spectator and becomes the major axis of the ellipse representing the circle. The portion behind this line on the sketch will appear from point *s* as exactly the same size at that portion left white; hence the ellipse must appear truly symmetrical about this line. At *B* the spectator stands closer and so sees less of the cylindrical surface.

Suppose we have two concentric circles representing the tops of two concentric cylinders as indicated at *C*, the spectator still standing at *s*. If we treat these independently as before, drawing tangents to the curves, these tangents will measure off visible surfaces from 1 to 2 on the larger and from 3 to 4 on the smaller. This shows that the eye will see relatively more of the cylindrical surface of the smaller cylinder. Line 3-4 is nearer the center *o* than line 1-2 but does not pass through it.

The easiest way to draw such circles in perspective is to assume that they are inscribed in squares. At *D*, two squares having a common center are shown in perspective. The crossing of the diagonals gives us the true center of the circle at *o*, correctly located in perspective. At 1, 2, 3, and 4 are points through which the larger ellipse must pass. Line *x*, just halfway from points 1 and 3, will be the long axis of the large ellipse, which will be drawn symmetrically about this line, passing through points 1, 2, 3, and 4. The smaller ellipse will be drawn in exactly the same way, passing through points 5, 6, 7, and 8, and drawn symmetrically about axis *y*, which is halfway from 5 to 7.

Study these circles at *D* and examine objects in which other concentric circles are found. Isn't it true that foreshortened concentric circles appear as ellipses? And shouldn't the short axis lines of these ellipses coincide? Notice, too, at *D*, that distances 3-7, 7-0, 0-5, and 5-1 on the short axis seem to decrease gradually, though actually at the same rate as the unforeshortened distances on the long axis, 2-6, 6-0, 0-8, and 8-4. So in drawing such ellipses, remember to keep the space between them widest at the ends as at 2-6 and 8-4, and a little wider between the near curves at 3-7 than at the farther side, 5-1.

When you feel able to do all the more common geometric forms individually in every possible position, combine several of them. Follow this by a practical application of the same principles to the drawing of objects of all sorts and sizes based on the same forms, as discussed in the chapters on object drawing. And as you draw, analyze and memorize. Also try freehand perspective sketches from memory or imagination.

In the last chapter, drawing on glass has been discussed. This procedure might be of great help to you in perspective studies, particularly if this subject proves difficult. Training in instrumental perspective is often of help, too, though instrumental perspective sometimes shows apparent distortions which are misleading. A certain amount of help is gained from it, however, and students who are familiar with the instrumental work usually advance more rapidly in freehand work because of this training.

Architectural Examples

Once skill is gained in drawing cubes and other simple forms, it is not difficult to apply the knowledge acquired to representing more complex subjects. The architectural student will be drawing buildings, for example, so let us consider the application of these principles to this type of work.

Assume that we are to draw a house 20'/6m wide and 40'/12m long, and 20'/6m from the ground to the eaves, the house turned in such a way that we look more directly at the long face than at the end. The land is assumed to be level. In Fig. 76 (Sketch 1) such a house has been drawn. As the eye is usually from 4 to 5'/1.2 to 1.6m above the ground, the horizon line has been drawn a quarter of the way up on the building. The nearest cube was worked over first until its proportion and perspective convergence seemed satisfactory. Then lines D and E were produced indefinitely (see A) and a diagonal line AC was carried through point B, exactly halfway from the ground to the eaves, automatically marking off at C the end of a second cube. When the two cubes

were completed, the roof was added. By crossing the diagonals of the square ends of the house proper, centers o and p were located. Through these, vertical lines s and t were erected, and these lines were taken to mark the height of the ridge F, which was converged towards its correct vanishing point at the right. Sketch B is the same, with the exception of the roof which is here hipped instead of gabled. The ends of the ridge were located by erecting A and B perpendicularly through the points of intersection of the diagonals of the tops of the two cubes forming the main house. Sketch C shows a different roof of the gambrel type, the gable having been drawn first just as at A as a guide.

The student may feel that these are unusual conditions; that few houses would be the proportion of two cubes, and this is, of course, true. It is not difficult, however, when a cube has been drawn as a unit, to add one or several more cubes in any direction, or portions of one. If the house just considered was to be 30'/9m long, for instance, instead of 40'/12m, the second cube could be easily cut in half, the correct perspective distance being judged by the eye. Or the diagonals of its nearest face could be crossed, which would give the correct point of intersection for the cut.

Once the main proportions have been established, the doors and windows, roof overhangs, etc., can be added and the whole completed. Experience will show many uses of diagonal lines in locating centers and measuring distances, and other shortcuts which will prove a saving of time and an aid to accuracy.

Sometimes it is desired to show buildings entirely above the eye, as on a high hill or mountain, and again, it is a part of the problem to represent them below the eye. Fig. 77 (Sketch 2) illustrates these conditions in a simple way.

Now whether buildings are above or below the eye or at its level, and whether simple or complex, the same general principles hold. But when a building is complicated in its masses or irregular in plan, it is usually best to think of it as enclosed within a simpler mass and draw this mass first; then subdivide it into the smaller parts. Fig. 78 (Sketch 3) was designed to illustrate this thought,

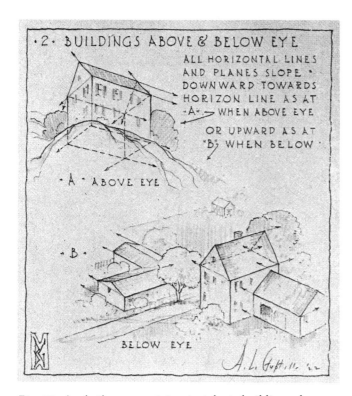

Fig. 77. Apply these geometric principles to buildings above and below eye level.

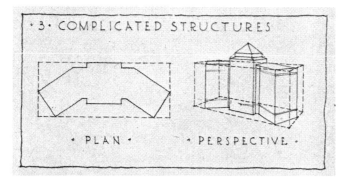

Fig. 78. Complex structures should be reduced to their simplest geometric components.

the dashed lines showing the simple mass, which was drawn first.

When the larger proportions of a building are established, there are many details to be added. Fig. 79 (Sketch 4) pictures a few typical ones in a very meager way. Many towers are based on pyramids and cones such as those shown at *A* and *B*. Practice these, then, and try your hand at steps, chimneys, arches, dormers, etc., until you feel able to sketch any of the more commonly seen details easily and well, either from the objects themselves (which is excellent practice) or from memory.

Sketch 5, Fig. 80, shows that when furniture is to be represented it is often preferable to first block it in very simply as far as mass is concerned, just as we did the building in Fig. 78. For the chair at *A*, two cubes were drawn as shown by the dotted lines, and the seat below was sketched within a square prism. When objects are enclosed within simple forms or "frozen into a block of ice," like this, you are less likely to get them incorrect in perspective. As a means of adding to your ability to do this well, cut out prints of buildings and pieces of furniture and sketch simple shapes around them with a few lines, preferably straight, for this will help you to realize that all objects are comparatively simple in basic form.

Photographs or prints can help us in another way in the study of perspective, for we can lay a ruler on them or a *T*-square or triangle, and produce with a pencil the various series of parallel lines moving towards their vanishing points, locating and drawing the eye level or horizon line first. This will help you to understand the perspective phenomenon more quickly, perhaps, than any other exercise.

Interiors

A brief word regarding interiors: these are done in just the same way as are exteriors, only we are looking at the *inside* of the cubes and prisms rather than the *outside*, which means that we simply remove those exteriors nearest to us. Rooms themselves are usually very simple in form; it is in the furniture, turned at various angles and of irregular shape, that you will encounter the greatest difficulty. A little practice, however, will give you considerable proficiency in all of this work.

Regardless of your subject, always look constantly in the same fixed direction until the drawing is finished. Although in practice this is not especially hard to do when an object is small, large objects or entire rooms or buildings require you to study details one at a time. Therefore it is not easy to keep from making a sort of composite sketch in which the various small parts may be correct in themselves, but wrong when considered in relation to one another and to the whole. When drawing a room, for instance, it is easy to go astray by looking first at a window and drawing that, and next doing a door, and so on, one thing at a time.

When this method is followed, the whole is quite sure to look distorted. For this reason, locate a horizon line on the drawing whenever possible and, if vanishing points would naturally come within the paper area, find them also. In sketching the main lines, try to give them the right proportion and perspective convergence; for if a sort of framework can be correctly built up for the whole, it will not be hard to add the detail. Therefore, spend plenty of time on this first work. If you find it too difficult to draw from actual buildings, sketch from photographs for a while, as this will be much easier to do. Then go on to portions of interiors and exteriors before attempting them in their entirety.

The excellent drawing by Ernest Watson in Fig. 81 shows a type of subject which would prove extremely difficult to block out because of the great number of converging lines, unless you are familiar with the perspective principles involved. If a subject of this nature is not correctly constructed, the errors will usually be glaringly apparent, regardless of the quality of the technique.

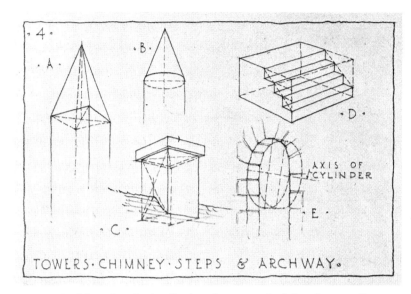

Fig. 79. Building details also display the same principles of perspective.

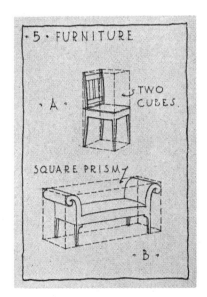

Fig. 80. Furniture is no different: reduce the objects to their simplest geometric forms.

Pennsylvania Station
from Grant Boulevard
PITTSBURG
Ernest W. Watson
June 1915

Fig. 81. Ernest W. Watson: Note all the principles of perspective involved in this splendid drawing.

10.
Composing Your Drawings

No matter how much technical facility you may have acquired through the kind of practice we have indicated, many of your future drawings will be disappointing unless you obtain considerable mastery over the art of composition. If you are approaching this for the first time, you may be one of those fortunate few who can compose well almost intuitively; otherwise, you are faced with quite a problem, because composition is not easily taught, especially through the pages of a book; you learn mainly through doing it.

Many draftsmen and students easily acquire the ability to represent small details of buildings, like bricks and shingles, and even larger parts, such as doors and windows. But the skill to compose these lesser units into a complete and well-balanced whole is not so easily gained. The student who is unable to arrange the smaller parts into a fine composition is seriously handicapped, regardless of cleverness in sketching every single detail, so it is well worth the effort to master this important art. As a compensating factor, everything you do learn can be applied again and again to any type of subject matter and to any kind of drawing, from the quickest sketch to the most highly finished rendering.

Selecting the Subject

The word "composition" means putting together things and arranging them in order, to make one unit out of them all. First, therefore, we must have good things to put together if the final composition is to be good. This means that in starting work we should use extreme care in selecting our subject, not only as a whole but in each of its parts. Students, especially beginners, seem to feel that any object found in nature is satisfactory for drawing, and they are led into this belief, perhaps, by hearing statements that all nature is beautiful. Although this may be true, it should be made clear that good pictures are not obtained ready-made by simply copying bits of nature at random. Amateur photographers know that a successful photograph is not made by simply pointing the camera in any direction and making an exposure; it is necessary to give some thought to the selection and composition of the subject.

Viewfinder

A little gadget we have already mentioned—a viewfinder—can be of amazing service in selecting subject matter, especially if you are seeking it outdoors. This is merely a cardboard, postcard size or so, pierced with a rectangular opening measuring, perhaps, 1.5 x 2"/4 x 5cm. By holding the card upright and peeking through the hole, with one eye closed, you can usually discover a wealth of good compositions, exactly as you might if using a camera viewfinder. The cardboard finder also helps determine whether the subject should go on the paper vertically or horizontally, and precisely how much of it you can best include in the picture. (The finder has another use, too. When you get around to constructing the drawing, you can estimate the correct slope of any doubtful line by comparing the line with a vertical or horizontal edge of the finder. If made of white cardboard, the finder can even prove of some aid in judging the value of any given tone in the subject, by comparing the tone in question with the white of the cardboard.)

The other commonly used finder or frame con-

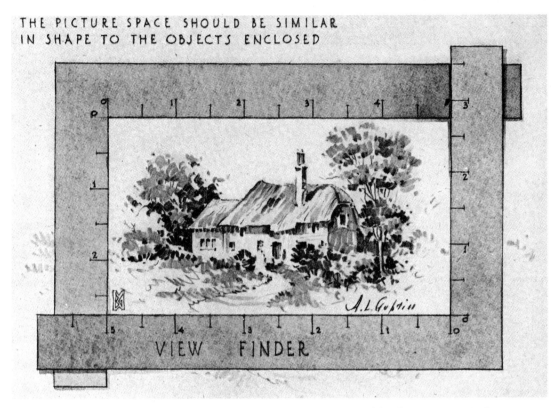

THE PICTURE SPACE SHOULD BE SIMILAR
IN SHAPE TO THE OBJECTS ENCLOSED

VIEW FINDER

Fig. 82. Take two L-shaped pieces of paper or cardboard and lap them like this for a viewfinder.

sists of two *L*-shaped pieces of paper or cardboard, which will give, when lapped as shown in Fig. 82, an endless variety of shapes and sizes, and it is, for this reason, much better than the other finder when working from photographs. As soon as a pleasing composition has been selected, this frame can be clipped or pinned in position on the photograph and left in place until the drawing is finished. This serves to hide the parts that have no relation to the sketch, freeing your eye from distraction.

Some art students constantly carry a viewfinder of the kind first described, continually studying different objects through its opening. In making such a viewfinder, you might try cutting several spaces of various shapes and sizes through your card instead of one. They need not be large, because the card can be held near the eye. In fact, two or three small openings or a single large one can be made in a finder of postcard size. Sometimes threads are fastened across the openings from side to side and from top to bottom as a

means of marking off the opening into a number of smaller rectangles or squares. This reduces the difficulty of laying out correct proportions when drawing from nature, just as in copying a photograph or enlarging a sketch, the work is simplified when the print or sketch is marked off into squares or rectangles.

Working from Photographs

You can usually find several excellent compositions for the same object or objects when viewed from one point, by showing more or less of the surroundings, just as a number of satisfactory photographs can be secured. Likewise, an infinite variety of compositions of any architectural object can be discovered by studying it from various positions and under different lighting conditions. When working from the photograph, several excellent sketches can sometimes be made from different portions of one print, especially if the picture is a street scene or a general view similar to that of the Wye Bridge and Cathedral, in Fig. 86. It is easy to frame a number of attractive compositions based on this photograph. Fig. 87 shows three sketches drawn from this very picture.

Notice that no attempt has been made to copy the values and details exactly as they appear on the print. The general effect is indicated in a broad, simple way. One of the best ways to learn composition is to make this kind of selection with the finder and sketches such as we have shown here. For this reason, the following exercises are offered:

First, obtain several photographs, such as street scenes or general views, each showing a number of objects which might make pleasing sketches. With the finder framing one of your prints, select one that seems to compose well, remembering that each composition should have a center of interest. Remember, too, that there should always be a pleasing relation between the shape of the picture space or margin line and the subject itself. If, for example, a very tall building, such as a skyscraper or church spire, has been chosen, it is probably best to draw it on paper placed vertically or to frame it in a vertical picture space, whereas a long horizontal building or mass of buildings can usually be represented to the best advantage when enclosed in a horizontal manner. This has been illustrated in Figs. 82 to 85. The English cottage shown in Fig. 82 seemed, when viewed in connection with the nearby trees, to demand a horizontal treatment. The church tower in Fig. 83 suggested a vertical handling. A group of buildings, such as that shown at Fig. 84, usually calls for a horizontal space, because if the horizontal masses are more prominent than the vertical, the fact should be expressed. Thus the church in Fig. 85 is given a long, low, frame, but the tower alone would be shown vertically. As a general rule, it is not desirable to use circular, oval, or triangular frames or margin lines on architectural drawings, because such shapes often have little or no relation to the form of the architecture itself. A square shape might work, but from an artistic standpoint, a square is usually less interesting than any other rectangle. It is even true that certain rectangles are more pleasing than others. One with a length just

Fig. 83. Proportion your picture space according to the subject.

Fig. 84. A group of buildings usually calls for a horizontal space.

Fig. 85. A long, low frame is required for this church.

twice its width is not as desirable, for instance, as a rectangle that is one and one-half times as long as it is wide. Even this proportion is less subtle and less satisfying to the eye than one about three parts wide and five long.

While discussing margin lines, we might mention that the line itself should never be so black that it draws the eye away from the subject. The width and tone of line should vary in different drawings in such a way that it is always in harmony with the sketch. Again, notice that sketches in some cases are carried to the margin lines, while in others they are allowed to fade gradually into the paper, "vignetted," as it is called. In either of these cases, if the exterior of a building is being drawn, the margin lines need not be far from the building itself. An exception here may occur with the line at the top, as all spaces will appear much greater after they are rendered than before, for surroundings add a sense of distance. If too much space is left in such drawings, the landscape and accessories may easily become too prominent in relation to the architecture.

When you have decided on your composition in the photograph, fasten the finder to the photo. On very thin tracing paper, with a soft pencil, make a simple tracing, not in outline alone but in values, trying to give the effect of the whole in a direct and simple manner, with sufficient accent at the center of interest. Don't spend more than five minutes on the sketch. Then frame the same object in a slightly different way and make a second tracing. Compare the two. Is one better than the other? Why? Is it because you have shown more foreground or sky, or because the frame has been kept of a size or shape better suited to the leading objects? After asking yourself these questions, make a third and even a fourth sketch, comparing them all with care. If one seems better than the others, make a larger and more carefully finished drawing, using this last sketch as the basis of your composition. Next try to find some entirely different composition in the same photograph, using a new subject, and make another series of quick sketches or tracings. Again compare them and analyze each, trying always to learn from this comparison why one composition is good and an-

other not. Select a different photograph and repeat the process. Or, if you feel that you have the ability to work in a similar way from nature, try this as well, choosing a comparatively simple subject so that each sketch can be done quickly.

Working from Nature

You will encounter more difficulty working from nature. Just as in the photographs the forms and values remain *constant*, in nature the values are always *changing*, and the forms are more difficult to represent. We have already mentioned that subjects that are full of interest and good in composition during some hours are entirely different under changed lighting conditions. And buildings that appear to good advantage at certain times of day are much less pleasing at others. This is largely because the areas of shade and shadow are never the same for long. Part of the time they nicely balance one another so that the lights and darks are all well related. At other times too much light or too much dark appears at one side or above or below, destroying the restful effect. At some hours, too, there may be patches of shade or shadow that become distracting because they are so oddly shaped. Therefore, it is preferable to do your sketching during favorable moments, if this is possible, returning, if necessary, to the same subject at the same hour during a number of days in succession until the study is completed.

Improving on Nature

If a subject that is otherwise good in composition exhibits a few unpleasant features—either in nature or in the photograph—it is perfectly legitimate to take certain liberties with them, if by so doing the drawing can be improved without sacrificing the truth of the main idea. Should a tree, for example, seem a bit too small in relation to a building, or too light or dark in value, or should some shadow be too dense and black or form a displeasing mass, feel free to make the changes necessary to improve the composition.

In landscape painting and decorative drawing, more such liberties are taken than may be pos-

Fig. 86. Three sketches drawn from this photograph of Wye Bridge and Cathedral are shown in Fig. 87.

sible in most architectural sketching or rendering. Architecture must, as a rule, be truthfully portrayed, and changes made here are largely in foliage and in shadow treatment. To illustrate this matter of changes, we have shown in Fig. 87 (Sketch 2), the dark boat in exactly the same position as on the photograph, Fig. 86. This spacing is not altogether satisfactory because the boat seems isolated in the center of the sheet, attracting too much attention. In this case, it would be better to improve the composition by moving the boat to the right or the left, or it might be tied into the scheme by adding extra lines or tones. Amendments like this are always advisable.

Principle of Unity

It is also wise to omit from a sketch objects that have little or no relation to the subject itself, and which, for this reason, detract from the main idea the drawing is intended to express. This means that we must observe the *Principle of Unity*. A composition must be a homogeneous whole, all its parts related and so thoroughly merged and blended together that they become a single unit. In order to secure unity in a drawing, we select only what relates directly to the subject of the sketch. Separate your subject from everything else that is visible, and think of it as a single harmonious whole. This rule applies if your subject is an entire building or some portion, such as a dormer window, or some still smaller detail, such as a door knocker.

Once you have determined which ideas are irrelevant, you must determine the relative importance of those that are essential, for unity in a drawing depends not only on the *selection* or rejection of material but on its *emphasis* or *subordination* as well. Unless each detail is given just the amount of attention that is proportionate to its importance, the composition will not count as a complete and satisfactory unit. Failure to give sufficient emphasis or accent to the leading parts of a drawing diminishes the force of a composition. In the same way, neglecting to properly subordinate the unimportant parts leads to confusion and complication.

To further illustrate this principle of unity, con-

Fig. 87. Notice how many variations in composition have been achieved simply from the single photograph in Fig. 86.

sider some simple objects found in everyday use. An ink bottle, a turnip, and a vase of roses might be arranged into a pleasing composition as far as variety of form, size, and value are concerned, but unity would always be lacking here, because these objects are not sufficiently well related by use to ever become a satisfying single whole. It would be equally difficult to compose a dust pan, a hairbrush, and cut-glass pitcher, but a comparatively simple matter to form an excellent composition of a loaf of bread partly sliced, with knife, plate, etc., or of a garden trowel, flowerpot, and package of seeds.

Fortunately, nearly all objects of an architectural nature are so closely related that little difficulty is experienced in finding things that go well together, so the architectural renderer has much less trouble in this respect than does the painter of still life. Unity in architectural work is often injured, however, because certain accessories are made too important in relation to the architecture itself. Although it is not inappropriate to draw an automobile at the curb in front of a Colonial doorway, if it is indicated so large in size or made so conspicuous that it detracts from the doorway, it prevents perfect unity. For this reason, in rendering architectural drawings, such accessories are often left in what sometimes seems an unfinished state. Trees are shown inconspicuously, clouds are often either omitted or only lightly indicated, and shadows are simplified.

Principle of Balance

This brings us to a discussion of the *Principle of Balance*, which is so closely related to the Principle of Unity that it is really a part of it. In fact, without balance there can be no unity. By balance we mean, as the name implies, the equilibrium or restfulness that results from having all the parts of a composition arranged in such a way that each receives its correct share of attention. Every part of a picture has a certain attractive force which acts upon the eye. In proportion to its power to *attract*, it *detracts* from every other part. If we find our interest in a drawing divided between several parts—if certain tones or lines seem too insistent

or prominent—we know that the composition is lacking in balance and likewise lacking in unity as well.

It is impossible to give concise and definite rules for obtaining balance in drawings, mainly because the attractive force of each portion of a drawing depends on an infinite number of variable circumstances. A short, straight line drawn near the center of a clean sheet of paper has the power to catch and hold the eye. But draw a figure 6 or some other curved line near the straight one and, even though they are of equal size, the curved line will prove the more powerful attraction of the two. In the same way, a star-shaped form or a triangle has more strength to attract than a square or rectangle of a similar area.

This power to attract depends on the value of light and dark as well as on shape. Draw two squares on paper, side by side, one dark and the other light. If the paper is white, the dark square will exert the stronger force; but if the paper is black, the white square will jump into prominence.

Again, the attractive power of an object varies in proportion to its *proximity* to other objects. For example, a man shown at small scale in a standing or sitting position near the center of the sheet, will receive considerable attention if by himself. But surrounded by other objects, he will seem much less noticeable.

Then, too, a moving object or one which *suggests* motion, will be more prominent than a similar object in repose. If a man is shown running, he is seen far more quickly than if he is at rest.

Objects near the edges of the sheet, or in the corners, usually arrest the eye more quickly than they would if near the middle of the paper. These concepts are illustrated more fully later in this chapter.

Check Your Work

These examples should show the difficulty of giving definite directions for obtaining good balance. The best suggestion we can offer is that you first make a preliminary sketch, as soon as a drawing has been blocked out in its main proportions. A painter is able to make many corrections as he

Fig. 88. Here the distance has been suppressed.

Fig. 89. Here the foreground has been suppressed.

progresses, until excellent balance in every part is gained, but in pencil sketching—where the nature of the medium and the limitation of time demand that the work be done very directly and with few changes—it is difficult to make well-balanced drawings unless the artist or student has had considerable practice or unless preliminary studies are made. Almost invariably, such studies save time and give results that more than justify the labor spent on their preparation.

As a drawing progresses and one area after another is developed, the drawing temporarily goes out of balance again and again. The artist expects this, and each time takes prompt action to remedy it, usually by giving added emphasis to some other area, so that ultimately all parts are adjusted to receive from the spectator precisely the right degree of attention.

One excellent way of judging whether or not your drawing is in balance at any given stage is to reflect it in a mirror. (If it is on tracing paper, look through it from the back.) If, when so viewed, some part or parts seem too insistent or too suppressed in relation to the rest, the picture is out of balance and a way should be found to improve it.

You should realize, however, that there can be more than one proper composition for any given subject. If a dozen equally capable artists were to draw the same subject from the identical point of view, they might develop twelve perfectly satisfactory treatments, each strikingly different from the others.

Center of Interest

One of the beginner's common faults, as we have already suggested, is that he overemphasizes things which at best can contribute little to the subject as a whole, while suppressing things which might well be played up by means of stronger contrasts of tone, sharper delineation of form, or some other expedient. Particularly when working outdoors, each thing catching the eye seems all important at the moment, and it is easy to overstress it in your drawing.

It is good practice, when analyzing a subject, to decide where you want the observer's attention to be primarily directed—whether to the foreground, the middle distance, or the far distance; whether above, at the center, below, or to the right or left. (Interest should usually be confined largely to areas at or near the center.) Having determined this, you can develop a "center of interest" at that point, making this area definitely "in focus" while deliberately throwing other areas "out of focus." This is illustrated by Figs. 88 and 89. Figs. 90 and 91 show how to place the center of interest in different areas on the paper.

Rhythm and Other Terms

Rhythm is another term relating to composition, for by *rhythm* we refer to the regular recurrence of similar features—bushes, buildings, or clouds, for example. Because, with occasional exceptions, related forms tend to be more satisfying than unrelated forms, the artist often seeks or accents them. There can be rhythm of value, too.

Many other terms are also used in connection with composition—*symmetry, repetition, opposition,* etc. If you are curious to know their meanings, or to investigate further any aspect of this subject, you should consult books that specialize in this important topic. However, here we shall confine any further discussion to practice rather than theory.

Creating a Focal Point

Earlier in our discussion of composition, we gave a few examples of how balance is created or disrupted by certain pictorial forces in the drawing. These devices can be used to advantage in drawing the spectator's attention to a certain focal point. Here are some ways to direct the eye:

1. Through the choice of subject matter. Any living subject—a person or an animal—catches the eye more quickly than an inanimate object. A few figures in front of a house, for instance, will draw attention to that area. (See 1, Fig. 92.) Interesting or unusual things, whether animate or inanimate, have more power to attract than do commonplace things. A bear in front of the house would be more compelling than the figures. (See 2, Fig. 92.)

Fig. 90. *The center of interest has been placed in the lower portion of the paper.*

Fig. 91. *The subject matter of a sketch often dictates its composition. Here the interest has been placed high. Nature will show the way.*

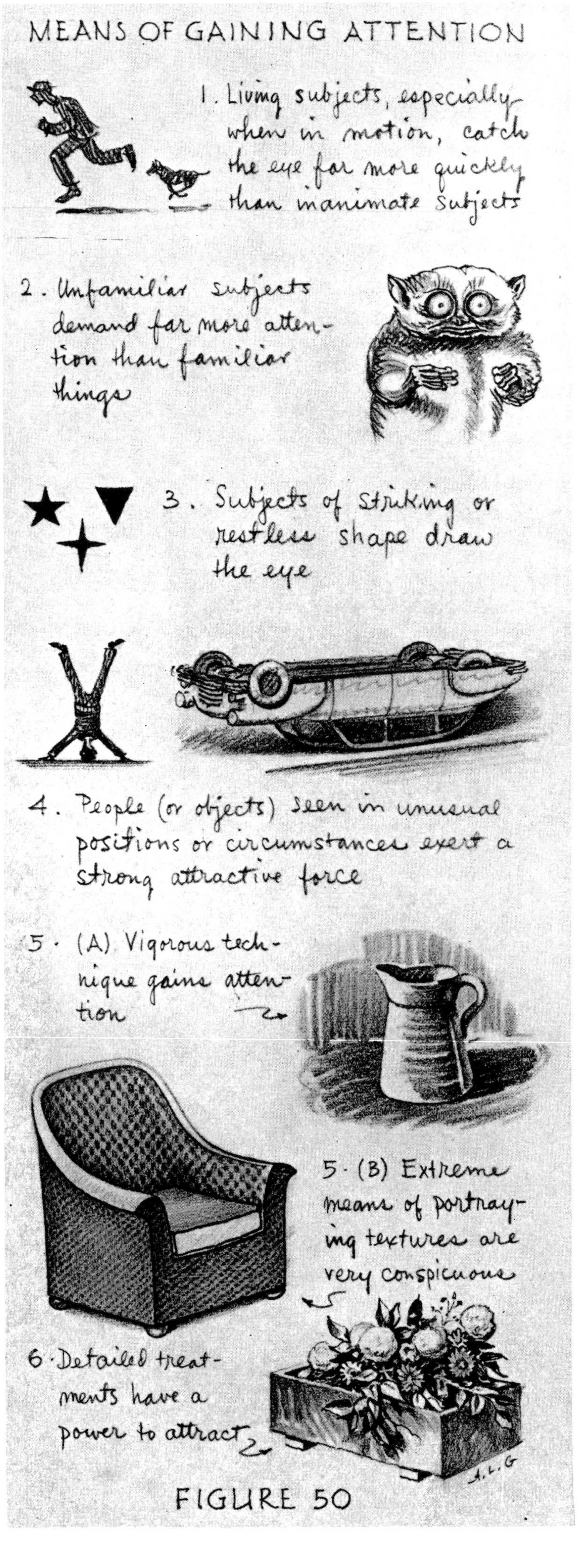

MEANS OF GAINING ATTENTION

1. Living subjects, especially when in motion, catch the eye far more quickly than inanimate subjects

2. Unfamiliar subjects demand far more attention than familiar things

3. Subjects of striking or restless shape draw the eye

4. People (or objects) seen in unusual positions or circumstances exert a strong attractive force

5. (A) Vigorous technique gains attention

5. (B) Extreme means of portraying textures are very conspicuous

6. Detailed treatments have a power to attract

FIGURE 50

Fig. 92. Here are several traditional methods of creating a focal point in your drawing.

Subjects of striking or restless shape will also draw the eye. A star-shaped mass, for example, or a triangle, teetering on one corner in suspended animation, attracts us more than a square or rectangle. (See 3, Fig. 92.)

2. Through unusual arrangements of subject matter. A man standing on his head, or walking on his hands along the ridge of a house, will gain our attention far more effectively than the same man normally occupied. An automobile wrong side up in the street will quickly catch the eye. (See 4, Fig. 92.) In short, many of the things that are conspicuous in scenes in real life are equally so in most representative drawing.

3. Through expressions of extreme activity. A man running will be noticed more quickly than a man walking or at rest.

4. Through vigorous or unusual technical handling. Bold strokes, or highly individual arrangements of strokes, stand out plainly. Extreme means of representing textures serve to draw the eye. (See 5, Fig. 92.)

5. Through particularly detailed handling. If some parts of a subject are treated more fully than the rest, they may become more noticeable. (See 6, Fig. 92.)

6. Through the addition of color. Even a single small spot of color, seen in the midst of neutral surroundings, is a great attention getter.

Often several of these devices are used in combination. Advertising artists in particular, whose drawings frequently are forced to compete with other artwork on the printed page, need to learn many ways of making their results conspicuous. They don't merely seek to reinforce a center of interest; they want their entire work to have strong pulling powers.

Composing with Values

It may not occur to you how many liberties can be taken with values, and how great an effect this can have on your overall composition. Study Fig. 93.

Here you will see how many possibilities there are in just a simple composition. Here we show six of many possible arrangements of the values of a single subject. Note that in all of these the forms remain substantially the same. In Sketches 1, 2, and 3, the tonal differences were based on normal fluctuations in the direction and intensity of light, as they take place at various times of day. In Sketches 4, 5, and 6, the differences result primarily from arbitrary readjustments of the local values. The artist merely lightened some tones and darkened others because he wanted to, and thought it would look all right. Many additional arrangements could utilize both of these procedures. In other words, the artist could deliberately manipulate, according to his own fancy, both the local tones and the values representing light, shade, and shadow.

Decorative or Conventionalized Values

We must not forget to mention those cases—somewhat uncommon, yet by no means rare—in which purely conventional or decorative values are employed, perhaps in combination with outline. In these, little if any resemblance to tonal truth is sought. The artist, instead of working for reality, is simply creating a design. The exact values of tones, and their "spotting" or arrangement in the composition, are dictated largely by esthetic considerations. Fig. 94 shows one of these highly conventionalized drawings.

Value Studies

Only after you have done quite a bit of sketching from nature, however, will you acquire both the confidence to take liberties as drastic as some of these, and the ability to do so convincingly. There is no reason, though, why you should not start to experiment in this direction right now.

One of the best approaches is to place tracing paper over a photograph, drawing upon it (with the photograph showing through as a guide) a series of experimental studies somewhat like those in Fig. 93. Then repeat the exercise with other photos. Try exterior subjects, interiors, still

Light downward from in front

1. LIGHT FROM LEFT

Light downward from the right

4. ROOFS LIGHT, WALLS DARK

Light

2. LIGHT FROM RIGHT

Light

5. WALLS LIGHT; ROOFS DARK

Light downward from behind

3. LIGHT FROM BEHIND

6. BUILDING LIGHT AGAINST DARK

Fig. 93. Value composition is an important compositional device. A single subject may permit many value schemes, perhaps more than you imagine.

life—anything you like. Just as the organist pulls out different stops in order to diversify the effects, this is your chance to pull the stops of white, gray, and black. Grade some tones; keep others flat. And as you work, think about textures, particularly if your drawings are fairly large.

When you have repeated this experiment with a number of photographs, substitute some of your own earlier drawings, again placing tracing paper over each in turn, in order to see how many effective value arrangements you can discover.

Then, when you work from nature the next time, apply the same method by laying tracing paper over your construction layout when completed. Do a series to trial sketches in which you substitute, for some of the values before you, others of your own choosing. Try at least three or four of these sketches for each subject. Then select the best ones as a guide for your rendering.

Fig. 94. Values can also be handled in a decorative manner.

Recomposing Forms

In attempting to recreate nature, the artist customarily constructs proportions of subjects quite realistically. Few liberties can be taken with form representation. This is especially true in the case of certain types of subject matter, such as the human face or figure. (To illustrate this latter point, to do a recognizable portrait of George Washington, you would scarcely elect to use the proportions of Abraham Lincoln!) With living subjects, errors in proportion are usually all too noticeable; they may even result in unintentional and unwanted caricature.

Granting, then, that you want your drawings to look realistic, you can usually do less recomposing of forms than of values. You nevertheless can often rearrange separate parts of your subject matter, one in relation to another, without stretching the credulity of the spectator. You may even take liberties with the sizes of individual objects. And if there is no reason for holding to the original shapes of objects, you can alter them too. If, in drawing a still-life composition, for instance, you feel that a jug, a box, or a book is the wrong size or shape to suit your purpose fully, you are usually free to alter it. Similarly, if you are drawing from landscape, you can shrink or expand a mountain, or change the shape of a tree, or add a chimney to a house. So long as the final result looks soundly constructed, you are well within your rights. (An obvious exception is when you are making what might be called a true portrait of some particular scene—possibly a noted landmark.)

Illusions with Values

If you surround a small and clean-cut area of pure white paper with very dark tone, you become aware that, because of the contrast thus created, the white area actually looks whiter than white.

In order to comprehend this very important point, study the little white disk at 1 (A), Fig. 95. Doesn't this actually appear whiter than the rest of the paper? The fact that the surrounding dark tone has been brought into crisp contrast with the disk, and has then been vignetted away from it, adds to the apparent whiteness of the disk.

Only by trying this on your own paper will you discover the extent of your ability to make things look whiter than white. Apply the idea to small circles, triangles, and squares, as well as to irregular shapes. You will soon see that it isn't the shape that counts, but only the dramatic contrast of light against dark.

At 1 (B) study the simple sketch, an application of this white-spot type of composition to the drawing of a house. Here the building, together with a bit of the lawn before it, forms the white spot, almost as though a spotlight had been thrown upon it. Surrounding this spot is an irregular ring or band consisting of black and gray tones, enough of them brought into sharp relief against the building and lawn to emphasize their whiteness. At the outer edges, the sketch vignettes into the paper just as does the spot at A. This vignetting is vital. It prevents the eye from being drawn away from the planned contrasts nearer the center. From this we derive a helpful rule: With rare exceptions, omit or suppress any rendering at the corners of your drawing. (For other simple applications of this rule, and of the white-spot arrangement in general, see Fig. 99).

Interpreting Sunshine

This white-spot type of composition applies especially to rendering light-toned objects—such as this building at 1 (B), Fig. 95—as seen in bright sunshine. It should be self-evident that your white drawing paper, as normally viewed in shade, can never look as light as a white wall (or other similar surface) exposed to the sun. One of the few ways in which the artist can make such a sunlit wall *look* sunny in a drawing is by forcing some of the adjacent dark areas into strong contrast with the wall, even if this calls for (a) representing the darks darker than they really are in nature, and (b) making their edges, as they come against the white, abnormally decisive.

Blacker than Black

Just as a white area surrounded by black (vignetted to gray) appears whiter than white, so a black area thrown into sharp relief against white looks unusually black. The effect of this contrast will be heightened if the white area against which the black is placed is surrounded by a soft-edged tone of gray. At 2 (A), Fig. 95, is a demonstration of this. Note what a striking contrast this scheme engenders. Take your own pencil and try it—this will dramatize and fix it in your mind. At 2 (B) we utilize this basic principle. Many so-called silhouette effects fall into this kind of composition.

Modifications

Inasmuch as few subjects have large areas of either uninterrupted white or black, very rarely do we see in their pure form either the white-against-dark composition, or the dark-against-white composition. Just as the white spot of the little house at 1 (B) has been punctuated by the grays of door, windows, and roof shadow, so almost all light and dark spots are broken by the artist by means of at least small areas of contrasting tone. We have demonstrated this at 3 (A), where a white disk like that at 1 (A) has been pierced by a black accent. Observe what a forceful compostion this gives us. At 3 (B) we have a simple application. Similarly,

1 (A) Whiter than white   1 (B) An application of A

2 (A) "Forcing" the black   2 (B) An application of A

3 (A) White, pierced   3 (B) An application of A
with small black

4 (A) Black, pierced   4 (B) An application of A
with small white

Fig. 95. Many optical illusions can be created with values. These diagrams demonstrate what can be done with black and white alone.

A · WHITE-SPOT COMPOSITION   B · BLACK-SPOT COMPOSITION

Fig. 96. Values can be recomposed with great freedom.

blacks are often pierced with white: see the disk at 4 (*A*) with its white accent, and the application of the same scheme at 4 (*B*).

Contrasts fundamentally like those at 1, 2, 3, and 4 in Fig. 95 are unlimited in kind and number, being subject to endless combination and adaptation. In fact, such vigorous utilization of black and white might be said to constitute the pencil artist's *tour de force*. Sometimes the artist adapts this basic plan of light against dark or dark against light to his overall composition. He then reserves such striking contrasts only for those particular sections that call for special attention.

For the overall composition, in a large number of cases, the same subject may be treated successfully either as a light spot against dark or a dark spot against light. Compare, for instance, the two chimney drawings in Fig. 96. Notice that there is little solid black in these drawings. This illustrates another modification of the use of contrast: the artist seldom needs extreme contrasts of light and dark such as we have used for our demonstrations

in Fig. 95. Almost invariably, where dark is desired, a deep gray will serve your purpose better than pure black. Similarly, your white can sometimes be toned down advantageously, though in pencil work, this is less often true.

Using Contrast for Focus

Returning to the matter of centering the interest, if your subject for a drawing is simple (as in the case of the chimney just pictured) or small, the spectator's eye easily takes in the whole thing and there is seldom any serious compositional problem. The composition almost automatically develops perfect unity. If, however, a subject is large or complex—perhaps made up of several unrelated or even incompatible elements—the artist must be very careful (as earlier pointed out in discussing the principle of balance) not to set up an opposition of two or more major centers of interest. (Such a scheme of clashing elements might conceivably be useful only in one of those rare compositions designed to interpret violent action, turbulent strife, or clamorous sound. This proves there are exceptions to all rules.)

If a subject is large or complicated, you are generally wise to focus attention on some limited area, just as in viewing a scene in nature you often concentrate, for a moment at least, on a given spot. In order to focus this attention, create some of your strongest contrasts within the chosen area, perhaps calling into play either the white-spot or dark-spot motive. Then be careful not to employ equally strong contrasts in other parts of the drawing to cause competition.

In Figs. 97 and 98 we see how the artist can focus on any given area of a subject by strengthening the value contrasts in that area and simultaneously restraining his contrasts in such other areas. Figs. 88 and 89 further illustrate this point.

(In connection with Figs. 97 and 98, if you focus your attention first on the top of the lighthouse (1), and next on the facade of the appended building (2), the perspective in the two drawings would not remain identical, as drawn here. For our purpose, however, it seemed best not to make the very slight perspective adjustment such a distant subject would ordinarily call for.)

Exercises in Value Composition

To put into use these basic concepts of white-spot and dark-spot composition, we urge you to make numerous experimental studies—they may be very small—to learn how much power you have to dramatize subject matter through deliberately playing one value against another. In Fig. 99 we reproduce (at the exact size of the originals) a number of spottings to suggest some possibilities. These have purposely been made extreme in value contrast; the basic idea would, of course, apply equally well to more restrained tonal schemes.

For further practice, study the work of other artists, isolating their basic value schemes. Forget all the small details and subtle variations of tone; merely see if you can reduce each composition to its simplest terms of black and white, or black, white, and gray.

In light of your recently acquired knowledge,

Fig. 97. Here the focus is placed at the top of the lighthouse.

Fig. 98. Here the focus is at the base of the lighthouse.

1. Dark against light

2. Light against dark

3. Contrived contrasts

4. View through archway

5. Frame of planting

6. A half-frame will do

Fig. 99. A number of spottings can illustrate the great variations possible in composing a drawing.

repeat the practice of selecting photographs of different types of subject matter, and recompose their values through the aid of tracing paper. You will find that you can soon gain considerable command over this art. Try a number of comparative sketches of each subject, varying the tonal composition.

We all know that professional photographers, in order to arrive at the best possible composition, like to study a subject from many viewpoints before snapping the camera. Realizing the frequent need for dramatic tonal relationships, they often "frame" a subject by viewing it through an archway, from between trees or, perhaps, from beneath a bridge. Or they may wander about until a branch is found which effectively hangs from above to give distance and to break their otherwise blank sky areas.

The artist has even more freedom; he can manipulate to greater degree both forms and values and at the same time move objects from place to place almost at will. Like the photographer, the artist often finds it advantageous to create frames—perhaps of extremely dark tone—on the order of those in Fig. 99 at 4, 5, and 6. Such contrasty frames are particularly suitable when viewing subject matter at some distance. As dark frames are very conspicuous against the light tones beyond, their shape and value must be designed with great care. In fact, whenever the artist uses strong contrasts of tone, any unpleasant tonal relationships will be far more prominent than when contrasts are less evident. In other words, using strong contrasts takes courage and skill.

Some Practical Pointers

In terminating this present discussion of value contrasts we offer eight pointers to keep in mind when making a drawing. Though not all of them relate directly to composition, they nevertheless should be grouped together for obvious reasons:

1. In a typical pencil drawing, try to find an opportunity in the outline before you to create a leading dark area. (There may, of course, be many subordinate dark areas.)

2. Strive for a compensating large light area. (Often this and the leading dark area will be adjacent.)

3. Employ at least three distinct values—white, gray, and black (or very dark gray)—but avoid too many scattered contrasts throughout your drawing.

4. Even if you are working for a very realistic final impression, don't be afraid to manipulate your values by methods such as we have demonstrated.

5. In building your tones, attempt to obtain not only appropriate values, but also a proper expression of surface directions and textures.

6. Use, in general, a free, spontaneous technique so that your complete work will express your confidence.

7. Stop when you arrive at a reasonably satisfactory effect. Many drawings are ruined through overwork.

8. If your final result is disappointing, try the same subject again.

Composition in Architectural Drawings

The principles of composition described all too briefly in the previous section, are most important, and apply to all forms of drawing and design. But we will now offer a few suggestions that relate especially to architectural work.

First of all, in making drawings of architecture, strive for an effect of restfulness and repose. A painter of birds and animals or of marine views may often desire the appearance of motion, but where drawing architecture is involved, care must be taken not to suggest much movement. Each building should look permanent and solid and should appear to rest firmly on the ground. Avoid, therefore, any effect of violent wind or of speeding automobiles or hurrying people.

If figures are indicated, have them walking quietly into the picture or approaching the center of interest. If they are shown walking away from the center towards the margin line, the eye follows them and the balance is disturbed. There are, of

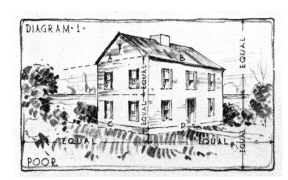

Fig. 100. Avoid centering a building in this way.

Fig. 101. This is somewhat better.

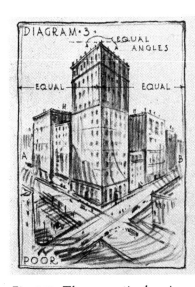

Fig. 102. The perspective here is too violent.

Fig. 103. Here is a better variety of masses.

course, exceptions to this. If many people are shown, as in a street scene, they may be represented as going in all directions, for the sense of motion in one direction will be offset by that in the other. Figures of any sort greatly injure a drawing, however, unless they are well drawn and naturally arranged into effective groups. Therefore, either omit them entirely or draw them very well.

Figs. 100 to 108 are designed to show certain displeasing effects often found in architectural drawings and how to correct them. In Fig. 100, notice that the foremost corner of the house is equidistant from the two end margin lines. It is seldom advisable to place a building in this position, a possible exception being a tower which is absolutely symmetrical. Fig. 102 illustrates the same point, while Fig. 104 applies the idea to an interior. In both of these, the effect is somewhat unpleasant. Do not, then, divide the picture space into two equal parts by having some important line directly in the center.

Look again at Figs. 100, 102, and 104 and you will find that the horizon line or eye level towards which all the receding horizontal lines seem to vanish is exactly halfway from top to bottom of the picture space; this division is unsatisfactory, too. Better results are obtained when the horizon or eye level is set either above or below the center of the sheet. In the same way, the sketch in Fig. 87, would be better if the top line of the bridge were not so near the center. Here the picture space is also divided into two nearly equal parts by this particular line.

It is usually preferable to avoid many opposing lines of the same slant or angle, for variety is always desirable. In Fig. 100 (Diagram 1), the lines at A, B, C, and D are all of equal pitch. This leads to monotony. The same fault is found in Figs. 102 (Diagram 3) and 104 (Diagram 5). It is better to place the building on the sheet in a way that avoids these difficulties. Figs. 101, 103, and 105 (Diagrams 2, 4, and 6) show a better placement than Figs. 100, 102, and 104. First, the perspective is so violent that the building has the unstable effect of resting on its lower corner, and the crossed lines of the streets form too conspicuous a pattern with a tendency to draw the eye away from the building towards points *A* and *B*. Fig. 103 has a more pleasing variety of masses and the interest plainly centers in the main building. Fig. 104 shows a fault in that the two visible wall surfaces are equal in size and shape, as are also the ceiling and floor, and here, too, there is no real center of focus, for the eye jumps back and forth between *A* and *B*. Fig. 105 is better, for the interest undoubtedly centers at *A*. Even though there is an important mass at *B*, it is toned down to seem unimportant. The floor, too, has been made larger in mass than the ceiling, but the advantage gained is largely lost, for the rug is unfortunately of the same size on the drawing as the visible portion of the ceiling, so that this sketch could be still further improved by adding either more rug or more ceiling. Fig. 106 shows that when a room is turned so that we are looking directly at one of its walls or is placed in "parallel perspective," as this is called, similar faults may develop. Here the main surfaces are all monotonous, the interest is divided and the drawing made still more unpleasant because the receding lines exactly meet the margin lines at the corners. In Fig. 107 an attempt has been made to avoid some of the difficulties found in Fig. 106.

The little sketch of the dormer (Fig. 108) is shown to illustrate an important matter of composition. When drawing small details, always take care that they do not seem to be merely suspended in the air. They should appear instead to be attached to a solid background or support. One of the best means of giving this impression is by allowing each sketch to fade out gradually into the sheet, showing enough of the adjacent surroundings to give the whole a sense of stability and strength.

This is only a brief introduction to the matter of architectural drawing and composition. We urge you to make drawings of your own to illustrate any of these principles.

Let us close this chapter by once again reiterating that the artist is a creator, not an imitator. Don't merely try to copy some bit of nature with photographic precision. Instead, use nature as a point of departure, relying on your own inborn esthetic ability as developed through experience.

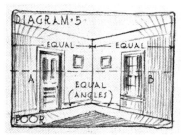

Fig. 104. The wall surfaces are too equal in size and shape.

Fig. 105. By placing the walls off-center, the composition is improved.

Fig. 106. Parallel perspective in an interior is dull.

Fig. 107. Shifting the perspective will help.

Fig. 108. Details should seem to be attached to
a solid support.

Exercise artistic license to select or reject, to rearrange, to substitute, to stress or suppress—to compose, in other words—until you translate your bit of nature into a satisfying drawing which may or may not bear close resemblance to its natural prototype.

No doubt you will, for awhile, choose to hold close to nature's appearances. You may rearrange minor details, and experiment with value adjustments, but that is about all. Gradually your increased skill will add to your confidence until ultimately, on an outdoor sketching trip, you may select a barn at the right, a hill at the left, a cow from the foreground, the clouds behind you, and recompose them into a picture. You may even compose from memory, far from the subject matter which you used in the picture. Your knowledge of composition will help make this possible.

11.
Graded Tones

We have already seen several uses of gradations: (a) In shading rounded objects, for example, graded tones are practically indispensable. You could scarcely do a figure drawing, a portrait—or, for that matter, a study of a jug or a simple sphere—without them. (b) Shadow (or other) edges, which tend to become too conspicuous, are frequently softened by gradation. (c) In focusing attention on a center of interest, great reliance is placed on gradation. (d) All of the white-spot and black-spot types of composition discussed earlier depend largely on gradation for their effectiveness.

Yet this frequent application of such modulations is not all an artist's whim. He is actually observing these effects in nature which generate tonal gradations of every sort with the utmost prolificacy. If you have never observed this, look about you!

Our present chapter deals with some of the naturalistic gradations of subjects before you, as well as certain with rather arbitrary uses of grades which the artist has learned to make. In fact, the artist even finds it advisable, on occasion, to substitute graded tones for some of the flat ones in nature so he can obtain certain desirable effects by the simplest and quickest means.

Substituting Graded for Flat Tones

To turn to a specific example, in Fig. 109 a plain barn is rendered largely in flat tones, much as it appeared in nature. In Fig. 110 graded tones are substituted in such a way that they emphasize value contrasts where most needed to express the subject effectively—as at *a* and *b* where light and shadow planes meet at right angles. (In drawing

the grades in Fig. 110, greater technical freedom was used than in producing the flat tones in Fig. 109. The grades have more character. But that's another story.)

Study Objects Around You

Careful observation and study of objects in nature, as well as objects created by man, will reveal one fact of great value to the student of drawing: although some of their beauty depends on the color, shape, and proportions of their parts, more of the beauty of objects in nature derives from a variation in light and shade and especially from a gradation of tones from light to dark or from dark to light.

There are, to be sure, some objects that seem to have no gradation of tone, each surface being apparently of one value throughout. In spite of these occasional exceptions, there are far more "graded" tones in nature than "flat" tones of uniform appearance. It is certainly true that a graded tone has more interest and variety than a flat one.

Rounded Forms and Graded Tones

It naturally follows that in representing nature by drawings, graded tones are generally more valuable to the artist than flat ones. Almost any object can be represented satisfactorily by graded tones, whereas many objects—especially rounded or curved ones—cannot be made to appear correct if flat tones alone are used. We can, for example, make a pleasing drawing of a square box, and still grade every tone if we wish. On the other hand, it is impossible to represent a sphere or an object of spherical form by flat tones only, unless we resort

Fig. 109. This scene is rendered largely in flat tones.

Fig. 110. Here graded tones are used to render the same subject.

to a succession of small adjacent flat tones, each slightly different in value from its neighbor. But such a combination really is, after all, a graded tone.

If we try to portray a sphere by drawing its outline as at 1, Fig. 111, we fail to give our picture any effect of convexity of form. Shading the entire circle with a flat tone, as at 2, gives no better result. Only when we copy the gradations found on such surfaces in nature, as we have done at 3, do we approach the desired effect. In fact, we would not even recognize a sphere when placed before us if it were not for this subtle grading on its surface tones. Without these gradations it would appear simply as a flat circular disk. In the case of the cylinder, cone, and similar rounded forms, it is perhaps a bit easier to suggest their shapes on paper without using graded tones, providing they are drawn in perspective. Then, at least, their forms can be fairly well indicated, even in outline.

A real feeling of solidity and roundness, however, is best obtained by using graded tones. If a cone or cylinder were shown in elevation, instead of perspective, you would find that graded tones are absolutely essential for identification. Take, for example, the cylinder shown in elevation at 4, Fig. 111, drawn in outline only. In this form it appears more like a rectangle and seems flat. A smooth tone added, as at 5, is of no help. It is only when we use the grades, as at 6, that we get the real appearance of roundness.

Architectural Moldings

Just as the surfaces of cylinders, spheres, and similar geometric forms depend largely on gradation of tone for a pleasing effect, so, in architecture too, much of the beauty of the moldings and ornament depends on similar gradations. After all, moldings are mainly combinations of curved surfaces, and if these curves are well designed, the light and dark will be graded in a pleasing manner. In fact, these gradations on moldings are so expressive of the profiles causing them that we are often able to judge the curve of each molding at a glance, even though its profile is not visible. If the light is favorable, we are usually

OBJECTS SHADED WITH GRADED TONES

A·L·GUPTILL·1920

Fig. 111. Graded tones may also be employed on architectural details.

able to identify every member composing a cornice and tell its exact form without once seeing its true profile. One of the main reasons why a designer works so hard to produce a good profile for a cornice, or similar group of moldings, is that he is seeking the most pleasing arrangement of light, shade, and shadow possible.

At 7, 8, 9, and 10, Fig. 111, are four sketches of typical architectural moldings, drawn in elevation, and with their tones graded. For convenience their profiles have been shown, but even if these had been omitted it would not be difficult to visualize the correct curves. Bear in mind, however, that without the use of graded tones it would be impossible to produce such effects of curvature.

Ornaments and Graded Tones

Just as it is necessary to use graded tones for a truthful expression of the curved surfaces of moldings, so they are needed in representing other rounded surfaces, such as those we so often find in ornamental work. Most ornament, in fact, consists largely of curved surfaces of every possible shape, difficult to represent on paper without some graded tones. At 11, Fig. 111, is a drawing of a rosette, nearly every surface of which is curved, and therefore represented by grades of light and dark. An object of such gradual curvature as this can be successfully portrayed only by equally subtle gradations of its values.

Balusters, columns, archways, round towers, and all sorts of similar architectural objects and details require a certain amount of graded shading. At 12 and 13, Fig. 111, a baluster and a capital are shown. Even though drawn in elevation, the rounded effect is very evident. Had they been done in perspective, less care would have been needed in shading to express roundness. For architectural purposes it is often necessary to work in elevation, so these sketches are done in that manner to prove it is not essential to show objects in perspective when a feeling of projection and curvature is required.

In order to illustrate the points under discussion in the clearest possible way, the drawings in Fig. 111 have been done with very evenly graded tones. By this means, the values on the objects could be more accurately represented than by using tones built up of separate lines. As a general rule, however, such smooth tones are not essential. You can also use a linear approach, and place your lines barely touching, to get a similar result. The result, being less mechanical or photographic is thus more desirable.

At 14 a few suggestions are offered for the formation of graded tones by individual strokes. (It is good practice to make a few drawings similar to these, trying some with the smooth tone and others with a more sketchy handling.)

Lighting Affects Graded Tones

Remember that, although the exact form the gradation of a tone takes depends largely on the curve of the surface, it really is visible because of the light causing it. If we had no light, the most perfect moldings would be lost in darkness—if we have too much light, their beauty is often destroyed.

I have in mind a certain, unusually beautiful, coffered ceiling. After this ceiling had been in existence a number of years and had been much admired, it was decided to install a new indirect lighting system in the room. The system was so arranged that the light was uniformly distributed over the ceiling so that nearly all of the shade and shadow was destroyed. The lighting engineers pronounced the job perfect—but from an artistic standpoint the effect of the ceiling was ruined. The moldings and detail were barely visible, while the few shadows that remained took weird and grotesque shapes. In this case too much light, or rather light distributed in too uniform a manner, destroyed the effect.

This proves that even a beautiful curve may lose much of its value through unfavorable lighting, and it shows also that the gradation of tone on any given molding or curve varies with changes in light. Spheres and cylinders, for example, do not appear the same at all times and hence cannot always be represented in the same way.

Surface Affects Graded Tones

Remember, too, that the gradation of tone on any given form—take a cylinder, for example—depends also on the material from which the object is made. A study of a number of cylinders of equal size and of various materials such as wood, plaster, polished white marble, sandstone, red granite, brass, silver, etc., will reveal, even under the same conditions, a surprising difference in the values and the method of tone gradation. Cylinders with highly polished surfaces will show a greater complication of values and much sharper and more sudden contrasts, as a rule, mainly because their surfaces serve as curved mirrors to reflect distorted images of other objects. Such surfaces usually have brilliant highlights in spots. On the other hand, those of the wood, plaster, or other dull appearing objects will not only lack these highlights, but will show throughout a more simple and gradual change in tone. Because of conditions such as these, there can be no definite rules how such objects should be represented. Only close observation will provide you with this knowledge.

Graded Tones on Flat Surfaces

We have, up to this point, spoken mainly of graded tones found on curved surfaces. Yet you should also realize that smooth, flat surfaces often appear to grade from one part to another. Prove this to yourself by observing objects around you. You will see this particularly on surfaces indoors, where the light is frequently coming from a number of sources and is all more or less diffused. Here you will find many graded tones. A ceiling, for instance, often appears light at one side and dark at the other.

In the shadow tones, especially, we find a great amount of gradation. As a rule, the shadows of objects indoors seem the darkest and have the sharpest edges near the object casting them. A chair leg, for example, usually casts a dark shadow where it touches the floor, but this shadow softens as it gets farther from the leg, soon disappearing altogether. The little sketch of

Fig. 112. On flat surfaces, the shadow is usually darkest near the object casting it.

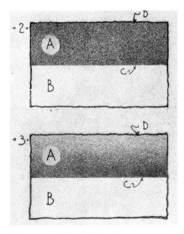

Fig. 113. Graded tones give a greater sense of separation than flat ones.

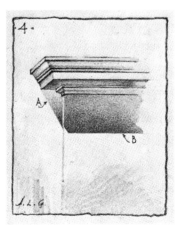

Fig. 114. In brilliant light the lower edge of the shadow seems darkest.

the pencil touching the paper at 1, Fig. 112, was made to illustrate this point, the shadow being the darkest at *A*, softening as the light becomes more diffused towards *B*.

In brilliant light, such as bright sunshine, the opposite effect is often found. Let an object project from the wall, like the little cornice shown in Fig. 111, and the lower edge of the shadow at *B* frequently seems sharper and darker than the edge nearer the object, as at *A*. Such an effect, is, as a rule, only an optical illusion. Unless there is something to cause a strong reflection of light into the upper portion of the shadow, the tone is usually of equal value throughout. What appears to be darkness towards the lower edge is caused by the sunlight which is so extremely brilliant that, when it falls on a light wall or similar surface, it produces a value so bright that we are unable to correctly represent it on paper. So when a shadow tone cast by some object similar to the cornice in Fig. 114 falls on this bright surface, the tone appears, in relation to the bright surface, darker than it really is. A shadow may be a medium gray when compared with black. But if its lower edge is thrown into sudden and sharp contrast with extremely brilliant light, it often actually seems black.

In drawing shadows, therefore, there is a legitimate reason for the gradation we have shown in Fig. 114, as this method causes the white of the paper to appear brighter than it otherwise would, and therefore more correctly represents the sunlit surface. The lighter shadow tone above also gains

a quality of depth and transparency by the use of this gradation.

Distance and Detachment

There is another use for graded tones that is of great importance—to give a sense of distance and detachment or separation of one object from another. We can perhaps best explain this by referring to Sketches 5, 6, and 7, in Fig. 115. Objects in nature, even when they are of the same value, can usually be easily distinguished one from another by their different colors, their motion, or in a number of other ways. In photographs, such objects, if the values of light and shade are the same or nearly the same, often seem lost or indistinct. Sketch 5, made from a photograph, shows at *A* just this condition: the roof and wall tones lack detachment—it is hard to distinguish one from the other. In Sketch 6 this same wall tone has been graded back to light from dark and at *A* the roof has been darkened. The result gives us a much greater feeling of separation—the roof seems to come nearer to us and the wall tends to recede—as it should. The edge at *B* still appears just as sharp as it did before the wall was lightened towards *A*.

In just the same way, edge *C* in Diagram 3 (Fig. 113) seems as sharp or even sharper than the same edge in Diagram 2 (because in 2 the edge *D* detracts from *C* to a greater extend that it does in 3). We have about the same relative contrast in Sketches 5 and 6 between the wall in light and the wall in shade, so that Sketch 6 is not injured in any

Fig. 115. Distance and detachment are obtained with graded tones.

way because of the changed values at *A*.

Sketch 7 (Fig. 115) is another and very emphatic illustration of the use of graded tones in securing detachment. The chimney has been lightened towards the bottom and the room darkened towards the top in order to gain a sharp contrast. This method brings the roof forward and carries the chimney back, giving an effect of distance. The idea is, therefore, useful to remember as it can be applied in many different places in nearly every drawing. In Sketch 1, for instance, the horizontal line is softened as it goes behind the pencil, thereby bringing the pencil forward.

Sketch 8 (Fig. 116) shows a similar application of a graded tone. By darkening the cornice shadow towards the nearest corner of the house, that corner actually seems to come nearer. This method is of even more value when the wall is turned at a sharper angle, making the foreshortening more acute.

Graded Tones and Emphasis

Graded tones are of great assistance in forcing the eye to any given portion of a drawing, and the little diagrams *A* and *B*, Sketch 9, Fig. 117, show two methods of bringing attention to a desired spot, in this case the dark circle. The sketches really explain themselves. Method *B* is perhaps the stronger one, for the dark tone at *C* in Sketch *A* detracts from the spot itself. Of the two little window sketches in Fig. 117, the second carries out the idea represented by method *B*, the dark shadow taking the place of the dark spot in the diagram. The eye here is forced to the bright upper portion of the window. The first window sketch shows in place of such strong contrast, a more gradual grading from dark at the top down to light.

Occasionally it is necessary to apply the idea of separation or detachment to such accessories as fences and tree trunks. In Sketch 10, Fig. 118, the fence is graded in such a way that it appears light againt the two dark masses of foliage and dark against the light background. You may apply the same idea to trees making the trunks and branches appear dark against the sky, then grad-

Fig. 116. Areas can advance or recede with the use of graded tones.

Fig. 117. Graded tones can be used effectively for emphasis.

Fig. 118. Particularly in landscapes, the idea of separation and detachment can be used to advantage.

ing them to a lighter tone against the background of hedge or other foliage, and sometimes having them reappear dark in contrast with the grass of the lawn.

Composing with Graded Tones

Just as graded tones prove of value in innumerable ways when representing small details, they are of use, too, in composing entire drawings. Occasionally compositions grade from dark at the top to light at the bottom as in Figs. 119 and 121. Sometimes they are light at the top and dark below, like Sketches 4 and 6 in Figs. 122 and 124. These are all rather extreme examples, however, though frequently drawings combine grades in two or more directions. Sketch 2 in Fig. 120, for example, shows dark masses of foliage behind the building which grade away to light. At the end margins there are opposing dark masses causing a sharp contrast which seems to set the building back into the middle distance. Sketch 3, Fig. 123, also shows two sets of grades, the one on the

building itself, going from light at the center to dark at the ends; the other on the hedge, which, by grading in just the contrary direction, gives contrasts which carry the eye towards the center of the composition. Sketch 7, Fig. 125, is a further example of forcing the attention to a given point, in this case the near end of the building. By grading the walls are left light at the end to form a strong contrast with the trees. Drawings are sometimes graded off into distance in just the opposite way—that is, they are carried from dark in the foreground to light in the background.

Graded tones can also be used to show the roundness of objects that show perspective, as in Fig. 126.

We might go on and on with such demonstrations, but our purpose is not so much to show you exactly what you can do as it is to direct your thinking along exploratory lines. We hope that this chapter will make you more observant both of the many ways in which nature employs gradations and of the equally varied devices artists perform with graded tones.

Fig. 119. Here is a larger composition that grades from dark at the top to light at the bottom.

Fig. 120. Dark masses of foliage grade away to light.

Fig. 121. This composition
also grades from dark at the
top to light at the bottom.

Fig. 123. The tones grade in one direction on the
building and in the reverse direction on the hedge.

Fig. 124. This drawing grades from
light at the top to dark at the bottom.

Fig. 122. This drawing grades from
light at the top to dark at the bottom.

Fig. 125. Emphasis is provided by tones graded to
contrast with the foliage.

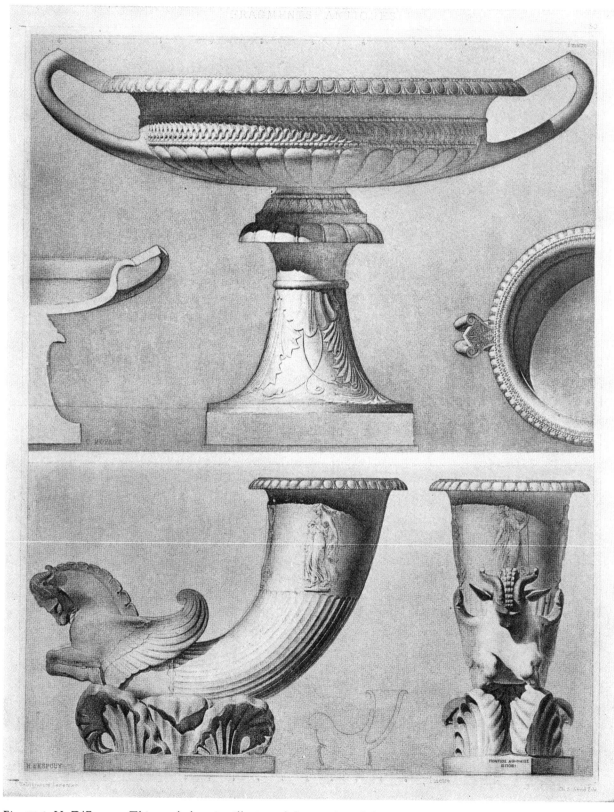

Fig. 126. H. D'Espouy: This wash drawing illustrated the use of graded tones in suggesting the roundness of objects that show no perspective.

12.
Outdoor Sketching

Moving from the studio into the outdoors is a stimulating experience for the artist. This chapter will provide some assistance in taking this important step, because there are some surprises to be found.

Outdoor Still Life

By way of preparation for outdoor work, a little transitional practice in drawing still life in the open might be particularly valuable. This practice will introduce you gradually to the different conditions than exist indoors.

Subjects normally associated with the barn, shed, garage, or garden are appropriate and offer a real challenge for this outdoor work. Among these are packing cases, barrels, fruit and vegetable baskets, watering pots, flower pots, jugs, wheelbarrows, bird houses, benches, lawn furniture, tools, and toys. At the shore, you can find dozens of such things as boats, fish traps, lobster pots, net reels, and buoys. In the city, you can draw fire hydrants, park benches, parking signs, and playground objects. All of these may be drawn singly, or grouped into compositions.

Try to determine at once the height of your eye in relation to your subject matter. Draw on your paper a horizon line to represent the eye level (or, at least, determine it in your mind) to help you correctly construct any objects which have definite geometric form—those based on cubes, pyramids, cylinders, etc. Make sure that whether objects are actually quite a distance below the eye level, at the eye level, or above it, they are represented in a way that describes that standpoint. (See Fig. 127.)

Shadows and Sunshine

Draw the same objects in two different lighting conditions, once in full sunshine (A, Fig. 128), and then in shadow—perhaps in the shadow of a house or under a tree, as in B, Fig. 129. Try it again on a rainy or misty day, with the objects exposed to the elements. (You can, of course, keep dry by drawing through a window or from a porch.)

Outdoor objects in shadow have more the appearance of indoor objects than do objects in sunshine, so they afford a logical starting point. Their lighting—and therefore their shade and shadow tones—will be governed largely, of course, by the nature and direction of the light reaching them. This light may be reflected onto the objects from the sky or from some neighboring light surface, or it may be filtered through the trees. Because of possible reflections, there may be evidence of light from more than one direction.

On the whole, however, you will discover in these outdoor objects in shadow much the same variety of light, shade, and shadow which normally prevails indoors. In your drawing, try to give the impression that the subject matter is in shadow. This might seem to call for graying your entire paper surface somewhat in all shadow areas, though the artist seldom does this. Only the conditions under which you draw, and your own feeling in the matter, can guide you.

Objects in direct sunshine (as shown in Fig. 128) pose new problems. The subtleties observed indoors are missing. The light, shade, and shadow areas are clean-cut, with shadow edges sharp, and the light so glaring that the shadows look very dark in contrast. Reflected lights, however strong (like those thrown onto your subject from the

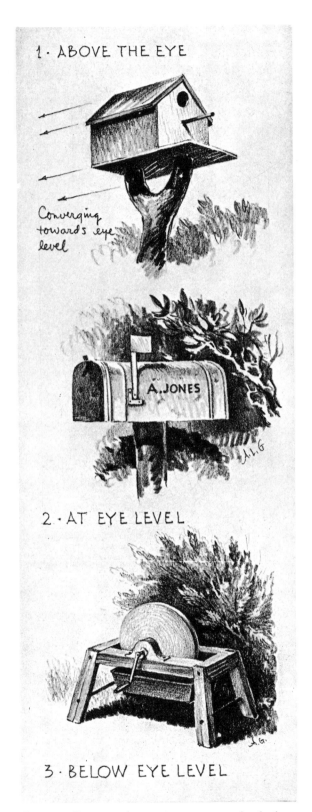

1 · ABOVE THE EYE

Converging
towards eye
level

A. JONES

2 · AT EYE LEVEL

3 · BELOW EYE LEVEL

Fig. 127. Pay special attention to your eye level when you draw outdoor still-life objects.

sunny wall of a nearby white house), will seem relatively dark when compared with areas exposed to the sun.

Direction of Light

As soon as you have arranged your objects in the sunshine and are ready to draw them, glance at the sun to determine the direction of the light rays. This direction is obviously expressed by the pattern of light and shade in your subject matter. You are more likely to represent your light and shade well if you keep in mind, as you work, this direction of the light rays. Remember that the rays coming to the objects the most directly will create the lightest tones.

Study your sunlit objects for a time before you draw them, then proceed much as you would indoors. Work faster, though, for the shifting sun is a hard taskmaster; the shadow shapes will change frequently. If clouds keep passing over the sun, the lighting effects—especially the degree of intensity—will be particularly inconstant. Whatever the conditions, don't try to keep up with every change in light or your work will never be done.

It is just as well that you can't work too deliberately outdoors. Haste results in spontaneous, vigorous effects, with emphasis on the essentials, and with nonessentials omitted or held down. There is no time to fool with fancy technical effects, no time to swap pencils or draw studied line or tone. You soon learn that you may be forced to quit at any time—perhaps unexpectedly. Therefore, always try to keep the whole drawing moving at the same pace.

Accidents

As you draw (especially if you work with considerable freedom), certain chance effects will develop that can sometimes prove very pleasing. That is part of the charm of the pencil—its strokes and tones can become very interesting in themselves. Unless such accidental effects are too conspicuous, don't suppress or obliterate them—be thankful for them and leave them alone, undeserved but not unappreciated.

Fig. 128. Draw objects in sunshine and study the shadow formation made by bright sunlight.

Fig. 129. Notice what happens to the values when the same objects are in shadow.

Moving to Landscape

Once you get outdoors, you won't be content with drawing inanimate objects. You will see a cat go by, and you'll try to record it, or you will be intrigued by an old man relaxed in a lawn swing, and you'll drop your still life in a hurry. That's all right. Who cares? You'll probably want to turn to larger subjects, too: that boat drawn up beside the wharf, that mountain in the distance, that elm tree hanging over the neighbor's garage. So go to it! You've had the patience to acquire the necessary background and can now begin to have some real fun and see some worthwhile accomplishment.

The novice at landscape drawing often finds himself in a bewildering world. First, nature offers an overabundance of subject matter; there's generally enough in sight for a thousand drawings. How can you, faced with all this embarrassment of riches, decide on a single subject? Also, unless you choose a subject at some distance from your position, you are in danger of focusing first on one detail and then on another. As a result, you may develop the same perspective inconsistencies mentioned in connection with room interiors. Also, each detail, in turn, may seem so important that you may over-render it.

Nature is capricious, too. In an hour, the shifting sun can wholly alter the shapes of the areas of light, shade, and shadow, as well as the intensity of the light. Other changes in effect may be instantaneous, as when a cloud obscures the sun, or mist blows in from the sea. During sunrise and sunset hours, it is next to impossible to catch one of nature's moods on paper before it has mysteriously merged with another quite different one.

Unlike still life, most landscape subjects are huge compared to your paper area. This means that you must indicate on a few inches or centimeters of paper a whole mountain, a tree, or a farm building—a fact that creates new problems.

And there are minor annoyances: you find, perhaps, that you have left your favorite pencil at home; a sudden shower comes up; hunger calls you from work; people gather to watch; the wind rips your paper from the board; the sun invades your shade or gets in your eyes; you are accused of trespassing.

Does all this sound like an argument against outdoor sketching? It's not supposed to be. Don't let a few things like these discourage you. To most people, outdoor sketching offers far more fun than drawing indoors.

Setting Out

In working outdoors, it is generally best to select the late afternoon when the rays of the sun are slanted, providing excellent contrast of light and shade and shadow. Sit in the shade, if this is possible, or at least keep the sunlight from falling directly on your paper, for a bright glare will be trying to the eyes and may prevent a correct judgment of values, especially if you are accustomed to spending the greater portion of your time indoors. In order to offset to some measure the brilliancy of the outdoor light, some artists use gray or straw-colored paper for sketching purposes. Besides having less tendency to cause eye strain, this paper also permits a pleasing use of white pencil or chalk for picking out some of the highlights. Any size paper will do, some of the pocket sketchbooks being very convenient. The smaller ones prohibit freedom of movement of the arm and wrist and can force you into unnecessary difficulties. The notebook proportion of 8.5 x 11"/21.5 x 28cm previously recommended seems practical, and some artists prefer still larger sheets.

As the main object of outdoor sketching is to record facts in a direct and forceful manner, don't use many grades of pencils. Have several pencils, of each selected grade, however, for they wear down rather quickly, and be sure to carry a knife because the pencils will need frequent pointing.

Make yourself as comfortable as circumstances permit, in order to have your attention free for the task at hand. A newspaper or magazine makes a fairly comfortable seat on the ground or on some stone or log or wall, if no better one is available.

Choosing a Subject

You may become tired of the constant admonition, "Pick a simple subject," but it's sound. Once you turn to subjects larger or more complicated than the outdoor still life discussed earlier, you must limit your viewpoint. Don't try to get all outdoors in your first sketch. Satisfy yourself with a single tree or group of shrubs; a bit of road or a path with the immediate surroundings; a quaint house or an old barn—even the barn door, for that matter. For example, in Figs. 130 and 131, the same subject is viewed in two different ways, with a variation in focal point.

One thing to remember is that the typical outdoor subject will reveal less interesting light and shade contrasts in the middle of the day, when the sun is directly overhead, than in early morning or late afternoon.

When you find something appealing, look at it through your viewfinder. Walk around; study it from different angles. Finally, pick a spot where you can sit and work unmolested, without a glare of light on your paper or in your eyes. And remember not to work so close to your subject that you can't see it all as one unit without shifting the gaze. A little distance will simplify your perspective problem (the perspective of distant objects is far less acute than in things near at hand), and will keep you from seeing—and so trying to indicate—every leaf in a tree, every stone in a wall, every shingle on a roof.

Thumbnail Sketches

If ever preliminary sketches are helpful, now is the time. As soon as you have found what seems to be a promising subject, immediately try a number of quick, small sketches, as in Fig. 132. Each sketch need be perhaps only an inch or two or just a few centimeters in size, which is why they are called "thumbnail" sketches. These sketches may indicate that you can get a better result if you shift your position somewhat. In selecting the point of view for the subject (shown completed in Fig. 133), for example, I wandered from place to place and visited the scene at different times of day. I then made a number of thumbnail sketches, followed by somewhat larger sketches as experiments in recomposition

Fig. 130. From this standpoint, the architecture is incidental to the entire landscape.

Fig. 131. From another viewpoint, the architecture and stone wall assume a more important position in the scene.

Fig. 132. Make many preliminary sketches to determine the most satis-factory composition and value arrangement.

Final Drawings

When you have made at least one promising thumbnail sketch, lay out your subject at final size on your selected paper. While you don't want to feel cramped, you can probably express most subjects well on an 11 x 15"/28 x 38cm sheet. Larger paper gives almost too much surface to cover when time is limited. The final drawing in Fig. 133 was done on kid-finished bristol, 11 x 15"/28 x 38cm. The penciling extended 9"/23cm across it.

After you have constructed your subject, you may want to determine on tracing paper the most effective value arrangement and the best directions for your lines. But don't spend so much time planning that you have no time left for drawing!

When you portray a well-known subject—perhaps some historic building or noted landmark—you shouldn't wander far from its true appearance. In this instance, limit your recomposition to value adjustments. You may make a light roof dark, for instance, or take liberties with the tones of the grass and trees. Landscapes or buildings of no marked individuality permit far greater alterations—trees and bushes may be moved about, or made larger, smaller, or different in form. As your experience grows, you will seldom be contented to leave any subject exactly as you find it; no matter how pleasing it is, a creative urge will cause you to change it.

While many of nature's details are pictorially very acceptable, this is not always true. And particularly when it comes to larger compositions, nature can often be improved upon. A quaint old house may have a too-perfect young maple tree near it. You may prefer to substitute a more harmonious tree—something rugged and wind-blown—or omit the tree altogether. For that matter, undesirable details can usually be dropped altogether or at least subordinated to something else in your drawing.

Practical Demonstration

In the accompanying demonstration, a comparison of the final drawing (Fig. 133) with the photograph (Fig. 130) taken at the exact spot from which the drawing was made, will show quite a number of readjustments. As the photo indicates, for instance, the roof of the house and the trees beyond were so nearly the same in value that they practically merged. For a more dramatic effect, in the drawing the roof was made lighter so that the house would count as a light spot surrounded by dark. The hill, trees, road, and fields composed rather well, so only incidental changes were required. Had these masses not been reasonably satisfactory, they could easily have been altered. The ledge in the foreground was pushed nearer to the house and made somewhat more rugged, with foliage added.

This subject has a major light area (almost surrounded by gray and black), and a leading dark area. Its values include white, near-black, and various tones of gray. An attempt was made to create an all-over pattern of pleasing shapes and tones, while employing lines well adapted to the proper expression of both tones and textures. The vignetting shows variety, and is designed to keep the eyes out of the corners.

Technique

We have already seen that, when working outdoors, you seldom have time to think much about technique. You must simply express the subject as directly and speedily as possible, knowing that the light and shade effects are changing every minute.

That's a good method. Important as it is for you to acquaint yourself, in first preliminary practice, with all natural means of drawing lines and tones, the less conscious thought you give to such things later, the better. Many artists—practically all—become at one time or another too technique-conscious, their work growing mannered and strained. This doesn't mean, of course, that a drawing shouldn't have technical excellence—it should. But technique should be subservient, used to make subjects appear convincing. Rocks should look heavy and solid; foliage, soft and yielding; skies, distant and ethereal. It doesn't take long, though, to acquire the knack of rendering all such things without much conscious effort.

Fig. 133. The final sketch, after touchup in the studio.

Retaining the Scene

You never know when you may be forced to stop working on some particular sketch before it is finished, so you should take a few snapshots of each subject. If later, in your studio, you decide to utilize the subject, you will have an adequate record.

After any outdoor sketching expedition, it is excellent practice—as with other types of subject matter—to try a memory sketch or two. It is highly important to learn to retain as many impressions of nature's effects as possible; memory sketching affords one of the best means.

Varying the Subjects

After you have sketched for a while from general outdoor subject matter, plan a definite course of study to acquaint yourself in a logical order with nature's appearances. For example, on a sunny day, concentrate for a few hours on striving to get a feeling of bright light. Make quick sketches rather than finished drawings. Striking results can be obtained by drawing shadows alone. Another day may be dull or foggy; see if you can express this condition. Or perhaps the wind is strong: draw trees as they bend, or attempt to catch the movement of rustling grass, or seek ways to indicate blowing smoke, or driven waves, or clothes flapping on the line—even people leaning against the wind or hanging onto their hats, their coats whipped into action. Or, from your window or an automobile interior, attempt to interpret rain or snow. Draw a wet street, a snow-covered roof. Skies with and without clouds will give you many hours of work. Sunsets are hard to handle successfully, but don't fail to try them—you will profit from the exercise. Later we will discuss some of these landscape features in greater detail.

Fig. 134. Here is a method of focusing attention on different parts of a building.

13.
Architectural Considerations

When you have obtained a sound fundamental knowledge of the subjects treated so far, you will probably find little difficulty in sketching buildings, street scenes, and other large subjects.

Yet every new subject presents its peculiar problems. There are many things the beginner hardly knows how to approach. A street scene, landscape, or building, for instance, needs a far different treatment from an old shoe. Among the following chapters you will find many valuable hints to help you draw buildings, both in whole and in part, as well as all sorts of accessories such as water and clouds.

If skill in representing buildings is important to the artist or art student, it is *indispensable* to the architect and his assistants, and it is mainly to meet the latter's requirements that the following chapters were originally prepared.

Selecting a Subject

In earlier chapters we placed great importance on selecting a suitable subject for each drawing, and this careful selection is equally essential for the work to be done here. It is as much of a problem to learn to select as it is to learn to draw. Since you will want to learn architecture as well as how to draw, it is usually best to choose some architectural object of merit. The drawing may be made directly from some interesting portion of a building, if you feel capable of attempting this, or from a photograph. In either case, don't attempt too much at one time.

Selecting a Viewpoint

When the subject has been chosen it is necessary to decide exactly how much of the object is to be drawn. If you work from the photograph this is comparatively easy, for by using strips of paper or cardboard as a frame, suitable composition can be found. You have more difficulty, however, when drawing directly from a building, for it is then necessary to determine the point from which the best view can be obtained. If you were to photograph the object you have selected to draw, the viewfinder of the camera would help you determine the best point at which to stand and would frame any number of interesting views from which you might select the best. The same idea may be carried out by the student of sketching, either by using a camera viewfinder or, what is more commonly done, by making a viewfinder by cutting a rectangular opening about 1.5 x 2″/3.8 x 5cm through a sheet of stiff paper or cardboard such as we described in Chapter 10. When this viewfinder is held near the eye, it will help you decide the point from which the drawing can best be made. Once the subject has been chosen and the point from which it is to be drawn decided upon, you are ready to block in the proportions of the sketch.

At this point, remember that it is more difficult to learn what to leave out of a drawing than what to put in. As you examine any object in nature you see an overwhelming mass of small detail. Even as you sit in your rooms and glance around you find, if you search, thousands of spots of light or shade or color. These tiny spots are the many lines of the delicate graining of the wood, the hundreds of partly visible threads from which the hangings and upholstery materials are woven, the myriad indentations and projections of the masonry and plaster.

It is hardly necessary to point out that it would be impossible to correctly indicate each of these spots on a small sheet of paper, even if this were desirable. Instead you must try to represent the effect of the mass as a whole. This is the effect you get *not* when you hunt for such details, but when you enter a room and look around in the usual way. If you do look directly at some object, such as a chair in a room corner, you see little detail except in the chair itself and in the objects adjacent to it. Even in these objects you are not conscious of each tiny spot, but instead notice only the broad general tone and effect. The chair, being directly in the range of vision, is the center of interest and the other objects become more and more indistinct and blurred the farther they are from this center. It really is surprising what a small area you are able to see plainly when looking in one direction only. We are so accustomed to shifting our eyes constantly from one object to another that we fail to notice this limitation. Stand within ten feet of a door and gaze intently at the knob. Without shifting the eyes, are you able to see the top of the door distinctly? If you raise your eyes and look at the top of the door, do you see the bottom plainly? Go to the window and look at some building across the street. Fix your attention on an upper window or chimney or some part of the roof. Aren't the lower portions of the building blurred and indistinct unless you shift your gaze to them? When you look at the foundation you don't see the roof distinctly.

Determining the Focal Point

In making a drawing, it is assumed that you are looking in one fixed direction. You gaze at some interesting object or, if the entire object is too large to come within range of vision, you select some prominent feature which then becomes the center of interest or focal point. In making the drawing, more detail is shown near this center of interest than in the other parts, which are allowed to become more and more indistinct towards the edges of the picture, just as they appear in nature. Every drawing should have this center of interest or focal point and everything else in the picture should be subordinated to it.

Now turn to Fig. 134. Cover the lower two

drawings and study the upper drawing, *A*. In this sketch, the spectator was looking towards that part of the old farm buildings nearest to him, so this becomes the center of interest or focal point. All else is subordinated.

Look at *B*, first covering up *A* and *C*. Here the spectator's eye has turned towards the center of the building and interest centers in the large doorway and adjacent walls. Here the details show most plainly and here are the strongest accents of light and shade. The two ends of the building become rather blurred and indistinct. They are subordinated.

Now uncover *C* and cover *B*. In *C* the spectator is looking still farther to the left and even though that portion of the building is some distance from the eye, it is the portion on which the eye is focused. The strongest contrasts and accents are there and the rest of the building is subordinate.

Turn to the street scene in Figs. 135 and 136. In Fig. 135 the spectator is looking at the upper part of the tower. This section becomes the subject of the sketch, the focal point or center of interest. The street is blurred, the detail is softened. In Fig. 136 the spectator is looking down the street. The archway becomes the center of interest and the tower is almost lost against the sky. In drawing such a subject from nature you are likely to get into difficulty. You look first, perhaps, at the tower and draw that. If you stop there, all well and good; the tower becomes the subject of the sketch. But if you lower your gaze to the street and add the archway to the drawing it is quite possible that this will form a second focal point which will compete with the tower. Then the drawing will be a failure, because the eye will jump back and forth between the tower and the archway and the balance will be destroyed. In this kind of composition, where there are two possible centers of interest, be sure that one is subordinated to the other.

Now turn to Fig. 137, the little interior. Where is the center of interest represented in the drawing at the top of the sheet? Where does the eye see the most detail and the strongest contrasts of light and dark? The window with its seat is outside the focus and it is only when the eye turns towards it—as it does in the lower picture—that it becomes

Fig. 135. The tower becomes the center of interest because detail and values are most concentrated in this area.

Fig. 136. Here the archway becomes the center of interest and the tower is almost lost against the sky.

· FOCUS AT MANTEL ·   A

· FOCUS AT WINDOW ·   B

A.L.Guptill. 1920

Fig. 137. The window is subordinated to the fireplace in A, while the reverse is true in B.

the center of vision or focal point. In this case the mantel is out of focus and might be omitted from the drawing. In fact, this room could be made the subject of two interesting sketches, one of the fireplace and one of the window and seat. In this kind of room we can well imagine that in the evening the fireplace, with the family enjoying a cheerful blaze, would be the center of interest in the room, while in the daytime the window with its seat would doubtless gain greater attention.

Now turn to the delightful sketch by Ernest Watson, Fig. 138. Notice that he has built up his center of interest very effectively, yet without forcing it upon the attention unpleasantly. Observe, too, that the drawing is allowed to soften or fade away gradually from those parts which come most directly within the range of vision.

It should be clear by now that in starting a drawing it is important to select something of interest to draw. Next, it is necessary to find the best point from which the drawing can be made. Then you must analyze your subject to determine the center of interest or focal point. Having done this you must use every care to subordinate all the parts having little or nothing to do with our subject, and which might detract from the center of interest.

Pointing the Pencil

Before sharpening your pencils, decide what you want them to do, and point them accordingly. Sharply pointed pencils are fine if a drawing is to be small or if much fine detail is to be shown. If the drawing is to be large, broad-pointed pencils will usually produce an effect equally satisfactory in a much shorter space of time. Many drawings combine both fine lines and wide lines with excellent results.

No special directions for forming a sharp point seem necessary other than those in Chapter 3.

Regardless of how the pencil is sharpened, take care that the point is wiped with a cloth in order to remove all dust. Otherwise it is difficult to get a clean, firm line and next to impossible to keep the paper from becoming soiled by the loose grit from the pencil. Another point to remember is that in

sharpening the pencil never remove the letters or numbers indicating the degree of hardness or softness of the lead.

The pencils pointed and dusted are now ready for use, though it will be convenient to mark each one so that its grade can be told at a glance. There are several ways of doing this. One is by cutting or painting the letters indicating the grade of the lead on several sides of the pencil where they can be seen easily, and another is by notching the pencils, increasing the number of notches as the pencils become harder in grade. Such letters or notches are perhaps most convenient if placed about 1.5"/3.8cm from the unsharpened end of the pencil where they will remain in view. If near the point, they will soon be cut away and if at the other extremity they will be hidden if a pencil holder or lengthener is used. Some artists, instead of marking their pencils, always lay them on the drawing board according to grade. By this arrangement, they can tell the degree of hardness of a pencil at a glance by its position on the board. When it has been used, the pencil can be returned to its proper place and another taken up. A still different way of marking pencils for identification is by dipping them into various colors, each color representing a definite grade of lead.

You may ask how many pencils are necessary for one sketch. This number will vary all the way from one, for a quick sketch, to seven or eight as used by some draftsmen for carefully finished work. Some well-known draftsmen never use more than one grade of pencil for an entire drawing, but as a rule, you can get better results by using three or four.

Quick Sketches for Practice

First try some simple drawings. Very often you can gain more from making a number of small sketches than from attempting one large rendering. Choose objects of architectural value and interest. The sketches in Fig. 139 are shown for two reasons. First, they illustrate a quick method of sketching, the drawings being very freely and rapidly made. Second, they suggest a means of obtaining a good deal of knowledge about archi-

Fig. 138. Ernest W. Watson: Notice how naturally the artist has built up the center of interest.

Fig. 139. *You can gain a good deal of knowledge about architecture by making many quick sketches.*

ALTERATION TO RESIDENCE FOR WILSON WEIR
A·L·GUPTILL · ARCHITECT · 30 EAST 42ND ST · NEW YORK CITY ·

Fig. 140. Here the same subject has been drawn first with broad lines and then with fine lines. The two effects are quite different.

tecture. You cannot fail, when making such sketches, to learn a great deal concerning the objects you render. Fig. 140 is also reproduced here for two reasons. First, it shows in a comparative manner two types of line, the broad and the fine, used side by side for representing the same building. Second, it is a typical presentation drawing frequently submitted to a client as a means of securing a commission. This particular drawing was laid out instrumentally. The original sheet measures about 10.5 x 14.5″/26.7 x 36.8cm to the margin lines. Fig. 139 was originally drawn about 9 x 12.5″/22.9 x 31.2cm, so allow for this reduction when studying these sheets.

Rendering Procedures

Remember that once a subject is selected for a sketch or rendering, whether large or small, it may be drawn in outline in either of two ways: the outline may be roughly blocked in with sketchy lines, to be erased when the final rendering is started, or it may be more carefully drawn directly with final lines, keeping them very light by using a hard pencil, and leaving them to become a part of the finished work. When the outline has been completed, there are several methods of procedure: you can put in the darkest tones of the whole drawing, later adding enough gray tones to complete the picture, or you can put in the gray tones first, later adding the dark tones and sharp accents to finish the drawing.

Many artists complete their work as they proceed, beginning at the center of interest and working out, or beginning at the top and working gradually down towards the bottom. The second method has one great advantage in that the drawing can be kept clean more easily than by the other methods, but it is difficult unless you are able to think very clearly before drawing or unless you make a preliminary sketch for the purpose of studying the values of light and dark. As a rule it is safer to start at the center of interest, making sure that the strongest contrasts of light and shade and the sharpest details are there, keeping the rest of the drawing properly subordinated.

In any case, it is wise to make a preliminary study of the values of light and dark as soon as the outline has been completed. This study is best made on tracing paper directly over the outline drawing. When completed, it will serve as a guide for the actual rendering. Once the values have been determined in this way, you are free to turn your attention to technique.

Regarding technique, remember to work for variety of line, for it is impossible to express all materials, and surfaces with one type of line. Smooth, straight strokes suggest smooth surfaces, while irregular strokes are best for representing rough, uneven surfaces. As we have mentioned earlier, it is usually advisable to let your strokes follow the structural lines of the objects represented. Thus, the strokes used on vertical walls should be vertical or perspectively horizontal. The roof lines should follow the slope of the roof or vanish towards a point with the other parallel lines. Curved surfaces, as a rule, can be best represented by the use of curved lines.

Methods of Indicating Architecture

Earlier in this volume we discussed the various approaches to drawing—outline, tone, and combined conventions. Let's now study how they affect architectural rendering. In Sketch A, Fig. 141 is a sketch of an old chimney done in outline only, but this outline is so accented that it suggests the textures of the various surfaces and a few tiny lines are added also as an indication of the shade and shadow. In Sketch B the same chimney is shown in full tone of light and shade but with the outline omitted. This drawing is much like a photograph of the same subject, in that the stone and brick and other materials have been given tones as similar as is possible to those appearing in nature. Though this type of drawing is used to some extent, it is not as popular as that shown in Sketch C, in which much of the white of the paper is left. Drawing C not only has more character than B but the method used is more economical. In this particular instance, the outline was drawn exactly as in Sketch A and then enough tone added to suggest the values of light and shade as found in Sketch B. For architectural work this method is

Fig. 141. Notice the varied treatment of this chimney: in accented outline only, in tone only without outline, and in outline with tone suggested.

quite satisfactory, for much of the form can be represented by the accented outline. The white of the paper answers for the lighter values and the darker tones can be drawn with the gray and black of the pencil.

Color cannot, of course, be more than suggested in any pencil drawing. A dark red brick wall can be shown dark, and light green shutters can be shown light, but unless explanatory notes are added or some color employed, there is no way of making it clear that the brickwork is red and the shutters are green. Because of these limitations, tints of watercolor are frequently washed over a pencil drawing and the results obtained in this way are often very effective, especially if the tints are light and delicate. Colored pencils are sometimes used, too, with considerable success.

Light and Shadows in Architecture

Fig. 142 illustrates the effect gained by using values representing the color and tone of the various building materials and accessories. Little attempt has been made to show shadows. It is sometimes possible to obtain a very pleasing result this way and you might try a few such drawings. The average subject demands some suggestion of the shadow tones as well. Many drawings can, in fact, be entirely made by the use of the shade and shadow tones *only*, the color of the building materials being largely disregarded. Fig. 143 illustrates this point. This method is especially useful when drawing objects are made of light-colored materials such as carved white marble, ornamental terracotta, white clapboarded, or stucco walls.

Although the natural tone and color of materials in buildings and their surroundings is of great importance, so much of the effect of a structure—both as a whole and in detail—depends on its shadows that the study of light and shade deserves special attention. When a sketch is in outline only, the light is either indicated in a simple manner or entirely disregarded, but when a drawing is to be done in full value, it is especially important to determine both the *source* and *direction* of the light before starting to render.

Students have been known to cast the shadows on a building in one direction and to indicate the shade on the trees as though the light were coming at a different angle. Such inconsistencies generally occur when students attempt to copy and combine parts of several drawings without thinking out the matter of lighting. There are, however, so many separate influences affecting the lighting of all objects—such as the condition of the atmosphere, the reflective or absorbing powers of different surfaces and materials, the constant shifting and moving of clouds and foliage—that we can only give the student a few hints to point the way for his further individual study.

Even in interiors the light often comes from so many sources and is reflected from so many surfaces that nothing but constant observation and sketching will teach you about these conditions. The opening or closing of a door may be sufficient to entirely change the appearance of an interior, and in the same way the shifting of a cloud may cause windows to appear very light one minute and almost black the next. Sometimes the lighting varies to such an extent that an entire building may appear dark against light at one time and light against dark at another, as illustrated in the example of the lighthouse, Figs. 97 and 98. Such an extreme change as this, though by no means unusual, generally takes place at morning or in the evening or under exceptional lighting conditions. But even the average building under normal conditions will vary greatly in appearance from hour to hour.

Because of these constant changes, most buildings appear to better advantage at certain times of day than at others, and so it is best to render them during these favorable moments. Buildings and foliage usually get the most satisfactory light during the late afternoon when the sun's rays are slanted in a way that causes an interesting variety of shade and shadow. There are, of course, exceptions to this, a great deal depending on the location of the building in relation to the points of the compass. Many architects fail, when designing buildings, to give sufficient attention to the fact that a design that will appear well when turned at a certain angle with the sun or other source of illumination, may be much less effective placed in

Fig. 142. Notice that the effect here has been obtained mainly by using values to represent the tones of various building materials and accessories.

Fig. 143. Here the effect depends more on the indication of shade and shadow than on the rendering of building materials.

some other position. It is not enough to make instrumental studies of buildings, with shadows cast at the usual 45 degree angle. The designer should also consider how the structure will appear under the vertical rays of the sun at midday, or the slanting rays of early morning, or late afternoon. The designer should, in many cases, make special studies with the shadows shown as they would exist in the completed building.

I have in mind one particular public building which was most attractive in the preliminary drawings, with its shadows cast in the conventional manner. Unfortunately, the building is so situated that for months at a time the sun seldom shines on the main façade. In the evening this façade is especially uninteresting when the bright light from the street lamps entirely eliminates the cornice shadows.

Obviously, it is impossible to foresee and prevent all such unpleasant appearances, but if you learn to study and observe light effects and have drawn much from nature you will find the knowledge gained from this work of great assistance if you are called upon to do original work in design. You will be able to avoid the kind of unpleasant results mentioned and you will be able to make the greatest use of the lighting conditions as they exist. Such knowledge is of great importance, too, when you are called upon to make renderings of proposed buildings or sketches from memory or the imagination.

Don't for a moment think we are condemning the practice of casting shadows on elevations in the conventional 45 degrees. This is not the case. Even the student of freehand drawing can gain considerable knowledge useful in sketching through a course in shades and shadows. What we do wish to make clear is that the draftsman or designer who studies light and shade directly from nature will not be handicapped by the man-made rules governing shades and shadows, but is able to supplement these with his knowledge of nature's own laws, and can apply them all with far greater intelligence.

We are told, for example, when studying the architectural subject of shades and shadows, that the surfaces in a building that are turned most directly towards the source of light will usually appear, all other things being equal, the brightest. From this you might conclude that a dark shingled roof receiving direct rays of light from the sun would appear very bright. In fact, it often does. Not infrequently, however, such a roof seems very dark under these conditions, even though the color of the shingles may be light, this appearance being largely because the horizontal lines created by the edges of the shingles—which are turned to receive little light—appear so black and conspicuous that they deepen and darken the effect of the otherwise light tone. The rule is worth remembering, however, in spite of such exceptions.

Also remember the rule that the darkest, sharpest shadows are cast by the edges of the surfaces receiving the most direct light. It naturally follows that surfaces turned at an angle that receives the light rays in a slantwise direction will be less bright than those receiving the direct rays. It is true, too, that a shiny surface generally appears brighter than a dull surface of the same actual value and sometimes even a black shiny surface will reflect some light tone and so appear practically white. There are exceptions to this: a shiny, light surface may reflect some very dark tone and appear nearly black. Likewise a smooth gray surface may appear either lighter or darker than it really is. In other words, glossy surfaces change in appearance with changes of light to a much greater extent than dull surfaces. Even light, dull surfaces, however, often throw much brilliance onto other objects, and white concrete walks, terraces, or driveways sometimes reflect enough light upon adjacent buildings to materially affect their appearance, as such lights soften the shadow tone or even cast shadows themselves.

One excellent way of studying constantly changing effects of light on a building is by making a series of snapshots from some one fixed point at intervals during a clear day and comparing them with care. Such photographs reveal much of interest and value to the observing student, especially if the building is rather small. You might make sketches from these photographs to help to fix the ideas in your mind.

We have mentioned that it is sometimes possible to make an effective drawing by using shadows only, and sometimes by suggesting the building

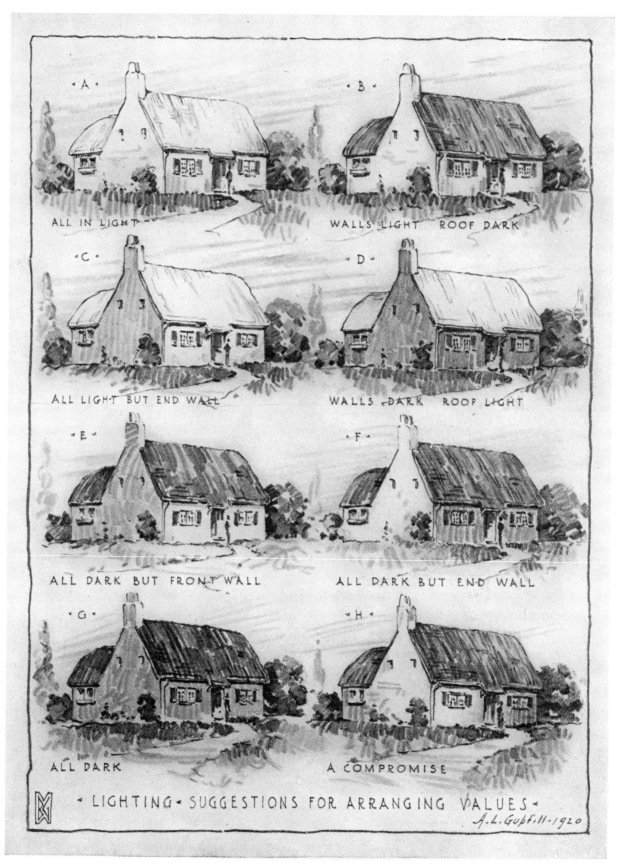

Fig. 144. As in Fig. 93, different value schemes can be employed for the same subject.

materials alone. It is more often necessary to represent both the material and the shadows to obtain a satisfactory drawing. It is not always easy, though, to decide just how much of each should be shown, especially when working from the imagination as the architect is often called upon to do. This can, perhaps, best be determined by making several rough studies on tracing paper directly over the outline drawing or by making two or three small sketches similar to those shown in Fig. 144. (You may recall that we illustrated some of these same concepts in Fig. 93.) These eight sketches illustrate that it is often possible to get many fairly satisfactory compositions of the same subject, but there are usually one or two that are better than the others, and one of these should be selected as a guide for the final larger renderings.

Make several similar small sketches of some object from memory or imagination as practice in composition. Remember too, that in making drawings from a photograph it is often helpful to try similar studies on tracing paper directly over the photograph to determine how much to omit and how best to compose that which seems essential to show.

Individual Style

Students of drawing often handicap themselves right at the start by attempting to produce sketches that show marked originality or individuality. They feel that unless their work is unusual in presentation, it is not good. Consequently they sacrifice truth in order to create drawings with a technique so peculiar and predominant that it detracts from the subject of the sketch itself.

It is impossible for you to practice drawing for any length of time without developing certain original mannerisms. This is most desirable. It would be unfortunate if all pencil artists were to draw in exactly the same way, producing work of monotonous similarity. But there is no danger of this. Just as most of us acquire a certain characteristic style of penmanship, entirely ours, we are also sure to attain a style of drawing having a character exclusively its own. But don't feel that you have to hurry this process. Focus instead on developing the skills necessary for sound draftsmanship. The rest will come naturally. Study the work of others and benefit by the lessons they have already mastered. But don't be intimidated by their skill. You will improve with practice.

Fig. 145. Here are two schemes for a small house drawn directly from blueprint plans and elevations. Notice that the structure of the house is basically the same.

14.
Rendering Small Buildings

The average client who comes to an architect's office is, as a rule, entirely unfamiliar with the drawings employed in carrying on architectural work. The instrumental plans mean little to him, though he can read them, perhaps, as far as the general layout of the rooms is concerned, and can understand the elevation drawings if the building is simple in form. Anything more complicated, however, and he finds it impossible to visualize its finished appearance.

Even experienced designers and architects are sometimes surprised when they see one of their own buildings taking definite form on the site. Despite their training, they are not always able to judge beforehand just how the complete work will appear in relation to its surroundings.

Undoubtedly, one of the main reasons clients are sometimes disappointed with their finished buildings is that the structure is entirely different from what they expected. Unwilling to admit this inability to understand the plans or overconfident because of the architect's words of assurance that everything would come out all right, clients approve the designs and give word to go ahead with the work, when they actually have little idea as to how the completed structure would appear. When such a building is finished, it is only natural, then, for the client to be displeased. But he is much more likely to condemn the architect than to admit any error or lack of understanding on his own part.

Largely because of this difficulty, it is common practice to prepare rendered perspective drawings that show, in a very clear manner, exactly how the completed structure will appear. These are of value to the architect in many ways, for they not only serve as a convincing expression of the problem to the *client*, but are of equal use as a means of studying the design.

Pencil rendering of architectural subjects is comparatively simple. You don't encounter the same difficulties as you would working in color, for there are only the values of light and dark to consider. Nor is it difficult to make changes, as in work with the pen. Originality is not a requisite as it is in some forms of artwork, nor is it necessary to strive for a decorative effect. As the small drawing does not often need figures or animals, it is not absolutely necessary to be able to draw them: Even if figures are shown, they are usually so small in scale that they need little detail.

Pencil Techniques

The most convincing sort of pencil technique for architectural subjects is the conventional type. You might study examples of these published in architectural journals. Notice the way in which the various details, such as the doors and windows, are indicated. Study ways in which draftsmen suggest different materials—shingles, clapboards, brickwork, stone, stucco, etc. Look at the way the foliage is shown. Copy either the whole or portions of some of these drawings, trying at the same time to memorize the methods of expression.

It is also valuable to compare the drawings with photographs of similar subjects, or even with buildings themselves, and sketch directly from the buildings, too, trying small drawings of doors and windows, or other similar portions first. Photographs of small houses will offer many suggestions for surroundings that you can copy.

To aid you in depictive details in the following chapters, a number of drawings show methods of representing details. Remember, however, that you will gain a great deal by studying the work of a great many different people, adapting the most appealing ideas.

Establish Station Point

After considerable practice has been given drawing details, a real rendering of some small house may be undertaken. Bear in mind that a rendering is a more carefully finished production than a sketch. Where a sketch is usually made rather hastily, a rendering is more in the nature of a study. In order to gain an accurate result, the subject to be rendered is first laid out instrumentally directly from the plans and elevations. This work demands some knowledge of instrumental perspective. The few facts necessary for drawing the usual building can be acquired easily, however, even though you do not go deeply into the theory of the subject. Many draftsmen learn simply a few "rule of thumb" methods which answer all general requirements. It is not within the scope of this volume to provide information regarding instrumental perspective, but there are a few points that are essential.

First of all, when starting a perspective, decide where to stand to obtain the best view. Though this position varies with different buildings, it is usually best to show much of the main façade. If the plot is flat it is usually best to take the eye level or horizon line about 5'/1.5m above the ground, as the eye is actually approximately this distance from the plane on which the building rests. If, instead, the building is to be on a hill, it would be natural to look up at it, and this is one way it should be drawn. In this case the horizon would be way below the house, as it is always level with the spectator's eye. On the other hand, if we are to look *down* on the building from *above*—as in a bird's eye view—the eye level or horizon will be towards the top of the picture. Seldom do we see houses from above, and even if we did, from a mountain or airplane, we would not show them that way. There are cases where the building is very irregular in plan, or where we have a complex group of buildings to picture, and under

these conditions there is sometimes no other means of expressing the entire subject adequately.

Determine the Distance

Another point worth remembering: it is best not to stand too close to a building when making the perspective, as this causes the receding lines to become so acute that they seem unpleasant. A little experience will teach the correct distances for various types of buildings.

The Surroundings

If you are to make a perspective and the plot has already been purchased, obtain either photographs or sketches of the site to help you in drawing the surroundings. A plot plan or survey showing the contours of the land, location of rocks, trees, etc., is immensely helpful, too, in getting a layout correct. If no plot has been selected, photographs showing houses of a similar nature to what you are drawing may offer valuable suggestions, especially for the surroundings. A pleasing relation should exist between a building and its environment—the house should seem to belong to the spot. If, for instance, you are drawing a little English cottage, don't arrange your landscape in too formal a manner. Have some curved walks, irregular hedges, a quaint garden, etc. A colonial house of dignified proportions demands, on the other hand, a more symmetrical treatment, with formality extended throughout the scheme. A rustic camp in the forest should show a real forest character and not look like a suburban cottage. And if a house is to be in Florida, don't use trees found only in the North, and likewise avoid hills and mountains if the location is in a level country. These are, of course, only matters of common sense and may seem too simple to mention. But they are, nevertheless, extremely important.

Composing the Rendering

There is something else that also helps a composition immensely: have some line or group of lines,

Fig. 146. *This is a quick sketch for a proposed house, done with a broad point.*

such as a path, drive, or shadows on the lawn, or perhaps a succession of bushes, to lead the eye into the picture. In Figs. 82 to 85, notice that all four sketches have paths directing the attention gradually to the center of interest. It helps a drawing, too, if there are little vistas to draw the eye out of the picture again. A glimpse of some distant lake, or down a pathway to the garage, or of a neighboring building seen through the trees will add depth to the picture. Avoid making these incidentals too prominent, however, or they will diminish interest in the house itself. In this connection refer to Figs. 145 and 146. The end of the distant house in Fig. 146 and the garage in Fig. 145 add to the effect. When a definite plot has been chosen, the buildings nearby that may be visible from that viewpoint should be correctly represented.

Establish a Scale

Leaving the subject of composition for the present, let's return to the practical points of laying out the drawing. After the station point, at which the spectator is to stand, has been decided and the eye level or horizon determined, it is time to locate the various vanishing points, before the work is underway. Since most perspectives are drawn directly from the working drawings, and since these are often at the scale of $\frac{1}{4}'' = 1'/$ 6.35mm = 30cm—this scale is frequently used for the perspective. There is no rule about this, however, but it can be difficult to show enough detail if a smaller scale is chosen. The English house in Fig. 146 was done at the scale of $\frac{1}{8}'' = 1'/3.175$mm = 30cm and is reproduced here at the exact size of the original.

This gives a fair idea of what can be easily done at that scale. The two houses in Fig. 145 were also made at the same scale, but are reproduced at about half that size.

Rendering Procedures

Once the scale is decided, you can push ahead the work of laying out the perspective. As soon as this is completed, you are ready for the rendering.

There are several methods of proceeding with this. Sometimes the layout is on common paper and then the rendering done on tracing paper placed over the other. This system means that there is no special need to keep the paper clean when drawing the layout. Again, there are no hard mechanical lines to show in the final result, and if the rendering is spoiled in the process, it is easy to begin once more. When the drawing is completed, the tracing paper can be smoothly mounted on heavy cardboard.

Another method, more common, is to make the layout right on the final paper, using a fairly hard pencil, such as a 3H, and drawing not only the outline of the large portions, but also all he window moldings, clapboard lines, and other details as well. When this is completed, go over the whole with a soft eraser until the lines are just visible as a guide for the freehand work.

The final rendering may vary in style, according to the subject to be drawn. An English cottage of hewn timbers and rough brick or stucco, roofed with thatch or uneven slate, can be done with a rather sketchy line, because this will satisfactorily express the irregular surfaces. If you are doing a formal house of cut stone, smoother tones and straighter lines are often better. This does not mean that it is impossible to represent this kind of house by a very sketchy sort of line, but it is certainly wiser for the beginner to render a building of this character in a painstaking way.

With these facts in mind, you are ready to start work, considering carefully the direction of the light, and so casting the shadows with care. Knowing about the shades and shadows is, of course, very helpful here, while photographs of similar buildings offer many suggestions. Then a preliminary sketch is often made on tracing paper and the values carefully worked out on that. If this preliminary work is done, it often seems best, when making the final drawing, to render from the top down, because it is possible to keep the paper clean quite easily. In theory, it is better to work from the center of interest out towards the edges, as we have stated in the preceding chapter, or to put in the darkest tones first, all over the drawing, later adding the halftones. If no prelimi-

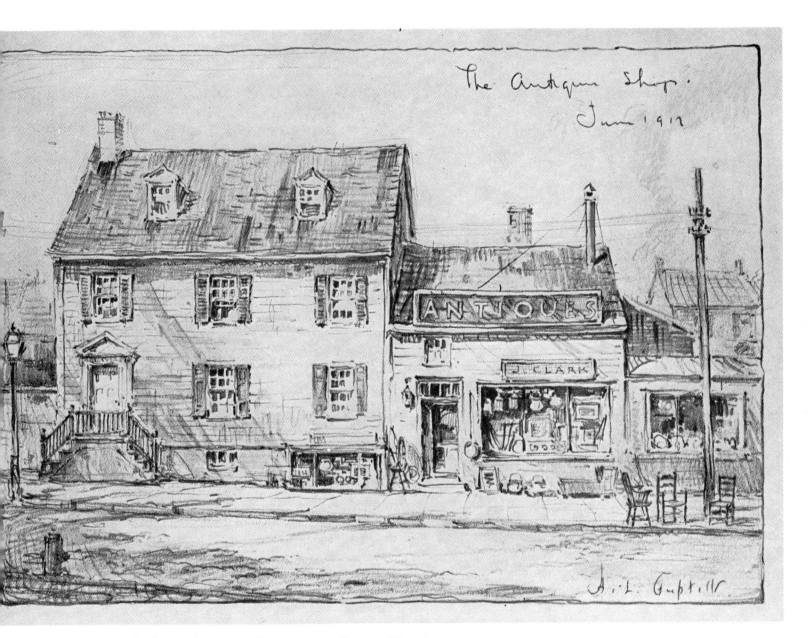

Fig. 147. This sketchy treatment is another way of handling small buildings.

nary is made, follow one of these methods. In any case, there is no excuse for untidy work, and if you take reasonable care, you should have no difficulty here.

Finish the drawing to the best of your ability. If you are not satisfied with it (and you are not likely to be), try another of the same or a similar subject. Only with this kind of practice and by learning to look for your own mistakes, will you become proficient.

The illustrations, Figs. 145 and 146, are typical examples of what can be quite easily and quickly done. These drawing show little individuality or originality. In fact, they are very similar to dozens of drawings that we see from time to time. In both instances they were drawn to accompany sketch plans before any definite site had been chosen.

Fig. 145 may have some additional interest because it shows two different compositions for the same house. Schemes A and B are both developments of the one plan. Fig. 146 is a sketch done directly from nature and by comparing this with Fig. 145, the difference between a sketch and a rendering of a similar building should be very evident.

The sketchy treatment in Fig. 147 is another approach to the treatment of small buildings.

15.
Architectural Details

We have now reached the point where we turn our attention to methods of indicating brickwork, stonework, clapboarded and shingled walls, slate and tile roofs, etc., and details such as chimneys, dormers, cornices, and doorways. Unless you learn to suggest these various component parts, you cannot hope to make an excellent drawing of a building as a whole, any more than a portrait painter can obtain a satisfactory likeness of a person without knowing how to draw the ear, the eye, and the mouth.

In previous chapters a few general instructions on drawing portions of buildings have already been given. This chapter is mainly an amplification of these earlier suggestions because certain points seem worth repeating.

Unfortunately for the beginner, there are few definite rules to help in this kind of sketching, for each artist develops methods that vary from time to time, choosing always what is appropriate to a particular problem. Naturally the manner of working differs, too, according to the size at which the details are to be drawn. It is obvious that a window, for example, shown at a scale of $\frac{1}{4}'' = 1'/6.35$mm $= 30$cm, requires treatment decidedly different from that demanded by the same object presented at a much larger scale.

Because there are so many methods of indication, it is not unusual to feel uncertain about how to approach a problem of this nature. Of course, in theory it is best to turn to actual buildings and landscape for inspiration and practice, observing and sketching the desired details directly from the buildings and their surroundings. However, the average student finds it rather difficult to work in this way without considerable preliminary preparation. For this reason, you can probably learn more at first by studying good drawings and copying portions of them over and over again, later applying the ideas to similar problems. If you supplement this work by sketching from photographs and from nature, using both broad and fine lines on all sorts of paper, using pencils of various kinds and grades, you will gain increased skill and a natural individual style.

Adopt some standard size sketching paper. The notebook proportion of 8.5 x 11"/21.5 x 28cm is appropriate for the smaller sketches, and you can also easily acquire a cover for preserving sheets. Retain all sketches, or at least the best of them. This gives you the opportunity to note your progress from time to time, and the drawings themselves may be helpful when you make finished renderings. Group a number of sketches of similar subjects on one sheet, arranged so they permit easy comparison. For example, group sketches of chimneys drawn with a fine line on one sheet, others done with a broad line on another, dormer windows on a third, details of stonework on a fourth, and so on.

Instrumental Elevation vs. Architectural Drawing

Never attempt to draw every tiny detail you know extists. It is difficult to avoid overemphasizing some of them, particularly if you are an architect or architectural draftsman. Your training to accurately draw each detail, whether large or small, when making an instrumental elevation of a portion of a building, acts as a hindrance when it comes to pictorial representation. Here we are striving to gain the effect of the whole in a broad, direct manner in a comparatively short

Fig. 148. Notice the difference between an instrumental elevation (A) and an architectural drawing (B).

Fig. 149. Here are various treatments of cornices and cornice shadows.

space of time. The two drawings, *A* and *B*, in Fig. 148 illustrate the difference between an instrumental elevation and an architectural drawing. *A* is done instrumentally at the scale of ½″ = 1′/ 12.7mm = 30cm and is a copy of an actual working drawing. Such a mechanical representation as this offers, of course, an accurate statement of certain facts of form, but it stops there. It gives us a wrong sense of the values. The numerous lines necessary to bound the various members form a dark mass on parts that might ultimately appear rather light, and there is nothing to show the difference in tone between the brick and wood. In a sketch or rendering, on the other hand, we usually work for an effect of reality. Even though certain details are slighted, by means of a free handling we are able to suggest the light, shade, tone, and texture of the materials, as well as the architectural form. In Sketch *B* we have attempted such an indication of the cornice shown at *A*, striving for the same relative values as found in nature. The brickwork is shown darker in the shadow than in the light, as is the white woodwork, too, while the shingles are given a tone which quite accurately suggests the color that might appear in the direct rays of the sun. This particular sketch is at a fairly large scale, so it has been possible to retain most of the fine detail shown at *A*, but if the drawing were smaller, it would probably be necessary to simplify it further.

This illustration is sufficient to show that the draftsman must work for a wholly different result in a sketch from that required in an elevation, forgetting or merely suggesting many of the tiny details in an attempt to achieve a broad effect. As a further example, in drawing a window, you must not allow your knowledge of the blind-stop, the pulley-style, and the parting-strip to interfere with the simplicity of the result. In fact, whatever the detail may be, avoid overemphasizing relatively unimportant portions of the subject.

Rendering the Cornice

Let us return for a moment to the subject of cornices. They contribute so much to the effect of a building that extreme care must always be used in their representation. First of all, do not overdarken the projecting portions. The contrast of the light corona against the shadow below gives the desired sense of projection. Remember the advantage sometimes gained by using a graded shadow below a cornice, allowing the tone to gradually darken towards the bottom, giving transparency at the top and a clean-cut contrast at the lower edge. (See Fig. 114.) Remember, too, that the cornice shadow is usually made darkest at the corner of the building nearest the spectator, lightening gradually as the walls recede, an effect that adds to the distance.

Just how much detail should be shown in a cornice shadow is not an easy question to answer, because everything depends on the size and purpose of the drawing. If it is large and designed for studying the proportions and detail, it may prove necessary to draw every modillion and dentil. If it is small or made simply to give the general effect, the less important parts can be omitted. Sometimes mutules, brackets, rafter ends, or any details with considerable projection are left white or nearly so, for if the sketch is small and these parts are drawn in their true values they may be lost in the darkness of the shadow. This point is illustrated by Sketch 1, Fig. 149, in which the rafter ends are shown lighter than they would probably be in the executed work. In some drawings, these details are made quite distinct, especially in those parts of the building nearest the eye, and then made less definite or omitted in other parts of the drawing. If well done, this treatment gives an excellent impression with minimal time and effort.

Three methods of building up a shadow are in general use. The first is illustrated at *B*, Fig. 148, where the lines composing the shadow are so merged together that they make it difficult to tell their direction. In fact, in a shadow where the lines themselves are so indefinite, this direction is unimportant and the tone may be formed in the most convenient way. In the second method, illustrations show, but sometimes they take the same value is "built up" by a succession of adjacent strokes, either touching or nearly so. The strokes are often drawn in a vertical position, as our illustrations show, but sometimes they take the same

Fig. 150. These roof treatments suggest shingles, slate, thatch, and tile.

general slope as the rays of light that cause the shadow. This method is frequently employed when the sketch is made at small scale.

If a drawing demands much detail, however, a still different method is popular. In place of the mass shading of the first and the parallel strokes of the second, the lines run in the direction or directions that best suggest the bricks, clapboards, or whatever the materials in shadow may be. Sketches 3, 5, and 6, Fig. 149, illustrate this third method and it is not difficult to tell, even by the shadow tone, which sketch represents brick, which one stone, and which shingle. In using this method, be careful not to get too "spotty" a character at the value, for it is essential to preserve a restful effect throughout the tone.

The subject of cornices also involves reflected light and reversed shadows. Frequently, bright light is reflected from some brilliant object into dark tones, such as those beneath a cornice. This not only means that the shadow value itself is neutralized, and so made lighter, but this kind of reflection may often cause "reversed shadows," which really are shadows within a shadow, caused by modillions or any such projections preventing the reflected light from penetrating some of the deeper corners. These reversed shadows are of particular value in rendering elevations in wash, such as that shown in Fig. 159. In this sort of drawing, where the shadows are cast in the conventional 45-degree method, the reversed tones are usually reflected in just the opposite way, as is the case in the rendering to which we have just referred. (Note particularly the reversed shadows cast by the dentils.) In nature, however, the location and form of the reversed shadows will depend on the direction of the rays of reflected light. This direction may vary from hour to hour as the sun or other source of direct illumination changes in position. As far as cornices are concerned, however, reflected light often causes the soffit to appear quite brilliant, so in many drawings the soffit value is represented no darker than in Sketch 5, Fig. 149. In tiny drawings these horizontal planes are sometimes actually left white.

Though we have spoken of reflected light mainly as it influences cornice tones, don't think

that it has no effect on other values as well! As a rule, however, the horizontal planes seem to catch more light than the vertical planes. A window soffit, for instance, is often quite brilliant, while even as large a surface as a porch ceiling is often visibly brightened.

Roof Treatments

Before we conclude our discussion of Fig. 149, study the variety of methods of suggesting roof shingles. You can never give too much care to this kind of representation, for so large an area is taken up by the roof planes that unless they are well handled the effect of the whole drawing may be ruined. First of all you must determine the values of the different parts of the roof. Some portions can be left white or nearly so, while others will appear quite dark. Next, you must choose the method of indicating the roof material, and here the sketches in Fig. 149 may prove useful, or—if the roof is of some other material, Fig. 150 offers some suggestions. Sketch A in Fig. 150 represents shingles, flat tiles, or slate. Sketch B indicates a rough textured slate in graduated courses. Sketch C shows shingle thatch, D straw thatch, E suggests tile, while F again shows slate, though a similar indication would answer for shingle. Good pen renderings are sometimes of great assistance when drawing roof or wall surfaces, because they offer a great deal in the way of material indication which can be adapted to pencil rendering.

There are several faults frequently found in representations of roof surfaces. If a drawing is small in scale, you should seldom attempt to show every course of slate or shingles. If this is done the value is almost sure to become either too complex or too dark. It is better to space the lines, separating the courses somewhat further apart than they would be in the actual building. In larger drawings this criticism does not hold unless the roof pitch is very low or the roof planes greatly foreshortened, in which case a small number of lines may prove sufficient to suggest many courses. When graduated courses of slate are shown as in Sketch B, Fig. 151, decreasing in size

Fig. 151. Here are various methods of indicating brick and stonework.

from the bottom to the top, an unpleasant effect of curvature of the roof sometimes appears. Such an effect, if conspicuous, can usually be overcome by throwing a shadow bounded by approximately straight lines onto the roof, such as from a tree or some neighboring building. In fact, adding any straight lines that follow the pitch of the roof will help to correct such distortion. Whatever material is used as a roof covering, avoid breaking the tone into too many conspicuous spots. One of the most common defects of beginners' drawings is the spottiness of surfaces, which in actual buildings would be either "flat" throughout or gradually graded.

Wall Surfaces

Wall surfaces also need to be represented with the greatest care. Here again it is seldom advisable to try to show every brick course or each stone. The materials should be indicated to leave no doubt as to their nature. Figs. 149, 150, 151, and 152 all give suggestions for the treatment of such surfaces, the larger drawings in Fig. 151 being of sufficient size to show the detail very clearly.

Windows

There is no great difficulty in acquiring the skill to render a wall of brick or stone, or a roof of slate or shingle, but when it comes to successfully representing any objects containing large areas of glass, the task proves less simple. Glazed surfaces are so complex and changeable in their appearance that they demand special care and skill in their indication. It is not hard to learn to draw a typical window or two, especially if shown at small scale. But if the scale is so large that it demands considerable detail, it is no easy task to render a number of adjacent windows in a way that is convincing and relates to the rest of the building. If they are made too dark or too light they may, even though good in themselves, attract more than their proper share of attention. If they are all drawn in the same way the result will be monotonous. If too much variety is shown, the effect of the whole drawing is almost sure to be destroyed.

Before attempting finished renderings of windows, acquaint yourself with the appearance of glass under different circumstances and conditions. Only then can you represent it to best advantage in any given problem Walk along a street and study the windows you see—not only those near at hand but those in the distance as well. Compare those on the sunny side with those in the shade, and those in the upper stories with those in the lower.

As you make these comparisons, ask yourself such questions as the following: What is the difference in the appearance of glass in sunlight and in shade? Do windows in the upper stories have the same general effect as those in the lower? How do windows in the distance compare with those nearby? Can you see the curtains or shades distinctly in all the windows? How much of the room interiors do you see as you pass? Is the glass always plainly visible? Is it hard to tell if panes have been broken from a sash? Is it easy to distinguish plate glass when you see it? If so, why? Do all the lights of glass in one window look the same? Does the glass usually seem lighter or darker than the sash itself? Do you see images reflected in the glass? If so, are they sufficiently definite to permit you to tell trees from buildings? Does your own image appear in the windows? Are images more distinct in glass in shade than in glass in the sunlight? Are reflections as clear on a rainy day as they are when the sun is shining?

A little observation will answer those kinds of questions and make it evident that ordinary window glass has two leading characteristics which relate especially to its appearance, and which are, therefore, of great importance: First comes its transparency. Under certain conditions glass seems practically invisible. This is especially true of clean plate glass favorably lighted. We are sometimes able, then, in representing windows, to neglect the glazing and treat the sashes just as though the panes were nonexistent, showing distinctly the shades and hangings within. Or, if the drawing is made from an interior, looking out, the foliage and sky beyond may be indicated.

The other characteristic, and one that causes much trouble, is the power that glass has to act as

Fig. 152. Study these door and window suggestions. Note that considerable attention has been given to representing the smaller architectural details.

a reflector or mirror. This quality very often produces a shiny effect to the window, and usually reflects images of objects as well, reflections that can appear almost as clear as those obtained in a mirror. One of the difficulties confronting the student who tries sketching directly from buildings is the complications resulting from these reflections. Often trees, buildings, skies, clouds, and people are all pictured in the windows, showing so plainly that they are confusing. The images are not only somewhat distorted, because of imperfections in the glass, but are crisscrossed by the sash bars and mingled and blended with the curtains in a most bewildering manner. It is not easy, therefore, to know just what to put in and what to leave out. Considerable experience will be necessary to teach what really is essential and what should be subordinated or omitted.

Remember that the two characteristics of glass appear in combination: the glass seems sufficiently transparent to enable us to see through it quite easily, yet has enough reflection to give it a shiny appearance. Sometimes, however, this power to reflect neutralizes the effect of transparency to such an extent that we find it impossible to look through the panes at all. This is especially true in windows near the top of a building where the reflection of sunlight or bright sky is frequently so strong that it makes the curtains within either invisible or very indistinct. Such windows, and particularly those of the upper stories of very tall buildings, often take on much the same color and tone as the sky. If the sun itself is reflected, the windows become dazzling in their brilliance. A reflected light cloud may make the glass almost white, while a blue sky may cause a blue reflection of a value similar to that of the sky itself.

If we observe the windows nearer the street level we find that most of them seem darker. In place of the sky reflections, we have those of nearby buildings and trees. Bear in mind, then, that the general tone of the glass, taken as a whole, may often be correctly shown lighter in the upper than in the lower stories. Even in the ordinary suburban home or country house, the windows of the lower floors frequently seem darker than those above, especially if the nearby foliage is comparatively low, reflective in the downstairs windows only.

It is true, too, that glass within shadow, or on the shady side of a building, usually seems much *lighter* than we would expect. It is by no means necessary to represent a window by a dark tone simply because it is within shade or shadow. Its light appearance is generally caused by its mirroring of the brightness of the sky or some nearby building in sunlight.

This power to reflect varies under different circumstances. If glass has black or darkness as a background, or is in shadow as we have just mentioned, it usually proves a stronger reflector than it does when in light or with light shining through from behind, or with a light background. Paint glass black on the back and it becomes a good mirror, reflecting objects very distinctly. When we look at a window from the outside, in the daytime, and it has no shades or curtains, its glazing may resemble this painted glass, the darkness of the interior being a deeper value than the outdoor tones and therefore taking the place of the black paint. Such a window shows reflections more distinctly than one with light curtains behind. If a window shows portions of a black, or any very dark windowshade and of a light one as well, the reflections will be more distinct on that portion of the glass having dark shade behind it. On the other hand, if a similar window has a light shade lowered to the sill in a way that fills the whole opening, the reflections will be comparatively indistinct.

As a further proof that glass is a good mirror when backed with black paint, stand facing a window in a lighted room at night, with the shade raised. If it is dark outdoors, your own image can be easily seen. In the daytime, however, if you stand in the same place and look out into the sunlight, your reflection will be quite indistinct or even invisible. When making a drawing of an interior as it appears in the daytime, therefore, you will not need to show any reflections in the glass of the windows or doors of the outside walls, as the brighter light outside renders them impotent. In fact, in architectural drawing definite reflections of objects are shown only occasionally. Unless extreme care is used to keep them inconspicuous, they may become so noticeable that they seriously detract from the result. It is not often advisable, for instance, to show the reflections of tree trunks or nearby buildings. If such images are indicated, they should be drawn correctly and kept subordinated. There are times, however, when a reflection reveals some adjacent part of a building and this may prove interesting. In Sketch 5, Fig. 152, a dark reflection of the shaded arch intrados is shown.

The images reflected in windows are so disguised by distortion that you are usually free to render them in whatever way you please. This means that if it pleases you to draw windows light, on the assumption that they are reflecting a bright sky, you are at liberty to do so.

First decide whether the glass is to be shown light or dark. This depends largely on the surrounding material. If the walls are of light plaster, and strong contrast seems desirable, keep the glass dark. If the walls are of dark material, light windows will attract more attention. There are many cases, however, where it seems wise to keep certain windows inconspicuous, as a matter of presentation. Under these conditions, avoid strong contrast.

The best way to determine which windows should be dark and which light is by making a preliminary study on tracing paper before starting the final rendering. As a rule, the windows nearest the spectator, or, in some instances, nearest the center of interest, should show, in sharpest contrast and in the greatest amount of detail. This gives us an opportunity to get a certain variety of treatment in the different windows, which is essential. At the same time, avoid provoking unrest by overemphasizing their differences.

Once a general scheme for the values has been determined, you must decide how much detail is to be shown through the glass. This will depend largely on the location of the windows and on the nature of the building. If a dignified façade is to be rendered, don't show much inside the glazing, as curtains sometimes detract from the architectural character of a formal building. An informal build-

ing, such as a suburban residence, permits greater freedom of expression, however. In a building of this sort you can show the shades and curtains quite distinctly. Stiffness is avoided if an occasional window is shown open, or with the shutters partly closed, while awnings and screens add to the feeling of reality. If shades are shown in a formal building, they are usually all lowered to the same point, generally about a third to halfway down from the top, or arranged in some uniform manner. Greater variety of spacing is permissible in less formal structures. Inside draperies harmonize better with the structural lines of the building if shown hanging vertically or nearly so. For this reason, it is better not to drape them in curves, as curved lines frequently attract too much attention. Nor is it desirable to show much detail or design in the hangings, though there is no harm in suggesting some simple pattern, as in 4, Fig. 152, especially if a sash is unbroken by muntins or other objects.

In rendering the sashes and windowframe, treat the woodwork very broadly, merely suggesting by one or two lines all the various members of which the whole is composed. The sash bars will usually be sufficiently well indicated if you use a single line representing their shady side and their shadow on the glass. Sashes are, as a rule, left white on renderings, but there are instances where the glass is shown so light that they cause dark sashes to seem essential as a means of producing proper contrast. In 5, Fig. 152, notice that the woodwork of the door is left light at the bottom where the glass is dark, but graded to dark at the top to count strongly against the light reflection. In 9, Fig. 154, the sashes are in shadow and consequently dark, but the glass here is catching a strong reflection of light, as in the previous example. Perhaps it seems rather extreme to leave the glass as white as it is in this sketch and in the doorway at 13, also in Fig. 154, but an effect of transparency is obtained in this way, and the light tone of the glass pleasingly breaks up the monotony of the shadow. Often, however, the glass in such windows is shown very dark, being a matter of choice, because both conditions are found in actual buildings.

Fig. 153. Simple window treatments can often be deceptively difficult to render.

Fig. 154. Windows frequently carry some kind of embellishment that may require your attention.

Fig. 155. Schell Lewis: This is an elegantly rendered detail of a country residence.

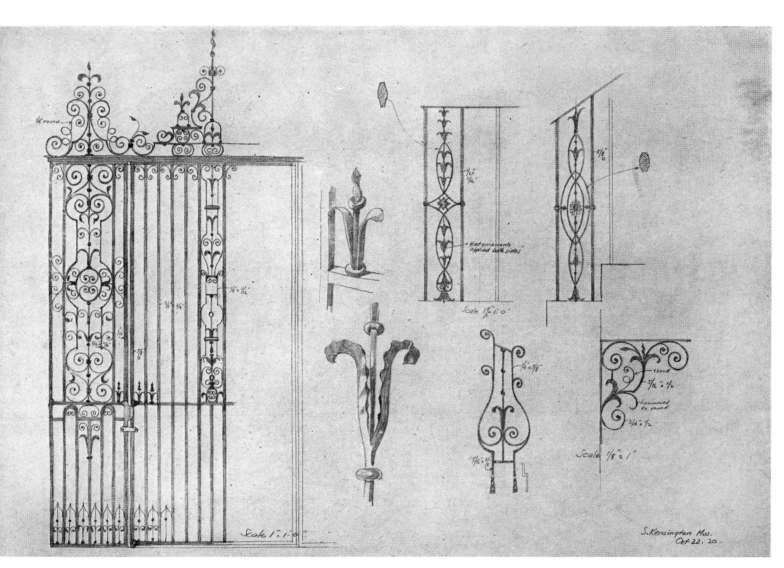

Fig. 156. Albert Kahn: *Great skill is required for a convincing depiction of even the smallest architectural detail.*

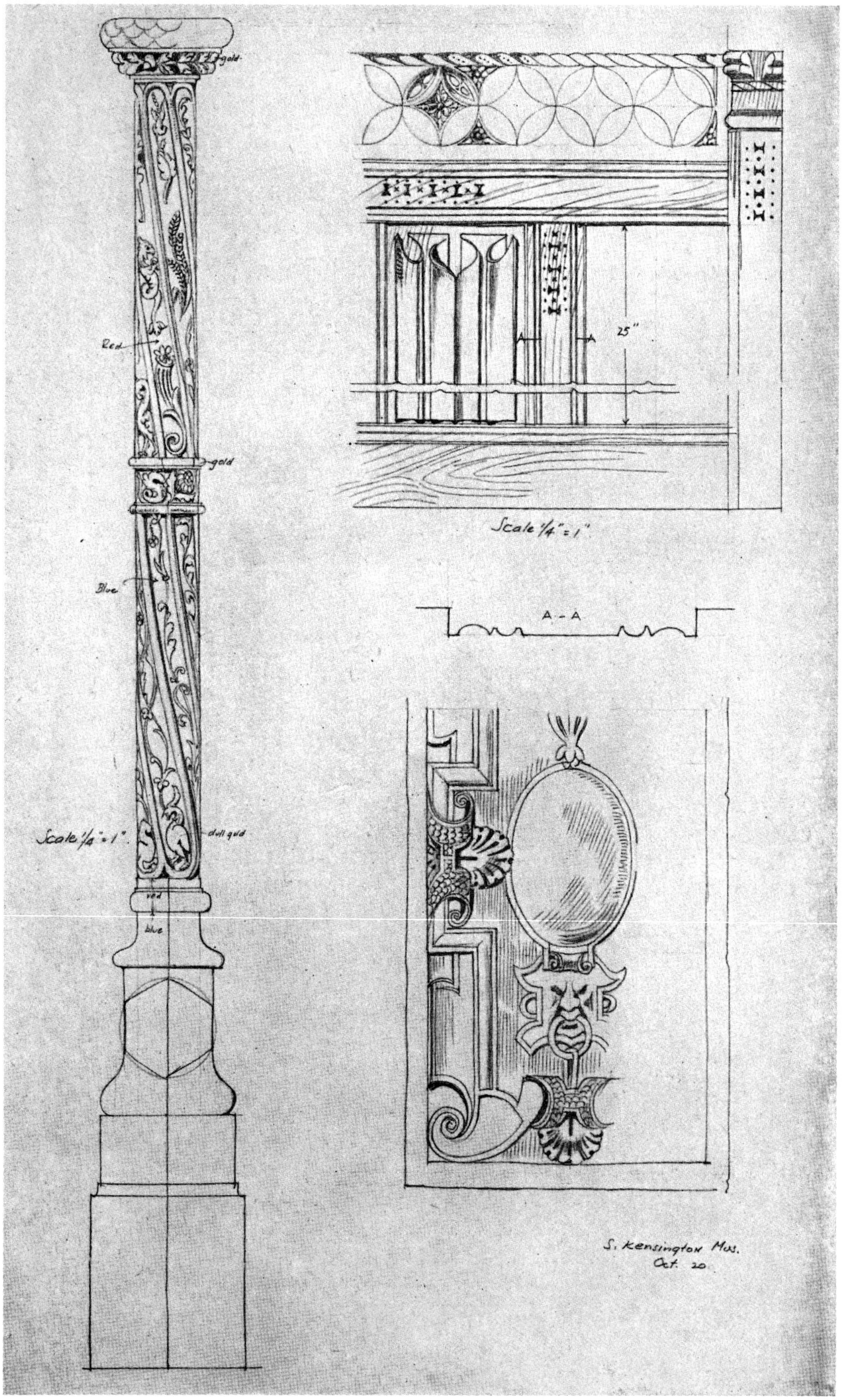

Fig. 157. Albert Kahn: These details of wood carving are in the collection of the South Kensington Museum in London.

Scale 1″=1′·0″

OAK·COFFER. S.KENSINGTON. MUS.

Scale ¼″=1′

Scale ¼″=1″

S.Kensington Mus.
Oct. 1920.

Fig. 158. Albert Kahn: Here are additional examples of Kahn's exquisite handling of the
fine pointed pencil.

Fig. 159. H. D'Espouy: This rendering in wash illustrates the effect of reflected light in shadows, particularly those cast by dentils shown in the drawing at the right.

In most drawings of windows the shadows cast by the frame and by the sashes on the shades and curtains are made quite prominent. This often adds greatly to the effect, and it is good to emphasize the shadows of the shutters also. There is another point worth considering: if there is a large dark shadow near the top of a window, don't have a similar dark tone at the bottom. This kind of duplication may injure the result.

Figs. 152 to 154 show a variety of suggestions for the treatment of windows. Fig. 152 was drawn at exactly the same scale as reproduced, but Figs. 153 and 154 were reduced from a larger drawing measuring 8x11"/20x28 cm. These seem to call for no special comment, except for Sketches 6 and 12 in Figs. 153 and 154. In 6, Fig. 153, note that the open sash is shown transparent, the shadow cast by the sash itself on the wall behind being visible in its entirety. In 12, Fig. 154, however, the sash appears as a reflector, the dark vine behind being invisible as though the glass were opaque. These two sketches illustrate the two characteristics of glass already described.

In the next chapter there are several interior sketches in which windows are featured. When facing a window or any glazed opening from the inside, you will notice that the sashes and frames usually appear dark in relation to the outdoor light beyond. Because of this strong contrast, even light woodwork often seems very dark if seen in silhouette.

When drawing an interior, you may show objects outdoors, providing they are not made too prominent. Unless these objects are quite near the glass, however, they should be drawn very simply and lightly.

Having studied the illustrations accompanying this text, as well as other reproductions you may have at hand, try some studies of your own, attempting to get a glassy effect to each window, and crispness of drawing as well, remembering that windows are too important to be slighted in representation.

Study Other Examples

The drawing by Schell Lewis in Fig. 155 is an unusually fine example of pencil rendering of a portion of a building drawn in elevation. This drawing shows that even without the aid of perspective it is possible to obtain a very truthful and interesting effect. A knowledge of shades and shadows is particularly desirable here, because the sense of relief and projection depends largely upon the form and value of the shade and shadow tones. Give particular attention to the handling of the smaller detail within the shadow of the cornice of the doorway itself.

The sketches by Albert Kahn in Figs. 156 to 158 are excellent representations of an entirely different sort of detail. These are measured drawings made directly from examples of wrought iron and carved wood in the South Kensington Museum. Apparently, a few of the main lines were laid out to scale instrumentally on a smooth-coated paper and the rest of the work done freehand. You can profit greatly by making such measured drawings as these.

Fig. 160. Here the light is behind the artist as he sketches the corner of a room in subdued light.

Fig. 161. Here the artist is looking directly toward the light. Note the striking contrasts of light, shadow, and shade.

16.
Interiors and Furniture

Inasmuch as many artists earn the major portion of their living portraying room interiors, furniture, and furnishings, this is a very important subject. Witness, for example, the advertising drawings in our magazines and newspapers. Illustrators of stories likewise use interiors as the settings for their figures. They would be handicapped if they lacked the ability to do them well. Architects, decorators, and designers are among the many others who have particular reason to delineate room interiors and their accessories, including furniture and furnishings.

Many of these professionals—whether they work in pencil or some other medium—utilize certain conventions of representation which have gradually been developed. Fundamentally, however, these representations must be based on the natural appearances of actual interiors, so you should first become acquainted with these appearances.

Interiors are Still Lifes

It is obvious that interiors are simply an enlarged type of still life. Therefore few problems are involved here that we have not already touched upon. Complete interiors are much bigger than most still-life subjects, however, and consequently demand a greater knowledge of drawing, and particularly of the principles and rules of perspective.

Perspective

When you draw a still life, the entire subject falls completely within the range of vision. It is not necessary to shift the eye in order to take it in. In dealing with any major portion of a room, on the other hand, you are forced, in drawing, to shift your gaze from moment to moment, unable to see the entire subject distinctly at one time. So first you look at some particular part and draw that; then you look at another and draw that, and so on. As a result, unless you are so familiar with perspective appearances that you can reconcile in your drawing all the conflicting shapes, you are likely to develop a sort of composite effect which may be all wrong. You are therefore much wiser to work into the matter gradually, by selecting as the subject of your first drawing only the corner, or some other limited area of a room. In subsequent drawings you can gradually take in more and more, until you feel qualified to embrace as much as can be viewed from any one point. If, perspective problems arise, review some of the information described in Chapter 9.

Interior Lighting

Indoor lighting is quite different from outdoor lighting. In the open, the light normally comes from a single source—the sun—in rays which can be considered parallel. So if the artist locates that source, knowing that all light rays will come from it in a single direction to cast shadows consistent in direction, the problem is half solved. Indoors, on the contrary, even in those cases where actual sunlight is pouring into the room through one or more apertures, a great amount of light will radiate at divergent angles, only to be reflected from surface to surface in a complicated fashion. This lighting will affect the value, form, and direction of shadows, some being light and others dark, with certain edges sharply defined and with others indistinct. A chair leg, for example, often casts several shadows on the floor at once and a lighting fixture as many more on the wall or ceiling.

This complication is further augmented by the numerous reflections, which we will discuss further in a moment. Notwithstanding all this, the fact that such a complex condition exists, frequently works to the advantage of the more experienced artist. The skilled artist is able to arrange values almost as he chooses.

As a rule, it is best not to begin by drawing every little change of tone that you see, but by simplifying the whole, working for the general effect in a broad, direct manner. When you enter a room you are not conscious of all this detail. So why draw it?

Because much of the illumination of interiors is indirect, and the light rays are diffused, the general effect is usually softer than in an exterior in direct light. The tones blend or merge into one another and the division between the light and shade is less clearly defined. This indefinite effect can be desirable in certain drawings, but it can be easily carried to extremes, a displeasing effect resulting. This kind of drawing can be so gray and lacking in contrast that it is hardly suitable, where a drawing with clean-cut edges and sharp definition of tone is preferred as a rule to a soft and vague interpretation.

If you work for a crisp result you will find that many objects found in interiors, being well polished and smooth, offer strong reflections and highlights which, if judiciously used, serve as a pleasing break in the grayness of the general effect. Outdoors we seldom find such shiny surfaces, with the exception of a few like those of smooth water and glass. The building materials used outside are usually rather dull in finish. Materials found in interiors, on the other hand, often exhibit the contrary characteristics. Floors are highly polished wood or marble; the trim is frequently varnished or given some enamel finish, and glazed tiles or similar objects are sometimes introduced. Especially in the furniture and in such accessories as the lighting fixtures, vases, etc., we find many surfaces of high reflective value. Table tops, for example, frequently act almost like mirrors, while the glass in the framed pictures on the walls has similar characteristics. Chair arms, door knobs, clocks, dishes, all add little highlights, often of extreme brilliance in relation to the surroundings. These sharply contrasting accents give life to your work, especially drawings of an architectural nature. Many otherwise "dead" drawings receive most of their character from just such accents as these.

Lighting and Composition

Many interior drawings fall into two categories: those in which the artist stands with his back to the light, drawing a lighted area (such as a room corner away from a window), and those in which the artist faces the light. This second condition usually results in more dramatic compositions. Not only are the window sashes and frames often thrown into sharp silhouette against the light, but objects near the window will exhibit striking contrasts of light, shade, and shadow.

These two basic conditions are illustrated by Figs. 160 and 161. In the former, we are looking into a room corner in somewhat subdued light, while in the latter the tonal contrasts are extremely vigorous. Note also, in Fig. 161 how the table top mirrors the light; it is shown practically white.

Textures and Details

Aside from these basic considerations, there are many secondary problems to which you should give attention. Take textures, for instance. Interiors offer an amazing variety. We have the roughness of stonework and brickwork, the smoothness of mirrors, window glass, and other glossy surfaces. We have the endless woven fabrics: rugs, upholstery, hangings. In brief, you must be prepared to portray nearly every material in almost every form.

In order to draw draperies, for example, or upholstery materials, it is necessary to carefully observe the various fabrics employed for such purposes, studying each one with care, looking at it close at hand and in the distance, in bright and in subdued light, laid out smoothly and draped in

Fig. 162. Notice the treatment of the various textures found indoors: brickwork, plaster, beams, and polished floor, in particular.

folds. Search always for its special characteristics under all these conditions, and try to retain mental impressions of these peculiarities for future use. Then compare one fabric with another, or drape several in such a way that they can be easily seen at one time.

It is surprising what differences you can discover by inspection and analysis of this sort. A piece of satin and a piece of cotton of similar color and tone will vary greatly in appearance. Even a light piece of cotton and a dark piece of the same material will show marked dissimilarity of effect, in addition to the contrast in color. Light-colored cloth usually shows more contrast in its values than darker material of a similar kind, because the dark color seems to absorb many of the lighter values of shade and shadow. A smooth material with a sheen will not look at all like some dull fabric of similar tone, since it will have many highlights and reflections. Certain fabrics, such as velours, will sometimes appear dark where we expect them to be light, and light where other materials would be dark. By rubbing the nap, you can change the effect from light to dark or from dark to light instantly. Many materials of a shiny nature grow dull and soft with age, but there are exceptions. Some others—leather, for example— often become smooth and glossy with wear. The smoother the material, the more complicated and changeable are its values, as a rule, and the stronger its highlights.

Among draping fabrics there is great variety in the way they hang, for some are stiff and inflexible and others, soft and yielding. Heavy materials usually hang quite straight and show fewer small folds and creases than the ones that are light in weight. Heavy materials, too, are generally opaque. For this reason, they are sometimes less difficult to represent than thin nets, scrims, and similar fabrics which are so translucent or even transparent that they show light, or occasionally objects, through them.

Drawings for Practice

As soon as you have carefully studied the appearance of all these things you are ready to attempt some drawings, giving special attention to surfaces and textures. Although there is no harm in sketching one single object, like an upholstered chair, it would be better to arrange compositions of several objects which are associated by use, and which offer, in addition, a variety of surfaces. Old objects are especially good for practice of this sort, as the textures of antiques are more varied and interesting than that of many modern pieces.

Arrange an easy chair, a table, and reading lamp, for instance, in natural position to form a pleasing group, adding, perhaps, a book, magazine or other accessories that might make the composition complete. Have the light coming from one direction if this is practical, to avoid complicated shadows. In making the drawing, use the greatest care in suggesting such things as the shine of the table top and the floor, the numerous touches of highlight, and the texture of the rug and the lampshade. Try to emphasize the center of interest. Pay special attention to the edges separating the light from the shade, having them clean-cut where they appear so and indefinite where such an effect seems called for. If this practice is too difficult, work from photographs, selecting those showing detail quite clearly.

Other Examples

Figs. 162 to 166, accompanying this text, require little explanation. Fig. 162 is shown mainly for the suggestions that it offers for the treatment of such textures as the brickwork, rough plaster, hewn beams, and polished floor. When drawing such a surface as a shiny floor or table top, show some lines representing the reflections of objects, and others, often in the opposite direction, indicating the surfaces of the boards themselves. A study of the floor shown here will reveal both these sets of lines and for additional examples see the top of the dressing table and the chair arms and the floors in Figs. 165 and 166. Figs. 165 and 166, by the way, are more conventional type renderings than Fig. 162, for the background is simply suggested, all of the attention focused on the furniture itself. Observe that in these particular examples comparatively little tone is used. Fig. 167 is a

Fig. 163. *The light coming in from the window is not strong enough to obliterate the details in the shadow areas.*

Fig. 164. Windows and doors can be treated in a variety of ways.

Fig. 165. Notice the conventionalized treatment of the reflection in the table top.

Fig. 166. The shadow areas in this chair have been rendered in a stylized manner.

A·L·GVPTILL ·1921

*Fig. 167. This stylized drapery study combines freehand and instrumental lines in a
highly simplified manner.*

Fig. 168. Otto R. Eggers: This drawing was designed as a proposal to a client for a rustic country livingroom.

Fig. 169. Otto R. Eggers: In this proposed treatment of a diningroom, washes of water-color were applied over pencil lines, and the final sketches were completed in lithographic pencil.

Fig. 170. J. Pauli: Many of the instrumental lines were allowed to remain in this meticulous drawing.

Fig. 171. This design for the decoration of a vaulted ceiling is a combination of freehand and instrumental work.

Fig. 172. Washes of watercolor were added to the pencil work in this drawing.

conventional rendering. The drapery itself receives all the attention, the architecture merely suggested by the fewest possible lines. Here much of the paper remains untouched.

The drawings by Otto R. Eggers in Figs. 168 and 169 were made to show the client how the rooms of his house, as designed, could be made to look—how the comparatively low ceiling and the simple window treatment would produce a dignified and homelike effect if the rooms were furnished in a suitable manner. These interiors were sketched lightly in pencil without being laid out instrumentally. Washes of watercolor were then applied roughly and, when dry, the sketches were completed with lithographic pencil. This procedure was necessary because watercolor cannot be successfully flowed over lithographic pencil lines.

The drawing by Mr. Pauli in Fig. 170 shows an entirely different handling, the whole being carefully blocked out instrumentally and finished freehand in pencil with infinite care, some of the instrumental lines being allowed to remain. Such drawings are often used for catalog purposes, where furniture, lighting fixtures, or things of that sort are advertised. The ceiling drawing in Fig. 171 also combines freehand and instrumental work, a typical vaulting development as frequently employed by interior decorators. From the same origin is the drawing of the side table in Fig. 172, which was done in pencil with washes of color added. This presentatition effectively shows the piece in a way that would give the decorator's client a clear idea. Now compare these drawings with others in order to learn different methods of obtaining similar effects, and—still more important—practice constantly.

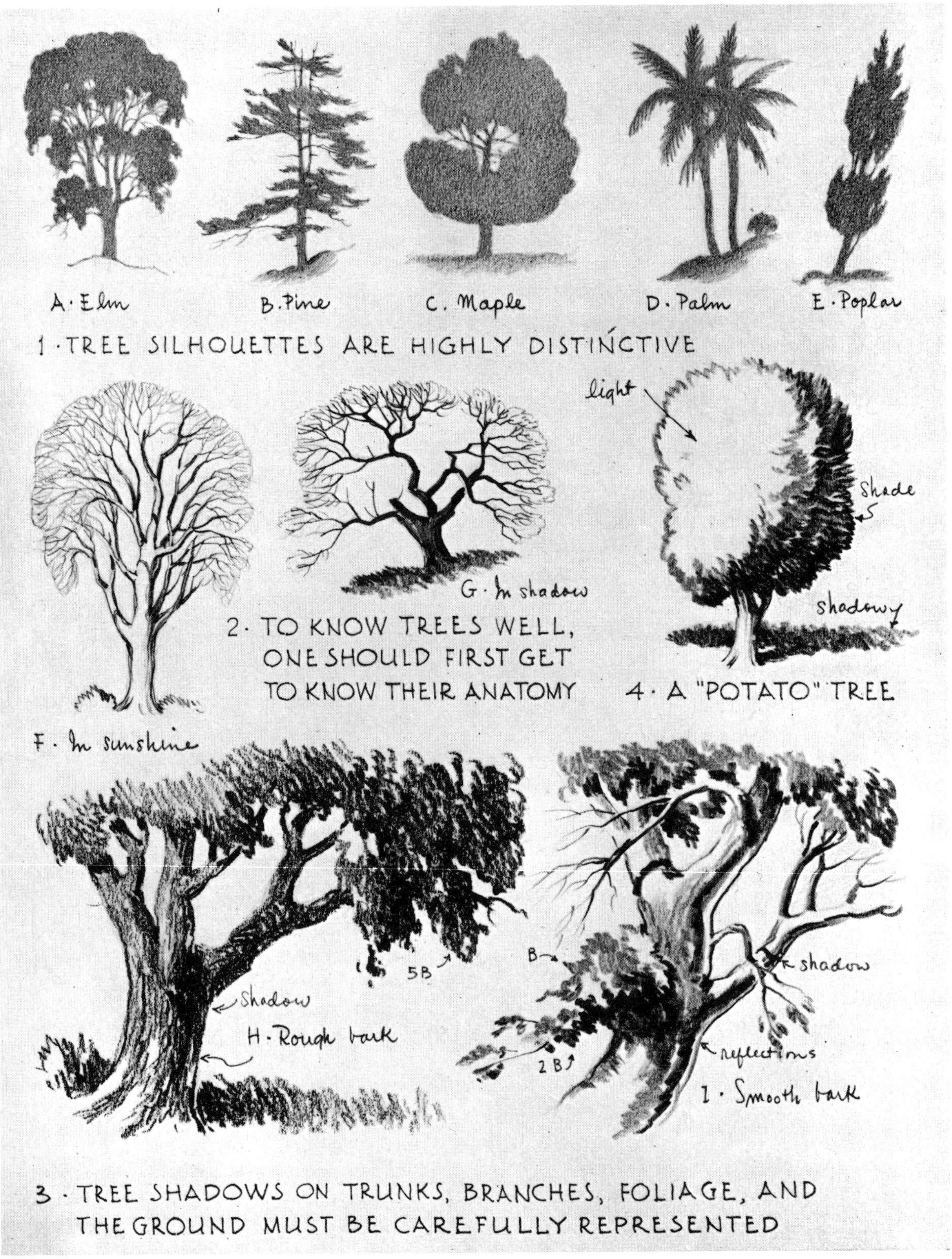

A · Elm   B · Pine   C · Maple   D · Palm   E · Poplar

1 · TREE SILHOUETTES ARE HIGHLY DISTINCTIVE

F · In sunshine

G · In shadow

2 · TO KNOW TREES WELL, ONE SHOULD FIRST GET TO KNOW THEIR ANATOMY

light

Shade 5

Shadowy

4 · A "POTATO" TREE

5B

Shadow

H · Rough bark

B

shadow

reflections

2B

1 · Smooth bark

3 · TREE SHADOWS ON TRUNKS, BRANCHES, FOLIAGE, AND THE GROUND MUST BE CAREFULLY REPRESENTED

Fig. 173. First get to know trees. Their basic form can often be depicted by silhouette alone.

17.
Trees and Other Landscape Features

In the last few chapters, special attention was given to representing minor portions of both exteriors and interiors of buildings. Now we will add the environment to this study, beginning first with trees.

Trees seem to be one of the most difficult landscape features to draw. They call for a somewhat special knack. The first step in learning to draw them well is to get to know them well. That is a large order.

A valuable preliminary would be to study books on botany, particularly field books on trees, in which examples have been rendered. Books of this nature will familiarize you with the names and leading characteristics of the more common varieties. It is by no means necessary to learn all the scientific terms employed by the botanist or to memorize more than a few of the essential facts, but it helps to know enough to answer such questions as the following: What are *evergreen* trees? What are *deciduous* trees? Name some chracteris-- tics of the pine family; of the maple family; of the birch; of the beech.

Do elms grow in Ohio? Are hemlocks found in Kentucky? Name five trees that are tall and pointed. Name five that are short and wide-spreading. Questions like these may seem unrelated to pencil sketching, but they really are not, for if you are a draftsman you may be called upon to make sketches for a building in Florida or Maine or California or in some part of the country you have never visited, using trees of an appropriate shape and variety.

It is, of course, especially important for you to be familiar with the foliage in your own vicinity. So as soon as you have gained a considerable amount of this "book" lore, you are ready to visit a park or the country, sketchbook in hand, look-

ing for actual examples to illustrate the things you have read.

Before starting to draw, take a walk among the trees, comparing one with another, observing the shape of the general mass of each, analyzing, also, its trunk, limbs, branches, and twigs. Search, meanwhile, for a suitable subject for the first sketch. This may be a whole tree, or simply some portion of one, or perhaps a pleasing group of several. In any case, the viewfinder will help in selecting an interesting composition.

Silhouettes and Skeletons

With rare exceptions, every type of tree has an easily identifiable characteristic form, one that can often be expressed through silhouette alone. (See 1, Fig. 173.) It's not a bad start, working from trees outdoors, to select typical examples of different species—preferably in the distance where little but the silhouette is visible—and to interpret them as simply as in the sketches at 1, Fig. 173.

The thing primarily responsible for the form of each of these recognizable silhouettes is the skeleton of trunk, boughs, branches, and twigs—yes, and roots. (Never forget the roots; from their hiding place beneath the ground they support and nourish the visible parts above. As you work, always remember that a tree is a living, growing thing; it comes from the ground and it reaches for the sky.)

The best time to study the skeletons of deciduous trees is obviously in cold weather when the leaves are off. We don't often see the complete skeletons of the pines, hemlocks, spruces, and other coniferous evergreens, though parts of these are generally visible through the dark surrounding masses. (See B, Fig. 173.) In summer you can find plenty of bare skeletons of dead trees of all types. Sketch some of these both in sunlight and in shadow (*F* and *G*, Fig. 173), not only to study their basic growth—every tree is consistent in growth throughout—but to observe details. Some bark is smooth, some rough. Some are light in value, some dark. The shadows limbs cast on other limbs or trunks (as indicated in Fig. 173 at *H* and *I*) are very expressive, also, as are the shadows cast on trunks and branches by foliage masses.

Foliage

When you have sketched some basic silhouettes and skeletons, concentrate on the foliage. Here you face a complex problem, for not only does each tree have a multitude of leaves, but each leaf has a number of shade and shadow areas, so if you stand at all close to a tree you can find these millions of tiny lights and darks very confusing. For this reason, you will be wise—at least for a time—to study each specimen from a hundred feet or so away. At this distance, instead of being acutely aware of these myriad details, you will notice primarily the larger masses of light and shade which give the tree its three-dimensional form. We know that a tree is not flat; it radiates in all directions from its axial trunk. Though it is a growing, yielding thing, far from solid, in one sense we can think of it as not wholly unlike a huge potato—perhaps a sponge offers a better simile—stuck up on a crooked stick. (See 4, Fig. 173.) One side or the top of this basic mass faces the light and therefore appears relatively light in value. Areas turned away from the light look darker. Certain parts, and especially cavities among the leaves where the light can penetrate very little, will seem black.

But to get this overall effect, we repeat, you must stand back, yet not so far back—at least at first—that the tree begins to flatten out. (In the extreme distance, trees often look almost flat, as though cut from paper. See 10, Fig. 174.)

Indication

Begin the shading, considering carefully the direction of the light, studying the subject through partly closed eyes to eliminate the less essential values, remembering the impossibility of drawing every leaf and twig (Fig. 175). Some foliage masses seem very sharp and clean cut against the sky, while others soften gradually into the surroundings, so it is necessary to choose the type of line best suited to the conditions at hand (Fig. 176). This choice depends partly on the individuality of the artist and the time available but mainly on the characteristics of the foliage itself. The line which would nicely suggest the leafage of the willow might fail, for instance, to represent the individuality of the pine (Fig. 177). Even at a moderate distance, you will probably see so much detail in a single tree that if you were to try to picture it minutely and realistically you would require an enormous sheet of paper and days of time, no matter how indefatigable a worker you may be. So, your paper being small and your time limited, you must learn to suggest—to indicate.

You must vary your strokes according to the distance of the tree from you, as well as according to the nature of the tree itself. (Compare those used at 10 and 11, Fig. 174.) When you have acquired reasonable mastery over trees at a moderate distance, try some close at hand and others in the far distance where, as we have just said, they tend to flatten. Use in each case the stroke which proves most effective. The greater the distance, the less the visible detail, and the more suitable the broad stroke or solid tone. On occasion, you may also wish to sketch a tree as a large mass of light or dark value against a simple background (Fig. 178), to aid your composition.

Tree Shadows

As already indicated, you must give great attention to shadows—the shadows of limbs on trunks or other limbs (*I*, Fig. 173); the shadows of foliage masses on other foliage masses or on the "bones" of the tree skeleton (3, Fig. 179); the shadows of one tree on another tree, the ground, or some neighboring building (2 and 3, Fig. 179). These tree shadows are very characteristic; their shapes, values, and textures need particular study.

Partly because trees are largely made up of

1 · "M" stroke   2 · "W" stroke   3 · Wandering strokes

4 · Radiating strokes   5 · Concentric strokes

6 · Branches left white

7 · Some branches white, some dark

8 - 9 · Coniferous evergreens are sharp, spiky, and very dark

10 · Distant trees are often "flat" in effect, and grayy

11 · Foreground trees show far more modeling, and strong value contrasts.

Fig. 174. The pencil is ideal for foliage representation. Notice how the strokes can be adapted to the appropriate forms.

Fig. 175. A typical outdoor sketch of a tree can portray the larger characteristics in a simple way.

Fig. 176. You can combine the tree with architectural elements, still retaining the tree as the center of interest.

Fig. 177. Each species of tree demands its own treatment.

rounded forms, and partly because of refraction (the deflection of light rays), the shadows cast on the ground or on neighboring buildings by foliage masses which are located a number of yards away—those towards the top of a tree, for instance—are often more or less rounded. If you study these shadows in detail, you will sometimes observe that they consist (in part, at least) of diffraction-created disks. Many of these disks are foreshortened to appear as ellipses, and overlapped and interwoven into highly complex patterns which, as the wind stirs the leaves above, live but a moment, only to be replaced by others equally complex and fleeting. Look for such shadow details (Fig. 179, 1) when you are under the trees, but don't confuse your delineated effects by playing them up too prominently.

As in the case of all other shadows, tree shadows help to express the contours and textures of the surfaces on which they fall. Tree shadows on a concrete walk may look smooth and simple; on a lawn, they will break to follow the inequalities of the cropped grass; in rough grass, they will assume still more ragged contours which will again be dictated by the grass itself. The values of tree shadows, too, depend largely on those of the surfaces on which these shadows fall, being dark on dark rocks, moderately gray on grass, and light gray on concrete or white woodwork. (See Fig. 179, 2.)

These drawings, and those in Figs. 180 to 182, speak for themselves. Study them and the many other tree delineations in this book. Then practice over and over the treatment of this subject. For a time, you may feel inclined to agree with the student who once paraphrased Joyce Kilmer by saying, "Only God can draw a tree." But persevere. Ultimately you are almost certain to a acquire reasonable skill, even in this difficult work.

Other Landscape Details

Important as trees may be, obviously they are not the only landscape details demanding attention. Grasses and many similar forms of vegetation are a constant challenge, while flowers alone could keep you busy for a lifetime. Water, both in mo-

A. Black against white

B. White against black

Fig. 178. Be sure not to neglect value representation. Here is a composition showing both black against white and white against black.

Fig. 179. Tree shadows require particular attention.

Fig. 180. M. R. Hermann: Notice how the artist has freely conveyed the texture of the surface on which the shadows fall.

Fig. 181. M. R. Hermann: This sketch made from life was drawn quickly but accurately.
Try making sketches like this of your own.

Fig. 182. M. R. Hermann: Notice how the artist has made use of a strong contrast in values in order to describe the bright sunlight in this outdoor scene.

Fig. 183. *The water in this photograph is absolutely motionless.*

Fig. 184. *The slight motion of the water disrupts the reflections.*

tion and at rest, also presents many problems, as do skies and clouds. Then there are fog and rain, smoke and steam, snow and ice—a whole host of things. So let's concentrate for a moment on some of the more important of these.

Water

Earlier we described the complicated effect of the appearance of glass. The characteristics of water present some of the same complications. In fact, water not only has the two important characteristics of transparency and the power to reflect images of objects, but adds a new peculiarity: its surface is constantly changing in form, smooth one moment, rippled the next, and disturbed a little later, perhaps, into large waves. Smooth water often gives as perfect a reflection as a mirror does, yet under slightly altered conditions the images are distorted, destroyed, or the surface becomes like a transparent pane of glass, the bottom plainly visible. Water can also appear opaque and lifeless, where the surface alone is visible.

Such appearance and changes are due in part to three conditions: First, the depth, color, and purity of the water. Second, the point from which it is viewed. And lastly, the angle at which the rays of light reach its surface. Deep, pure water, for instance, is usually an almost perfect mirror if it is still, especially if we look *along* it rather than straight from above. But in a shallow or muddy pool the reflected images are often merged or blended with the tone of the water itself and with the tone of the bottom showing through, distorted by refraction. If we look directly down upon water it seems far more transparent, as a rule, than when viewed in a more nearly horizontal direction. This is true whether it is smooth or rather rough. When the light rays reach the surface at some angles, reflections which otherwise exist may disappear, and the effect of transparency is lost also, the surface becoming apparently opaque. This refers to calm water. Let the slightest breeze ruffle the surface and the complications are still greater. And each change in the force or direction of the wind causes a still different effect. These things all show how impossible it is to give definite rules on rendering water. Only personal observation and practice will bring any real proficiency in its treatment.

There are, however, a few suggestions that may be of help. First, be sure to correctly draw the lines bounding any body of water. Unless this is done, distortion may appear, the water seeming to slope or bend in an unnatural manner. In a large lake or sea, where the farther shore is invisible because of distance, the horizon line for the water coincides with the eye level for any visible buildings. Occasionally, however, this line is moved up or down a bit, if by doing so a better composition can be obtained. In smaller bodies, the distant shore lines, unless viewed from a very high point, also appear practically horizontal. Once the outline is correct, block in whatever definite reflections there may be, drawing them with the greatest care.

Calm Water

We might expect that calm water would be easy to represent, but this is not necessarily the case. In fact, calm water can be very difficult, for it often acts as a mirror to reflect the sky, nearby trees or buildings, boats, people—each of these things demanding to be drawn in duplicate. If the water is perfectly calm and clear, these reflections may be so distinct that they can prove as hard to do as the objects reflected—possibly harder, because perplexing perspective problems are often involved, the reflections seldom being *exact* facsimiles of the objects reflected (Fig. 183). Such inverted images must be represented with a certain dash, too, in order to indicate the flatness, smoothness, and liquidity of the water. Sometimes horizontal strokes seem called for, as a means of indicating the flatness of the surface; see Fig. 185. Again, vertical lines can be successful; see Fig. 186. In the latter case, a few horizontal pencil lines or erased streaks (to interrupt the reflections slightly) can suggest both the flatness and the mobility of the water. As to values, reflections sometimes match almost exactly the tone of the objects reflected (Fig. 184), though more often they are slightly darker (Fig. 183). Occasionally they may be lighter.

Fig. 185. Horizontal strokes indicate the flatness of the water's surface.

Fig. 186. Vertical strokes can also be used to successfully represent reflections on the water's surface.

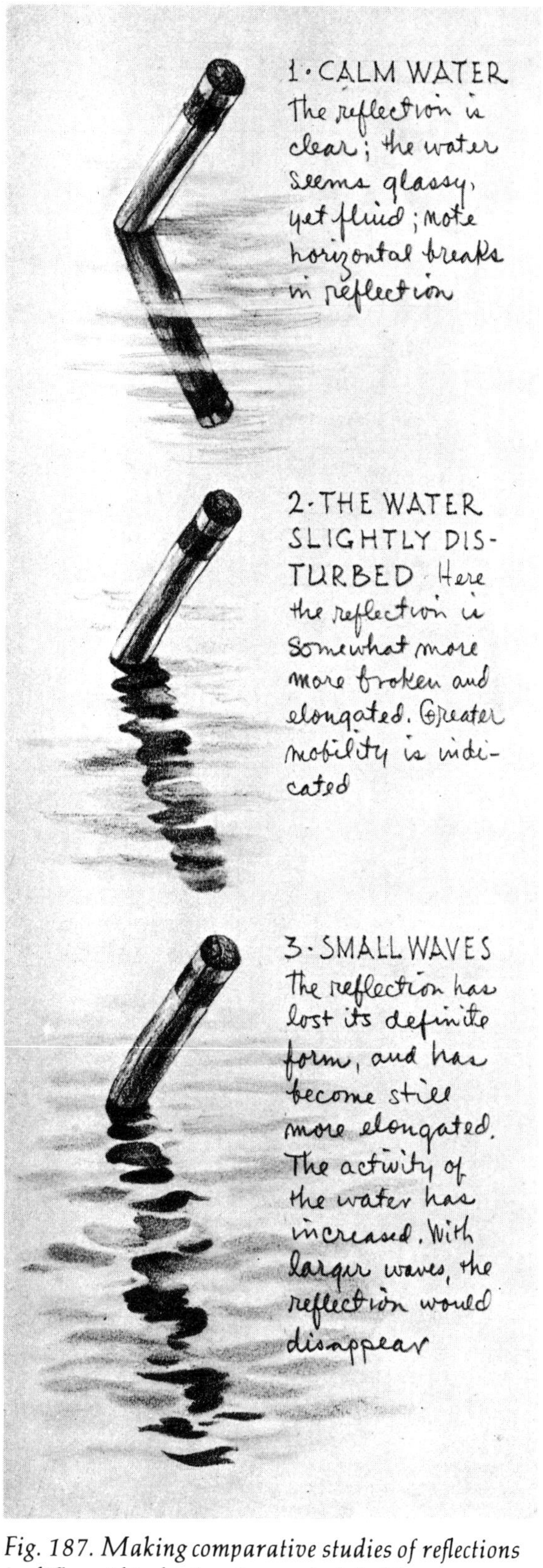

Fig. 187. Making comparative studies of reflections in different kinds of water can be helpful.

Although the customary way to master these reflections in calm water is by sketching them outdoors, certain basic appearances can be learned indoors by laying a mirror horizontally to simulate a body of water, then placing small objects upon it and studying the shape and values of each object and its reflection. You can even make a rather realistic model, using sand, wax, plaster—anything at hand.

The little sketch at 1, Fig. 187, is typical of smooth water indications. Here the reflection of the wooden pile was drawn mainly with slanting strokes, while the water as a whole was dashed in with horizontal strokes or bands (done with both pencil and eraser) to represent the surface.

Ruffled Water

The minute the least bit of movement is set up in water, reflections become distorted, much as they would be in a series of slightly curved mirrors. Yet these reflections are far from quiescent, and are constantly in a state of flux. Often they appear elongated and curved, but they never assume the identical form twice in a row. You must learn these complex appearances directly from observing moving water.

At 2, Fig. 187, is a drawing of how the reflection is affected by water that is slightly disturbed. The challenge here was how to suggest the mobility of the water with a minimum of modulation in the surface flatness. Note that the total vertical length of the reflection has become longer than before.

Distortion increases, and changes from one effect to another become more rapid in proportion to any acceleration of the water movement. Often the wind creates sudden and short-lived ripples which, as they scurry over the surface, briefly corrugate the elongated distortion. (Such ripples may, of course, affect calm water also.) If tiny waves start to form—waves not large enough to destroy the reflected images entirely—some of them may be tipped in a way that catches momentary reflections of the sky or distant objects. These new reflections, merging with the old, can easily result in a sort of jigsaw puzzle of variegated and constantly altering patterns. This effect is as though several series of flexible curved mirrors were rhythmically tipped first in one direction and then in another.

Waves

As water breaks into waves, any definite mirrored images of nearby objects tend to fly to bits. The waves masses now grow conspicuous. Each wave comes into being only to vanish again, its form, as emphasized by light and shade, constantly varying throughout the wave's brief existence. Not that the water ever entirely loses its reflective quality during this process, for its general values (and color) will still be affected by such influences as the sky. Although there are exceptions—according to the angle of illumination—waves are quite certain (despite their light and shade) to appear generally dark when heavy clouds hang low, light when light clouds float high, and brilliant as sunlight itself when direct sunlight is mirrored. But any definite reflections of nearby objects, such as those that exist when water is calm or slightly ruffled, are transformed as soon as waves form. The reflections become indefinite, broken—perhaps kaleidoscopic—alternately merging with and separating from the ever-changing tones of the waves' light and shade. (At 2, Fig. 187, we have one expression of wave formations.)

Does all this sound complex? Well, it *is* complex. But we aren't through yet. Water, whether rough or smooth, also has its own intrinsic tone—its local value. And, when water is shallow, things beneath may show through to modify it. Complexity is added to complexity. So many factors are involved here that you can't learn much about it from words or from teachers, or even from studying work by other artists. Instead, you must rely on your own keen observation of water itself, coupled with a lot of practice in drawing it.

True, you may chance to be one of those rare people who, without much practice, can acquire a certain knack for making water look convincingly real. All power to you! If, on the other hand, your progress seems slow, you can take some consolation in the fact that the marine painter, with a full gamut of pigments at his command, sometimes strives for a lifetime to master water of every sort—waves in sunlight, at sunset, in moonlight, beneath the clouds, dashing into spray, breaking on the beach—and still feels that he has a lot to learn. In fact, in the whole field of representational art there is perhaps nothing more difficult than water. It is not enough to portray its surface as it may appear at some one moment; you must strive to suggest the mighty power of the shifting mass beneath, as well as its weight, its depth, its fluidity, its rhythmic motion.

Running Water

In drawing running water you must observe rapids, waterfalls, etc. Usually swift water can be interpreted with quickly drawn strokes, dashed in to suggest the rapid motion. At 1, Fig. 188, we see a simple demonstration.

In rendering this drawing, incidentally, a little technical trick was utilized which has many applications. In order for the water to appear clean-cut against the background beyond, a sheet of heavy tracing paper was cut with a curved edge to fit curve a exactly. This tracing paper was then laid over the water area as a shield. The pencil lines used to build up the background tone b were drawn off over the edge of this shield, which was protecting the water area underneath. A similar shield was next fitted to curve c, and tone d was drawn. By the simplest of means, therefore, the water was made to stand out sharply against its background.

Wet Surfaces

The pencil artist is concerned not only with mobile bodies of water like the lake, sea, or streams; but with all sorts of wet surfaces. A wet sidewalk, roof, or awning takes on much the character of a mirror—see 2, Fig. 188. The problems involved are basically the same as have already been discussed under the heading "calm water," though, in the case of the awning in our little sketch, the tipped canvas introduced a new perspective consideration: the reflections tip accordingly.

Fig. 188. Running water, rain, and fog are landscape features that are important additions to your range of skills.

Fog

We all know that when mist (or smoke) veils the landscape, the thicker the mist, the less the eye can penetrate it. Therefore, as objects become more and more distant, they grow progressively less and less distinct until they disappear from view when they have become entirely enveloped. The objects that are visible through mist (or smoke) show no strong contrasts of value. And the greater their distance, the lighter they become, and the flatter in effect. Their edges are soft and blurred, scarcely distinguishable, in fact.

The little sketch at 3, Fig. 188, gives a simple illustration of this phenomenon. In making this, powdered graphite (scraped from the pencil) was first rubbed into the paper with the finger. (A stump would have been good also.) Then the pencil was used for the detail, care being taken to keep all objects—particularly those receding into space—light and indefinite.

Skies

As a light sky is far more brilliant—far lighter—than the whitest drawing paper, you will soon become aware that you can only *suggest* this. You can ignore the exact tone of the sky, leaving white paper for all sky areas. A clear blue sky, no matter how luminous, gives the impression of being darker than a white house, a sail, or some other light object. Cloudy skies, of course, vary greatly in tone from the extreme lights of sunlit white clouds to the near-blacks of heavy storm clouds. In brief, skies are so variable that you can safely utilize them according to your purpose.

Clouds

The person who is an expert on cloud formations, and who doesn't realize that the artist is allowed considerable license, can be amused, in a superior sort of way, at the artist's flaunting of natural laws. In fact, the artist undoubtedly should learn more of clouds than he normally knows, especially if he plans to draw skies conspicuously again and again. (There are numerous sources of informa-

Fig. 189. Clouds and water are always related to each other.

tion, such as those used by the weather bureau and in aviation.) On the other hand, there can be danger in knowing too much about clouds and other sky effects, unless you learn to control them in your compositions so that they nicely complement other types of subject matter.

Clouds are hard to draw, because they move so fast and change their shapes so often, even melting away before the eyes. Many artists—particularly in the commercial field—work up some good sky effects (perhaps based on photographs), incorporating them in their drawing when the actual sky effects are not too favorable.

(Skies and water, incidentally, must always be consistently related to each other. As we have already seen in discussing reflections, water almost invariably reflects, to some extent, the sky above, whether clear or cloudy. See Fig. 189.)

In drawing clouds, you may choose to rely, in part at least, on outline. In such a case, avoid black, inklike lines (though much will, of course, depend on the technique throughout the drawing). Gray lines are customarily better. Tone is often superior to even the grayest of lines, with soft, light effects of tone less obtrusive than bolder ones. Medium or fairly hard pencils (used with firm pressure) are generally the best choice, as the granular quality of a soft lead is far from ideal when trying to express clouds or water.

Skies in Architectural Drawings

It is by no means necessary to attempt more than a simple sky treatment in the average architectural drawing. As described earlier, it is permissible simply to leave the sky area untouched altogether, or to cover it with a uniform tone of gray or to grade it in the simplest manner from dark above to light at the horizon.

The value selected usually depends on the tone of the building illustrated. When it is dark in color or has a dark roof, the sky is left light, but if light it is sometimes shown against a dark sky to secure a satisfying contrast, as in 1, Fig. 190. These simple treatments are especially appropriate in rendering formal buildings where many clouds might prove distracting. Picturesque buildings permit greater freedom, for the accessories should have a charac-

ter similar to that of the building. But even these informal structures may be left with white paper for the sky if there is foliage or other landscape details to add interest to the whole.

In representing very plain buildings, with a rather monotonous setting, clouds serve the best purpose. Even though restrictions may prevent the use of trees or other accessories, there is seldom an exterior drawing in which clouds cannot be employed if you wish. Nature gives us so many kinds and arranges them in so many ways that there is always opportunity for an appropriate selection. A building of awkward proportion or displeasing contour can be disguised by skillful sky treatment. Perspective distortion can also be hidden in many cases, or made less conspicuous, while the shadows cast by clouds can be used to great advantage, thrown across a monotonous roof or wall surface or upon the ground.

Clouds, like other accessories, should never be made too prominent, however. Some students draw the masses so round that the curves fail to harmonize with the straight lines of the architecture. Other students employ such "woolly" strokes or such rough textures that no sense of distance is obtained, the clouds seeming nearer perhaps than the architecture itself. Each line and tone should quietly take its place. Unless a drawing is large or done with a very bold, vigorous technique, rather light but firm strokes are best, strokes made with a medium or hard pencil and striving for a silvery gray line, for smoothness suggests distance.

As skies seem softer in effect and the individual clouds smaller in size and less definite as they recede towards the horizon, it is best, as a rule, to have the boldest strokes and the largest and most definite masses near the zenith. Storm clouds, especially those showing strongly contrasting forms and values, are seldom desirable in architectural work, and sunrise or sunset effects detract from the architecture itself, unless they are skillfully handled.

Snow and Ice

A leading painter prominent for his landscapes once confessed that, although he had often tried

Fig. 190. Skies are important for providing contrasts in your drawing.

Fig. 191. A paper stump was employed here to "paint in" the snow.

to paint snow scenes, he had never had the slightest success. Certain other painters, on the contrary, have built their reputations on their portrayals of winter.

To the pencil artist, representing snow should be easy—at least in theory. All he has to do is to leave the paper white—or nearly so—wherever snow is to appear, drawing elsewhere only the things not covered with snow. In practice, it's not that simple. In fact, in one respect, the snow painter has the better of the pencil artist: just as snow is laid onto the earth in nature, so the painter can brush white (or light) pigment onto the canvas. The pencil artist, on the contrary, is forced to work in reverse by leaving the paper white, or light, fitting all of the other tones around these snow areas.

The beginner's most common fault is in making individual pencil strokes intended to represent snow too prominent. The natural tones of snow are by no means linear in effect, so it is hard to interpret them in line. Therefore, some of the best interpretations utilize tone. This tone is either built up with extreme care—often with a sharp point, which gives it a desirable vibrant quality—or rubbed in with the finger or stump. In Fig. 191, for instance, a portion of the snow was "painted" in with a stump which had previously been rubbed on a blackened sandpaper pad. The lights were then erased with a kneaded rubber. When lines are used, broad strokes of fairly hard pencils, touching or overlapping to minimize their linear quality, are generally the best.

A second fault of the beginner is in thinking of snow as pure white in value. In the sunshine snow may be dazzlingly white, but in shade and shadow it may appear surprisingly dark. Therefore, a full gamut of tone may be needed for its proper expression. But try it for yourself, either from the photograph or, better yet, from nature.

Ice, whether solid or broken, offers relatively simple problems. There is normally no restless movement to demand the skill required by water in its liquid state. Smooth ice exhibits reflections that are customarily indistinct and diffused.

18.
Rendering Large Buildings

In the preceding chapters most of the space has been devoted to describing methods of sketching or rendering small buildings such as the average student or draftsman usually desires to draw, although much of this relates also to larger subjects, such as office buildings, hotels, theatres, churches. In this chapter we will offer some suggestions that apply especially to their handling. Obviously, much of this material will be of interest primarily to the architectural student. But any pencil artist can also gain a good deal by studying this important subject.

The Use of Pencil in Renderings

When a proposed building of great magnitude is represented in perspective, there are many architects and clients who prefer to see it done in watercolor, wash, or in pen and ink. Pencil is less in demand as a medium for large subjects than it is for smaller ones. There is, nevertheless, enough call for it to make its study essential.

Bear in mind that the pencil plays a most important part in the preliminary laying out of subjects to be rendered in watercolor, pen and ink, and other media. In fact, it is difficult to make an excellent color rendering unless the instrumental penciling has been very carefully prepared, and it is quite an art to do this well. Certain profiles, lines of division between light and shade, etc., are often best if accented or strengthened, while subordination is necessary in other parts. When such a layout is complete and before the color is applied, freehand pencil lines are often added to indicate the brick courses or other details, a texture being obtained here which could not be gained with the brush alone. Even for a pen drawing,

where the pencil layout simply serves as a guide for the ink lines, this guide must be prepared with care, although no great attention need be given to the neatness of the draftsmanship because the lines will be erased or obliterated as the pen work progresses.

The Layout

This pencil preparation for rendering in other media is not what especially interests us at this time, however, but rather the freehand completion of a pencil rendering after the instrumental layout has been made. Just a word regarding this layout: To begin, select a paper or board that is satisfactory for freehand pencil work. In drawing the instrumental lines, use a hard-enough pencil to permit later cleaning of the paper with a soft eraser without entirely effacing them, a 2H or 3H being well suited for such a purpose. The choice depends, of course, on the nature of the paper: too hard a pencil or too much pressure forms deep grooves that mar the finished work; too soft a pencil will leave barely enough of a guide to be easily followed after the paper is cleaned. Although this layout must be accurate, it does not need to be quite so carefully drawn or so fully completed as would be necessary for wash or color work.

Preliminary Studies

Once the layout has been completed, make a preliminary study or two as a means of deciding the values and working out a pleasing composition of the surroundings. Because of the amount of time and labor involved in making a large rendering, these preliminaries are even more essential than for smaller problems. An hour or two spent making them will usually result in saving several hours in the end and, at the same time, in better work. These studies are usually made on tracing paper directly over the layout. Select the best one and save it as a guide for completing the drawing. On work of such great magnitude, a reducing glass often helps in making both the layout and the final, because you can reduce the whole drawing to a size small enough to be easily seen without shifting the eye. Setting the drawing back a distance of several feet or a meter will accomplish the same result.

The Finished Rendering

If the preliminary sketch is well done you can start the finished rendering at the top of the sheet and work down, completing the drawing as you go, except for a few final touches at the last moment. In order to do this successfully, however, the preliminary must be carefully worked out, special care being taken to see that there is a center of interest for the entire composition and that unity and balance are obtained. It is generally true that the larger and more complicated the subject, the more likely you are to over-accent relatively unimportant parts.

As soon as this sketch is completed and "fixed" for preservation, you can start the rendering of the final, having prepared pencils of several grades beforehand as described earlier. Beginning at the top, then, and working from left to right, complete a strip 1 to 2"/2.5 to 5 cm in height at a time. For instance, if a balustrade forms the crowning feature of a building, this and the cornice beneath might be finished first, next the upper story, then the story below, and so on down until the street is reached, adding the surroundings as the rest progresses or completing them after the building itself is finished. Finally, if necessary, go back to touch up here and there, adding a bit of tone in one place, lifting a little in another, until the results are satisfactory.

Some teachers and artists would probably criticize this method as not being conducive to the best results, but it does offer the great advantage of helping to keep the drawing crisp and clean, which means much to the architect, who takes little pleasure in smeared or soiled drawings. A more logical method, however, would be to render the center of interest first, gradually carrying the work towards the edges, building up the entire drawing as a unit, and going back over the different parts as often as necessary, to change or correct them.

Whatever method is followed, however, perseverance is the one thing most needed. There are many draftsmen willing to render comparatively small subjects and succeed with them nicely, yet shun rendering such large buildings, although mere size seldom brings difficulties greater than are found in work of less magnitude. In fact, small residences with their irregular plans, sloping roofs, numerous chimneys and so forth, to say nothing of the variety of building materials, are often far more difficult in proportion to their size than the bigger structures.

Again, the smaller the building, as a general rule, the larger the scale at which it is drawn. Simple residences are sometimes done, for instance, at a scale of $\frac{3}{8}$ or $\frac{1}{2}$" = 1'/9.5 or 12.7mm = 30cm and seldom at less than $\frac{1}{4}$"/6.35mm, whereas larger buildings are more often $\frac{1}{8}$ or $\frac{3}{32}$"/3.175 or 2.38mm, reducing such details as windows to a size too small to require much labor. Of course, the greater mass of a big building makes it necessary to spend more time and patience than usually demanded by the small one, because of the mere effort needed to cover the paper. Some complicated subjects, such as Gothic cathedrals, call for more skill as well. It is usually lack of persistence rather than lack of skill, however, that causes the failures in rendering large subjects. Paradoxical though it may seem, however, renderings completed by students or draftsmen attempting large subjects for the first time often show as their greatest fault overstudy rather than lack of study, and too much detail rather than too little. Too often every window is indicated with painful precision, as is every course of brick or stone. Meanwhile, too little attention is given to the effect as a whole. For this reason, we lay such stress on the preliminary study.

Fig. 192. Otto F. Langmann: *The artist used lithographic pencil on white paper for the drawing of lower New York.*

Function of the Rendering

The amount of time spent on a drawing should depend largely on its purpose. A few hours work provides answers for some problems, while several days or even a week may be required for others. Remember that most renderings are drawn for a practical reason, to show the architect or client how a building will look when completed. The drawing has, therefore, a limited and a somewhat temporary value. Naturally, the person paying for it can seldom afford a larger amount than the drawing is expected to be worth to him, and this will depend on its purpose. Some renderings are simply studies to help the architect to visualize the design. Many renderings are used to make its appearance clear to the client. Others are submitted to banks as an aid in obtaining loans for building purposes. Some are drawn for publicity or advertising, perhaps reproduced in circulars or magazines, the original exhibited in a show window or other conspicuous place.

It is evident, then, that the delineator must prepare the kind of drawing demanded by the particular problem. If a rough, quick sketch answers as well as any other, this is the ideal drawing. It is necessary, therefore, to ascertain all the requirements right at the start. It may be necessary to be familiar with several kinds of technique. Sometimes very bold drawings will be demanded, strong in contrasts and vigorous in treatment. At other times, preference will be shown for a more delicate type, with the detail more accurately handled. Bold drawings are often on rather rough paper, while the others are more frequently done on a smoother surface.

Two Technical Tricks

Some architects want the rendering to be rather bold, but also want greater accuracy, even in the smaller parts, than can be obtained easily on a rough-textured paper. Here's a trick for doing this: First lay out the building in the usual way, instrumentally, on a good quality tracing paper, and render it quite carefully and completely with the desired attention given to the smaller details.

Do nothing to the surroundings, however, at this stage. Before they are rendered, loosen the tracing paper from the board and place a rather rough sheet of cardboard, paper, or even cloth beneath the drawing. When the rendering of the environment is then done, the pencil lines on the tracing paper take an impression of the rough surface below. The building itself can then be touched up a bit, enough to bring it into harmony with the surroundings, and the tracing mounted on a stiff board, which, if rather rough will add to the effect desired. This technique can be utilized in making drawings of less pretentious subjects.

While we are on the subject of tricks, here is another one I stumbled upon just by chance. Muntins and meeting rails of windows, as well as other similar architectural members, are usually left white on small-scale pencil drawings. Considerable labor is sometimes involved in darkening the glass or adjacent members to leave these white areas sharp and clean cut. If a pencil drawing is done on a fairly thick board, such as illustration board, it is possible to rule these small members with a clean ruling pen, dull knife point, or anything of that nature, pressing a groove into the surface for each white line desired. Be sure, of course, that the instrument employed is perfectly clean and that the lines start and stop at just the right points. Then, with a little practice, you can learn to pass two or three strokes of the pencil over each window, grooves and all, toning the various parts to the desired values. Use a similar process wherever the grooves are employed. If the pressure is not too great and the point is rather blunt, the pencil will pass over the grooves without darkening them, leaving them to appear as white lines. After a day or two, or as soon as the paper has become damp (it may be lightly washed or sprayed with water if desired), the grooves themselves practically disappear, simply leaving the white lines. The greatest objection to this way of working is that the lines sometimes seem a bit too perfect in relation to those drawn more freely with the pencil. Yet, on drawings at small scale, enough time can frequently be saved by this technique to make it worth using.

Fig. 193. This is a quick sketch done in lithographic pencil on tracing paper as a preliminary study.

APARTMENT HOUSES
AT 115 TO 137 WEST 16TH ST
NEW YORK CITY·

G·A·&·H·BOEHM ARCHITECTS
7 WEST 42ND ST·N·Y·C·

Fig. 194. In this drawing of New York apartment houses, pencil on kid-finished bristol board was used.

Casual Treatments

Before closing our discussion, we should mention rendering large buildings in a sketchy, rather impressionistic style, one more common to the fine artist than to the craftsman. In drawings of this type, the whole is treated very broadly. Some of the windows may be merely suggested, perhaps, or omitted entirely, while practically all of the tiny members, such as dentils, left out. Such drawings are usually more interesting than the architectural type, partly because more is left to the imagination and partly because of the absence of mechanical perfection of line. The accessories may be treated with greater freedom, as no reason exists for suppressing them. When the artist draws architecture the results are better, from a purely esthetic standpoint, than those obtained by the average architect or architectural delineator, who is usually forced to show so much detail that artistic results are forfeited.

There is another form of work in which large buildings are shown, but subordinated to something else. As examples of this, we have advertisements of automobiles and clothing, let's say, where the buildings are simply a setting or background. Here, of course, the greatest freedom in their treatment is permissible, the slightest suggestion of the architecture being sufficient.

Regardless of how you intend to use your skill in rendering large buildings, there is no better training than to sketch directly from the buildings themselves. It is by making many sketches, such as the one by Otto F. Langmann (Fig. 192) that you get a strong grasp on how to handle them.

Study Other Examples

We selected architectural drawings for our illustrations in this chapter. Fig. 193 is a very quick sketch of a proposed building done on tracing paper with a lithographic pencil. Unfortunately, this reproduction is reduced from so large a drawing that the values show stronger contrasts in many ways than on the original, making the whole lighting seem somewhat unnatural and artificial. It serves to show, however, that such a drawing,

even though hastily done without preliminary study, conveys the general impression of the proposed structure.

Fig. 194 was done at much smaller scale (⅛″ = 1′/3.17mm = 30cm) with ordinary graphite pencils. Both of these illustrations show comparatively simple buildings, as far as general mass is concerned, and in presenting them we point out a truth not commonly recognized by the beginner: it is more difficult to get an interesting representation of simple masses of this type than it is in drawing a building having towers, domes, pediments or, in fact, any irregular-shaped features. Even the outline drawing of a domed structure is full of interest before the rendering is started, whereas the block forms or skeletons buildings shown here here seem very commonplace, which means that greater care must be given to the rendering. Choose, then, for your early practice, structures with domes or towers which will form interesting silhouettes. You will find it less difficult to obtain good results, saving the more simple forms for later practice. This seems strange, perhaps, but it is true.

Fig. 195 was also made at the scale of ⅛″ = 1′/ 3.175mm = 30cm on kid-finished bristol board. In this case, the main lines were drawn instrumentally and left to show in the final result, the freehand work being added to them. This building, like the others, is very simple in general mass, but because of the trees, it was possible to avoid the rather hard and uninteresting outline against the sky that we find in Fig. 194.

The admirable rendering by Hugh Ferriss of London, England, in Fig. 196 was done after the designs for the building had reached a definite stage. Since the surroundings were well known, it was possible to produce a drawing that conveys a very convincing and realistic impression. It shows both detail and atmosphere. A carbon pencil was used for this rendering, which was made on a fairly smooth, heavy drawing board.

Fig. 197 is an exceptional example of fine-line treatment by Chester B. Price of a large building. The subject is the building for S.W. Straus & Co., Fifth Avenue, New York City. Although a close inspection of this reproduction reveals that every

Fig. 195. This is a pencil rendering of a building for Harper College, Wichita, Kansas.
The scale was ⅛″ = 1′/3.175mm = 30cm.

Fig. 196. Hugh Ferriss: Bush House, London, England. The rendering was accomplished after the designs for the building had reached a definite stage.

Fig. 197. Chester B. Price: This is an exceptionally good example of fine line treatment of a large building.

*Fig. 198. Chester B. Price: This drawing for the Hartford Connecti-
cut Trust Company incorporated landscape features to suggest the
surroundings.*

Fig. 199. Chester B. Price: Building details of the Heck-
scher Building in New York City have been rendered accu-
rately but freely.

Fig. 200. Robert A. Lockwood: It is a good idea to draw buildings in the process of being constructed.

essential detail of the architecture has been shown, the drawing has, nevertheless, a remarkable breadth of effect and simplicity. Two other drawings of large buildings done by Mr. Price have been reproduced in Figs. 198 and 199, and these, too, are worthy of careful study.

The sketch by Robert A. Lockwood in Fig. 200 is a very virile interpretation of a building under construction. Subjects of this sort are excellent for the student to attempt.

We have already mentioned the delightful sketch by Otto Langmann in Fig. 192. This is one of a series he made of interesting groupings of New York buildings, old and new. Mr. Langmann approached his subjects in much the same way that the traveling student of architecture sketches buildings and groupings abroad. The original from which this particular reproduction was made is in lithographic pencil on white paper.

Study and analyze all these various examples carefully and try to obtain others of your own. Copy parts of them, if you wish, but in doing so, remember that the amount of reduction in size is considerable, so allow for this while doing your copying. Next go ahead with larger subjects. You might first make a number of sketches from photographs. When you undertake original drawings, remember what we said about the importance of the preliminary study. It is often a good plan, for the first time, to select photographs and reproductions of renderings of similar buildings viewed from about the same point, and to keep these around for study and comparison while you are working on your preliminary study and on the final rendering. Above all, don't lose your confidence and patience simply because the subject is large.

19.
Special Materials and Techniques

Throughout this book, our main stress has been on the customary or orthodox methods of drawing with the graphite pencil. Here our primary aim is to offer an assortment of suggestions to aid you in acquiring increased technical virtuosity. Most of the techniques and materials presented are commonly known to professional artists; others are rarely employed, though they have intriguing possibilities if they are properly used. A few are admittedly on the "tricky" side, more fascinating than useful.

The suggested experiments will lead you in four somewhat different, though parallel, directions:

1. We have by no means exhausted all of the possibilities of graphite as a drawing medium. We will now see graphite in new forms—oversize leads, flat leads, and powder—and in novel applications: scumbled in place, "rubbed" over rough surfaces, applied with a solvent, and combined with wash and watercolor.

2. We will be introduced to a number of pencils and crayons which contain little or no graphite. These are made of carbon, wax, or other materials, possessing individual characteristics which call for appropriate handling.

3. We will briefly discuss various colored pencils: (a) those which, being water soluble, are sometimes called "watercolor" pencils, and (b) the more common types that are insoluble in water.

4. We shall discuss some of the rough-surfaced and tinted papers.

The drawings that illustrate these special materials and methods have been made to vary in kind, size, and handling, and we hope you will experiment in the same way. Far too many pencil artists fall into ruts, their work becoming stereotyped.

This chapter is by no means all-inclusive. On the contrary, the inventive artist will ultimately discover many things for himself. I have seen interesting drawings made on window shade fabric, sandpaper, sheet metal, plastics, and glass. Novel results may likewise be obtained by drawing on the back of translucent tracing paper (with either black or colored pencils), so that the work appears softened when finally viewed through the paper.

Finished drawings may also be varnished, waxed, or oiled. (Always try a sample first!) Or they may be spattered or sprayed with opaque white or color. If done on smooth paper, finished drawings may be run through the pebbling and deckling machines used by printers to give them any of several rough surfaces: eggshell, canvas, ribbed, etc.

Not all experimental results will be good, of course, but if you play around long enough you are almost certain to find ways and means adaptable to your own requirements.

Special Graphite Pencils

Although you will probably do most of your work with the regular drawing pencils described in Chapter 2, you should have at least a speaking acquaintance with certain other graphite pencils, notably those with unusually large leads, generally soft. Practically all manufacturers offer these pencils. As typical examples, we picture at actual size at *a*, Fig. 201, layout (not the ¼"/6.35mm lead), and at *b* another layout pencil. Somewhat more unique is the *Allkore* by Koh-i-noor, indicated at *f*,

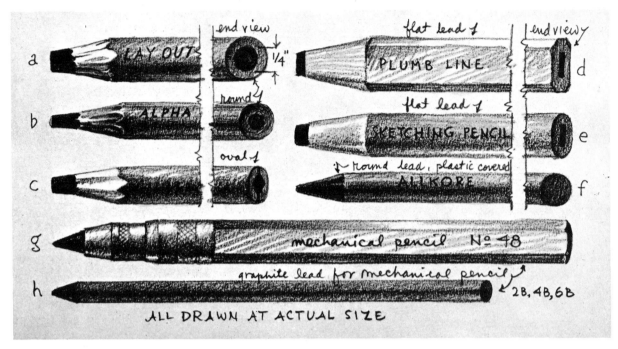

Fig. 201. Special graphite pencils for large work.

Fig. 202. Here are some of the possibilities that can be obtained with flat-lead pencils.

for in place of the customary wood casing this has a plastic covering to give the 5/16" or 7.94mm solid stick of graphite added strength. Another highly practical item is the mechanical holder shown at *g*, designed to accommodate huge leads.

In addition to all of these round leads, there are pencils with flat leads, such as the chisel-pointed pencils. Some makes of these flat leads are mammoth, ¼"/6.35mm or more wide. Often they are encased in wood which is hexagonal or oval in form, as shown at *d* and *e*. See Fig. 202 for some of the effects these pencils can produce.

Carbon Pencil

Despite the popularity of the various graphite pencils, there are numerous artists who prefer other types. The leading objection to graphite work seems to be its shine, often considered unpleasant in appearance. Among the media capable of results that are free from this objection, two are outstanding: charcoal and carbon. The latter is a greaseless medium which comes in leads of different sizes and degrees of hardness, making possible a full range of tones up to an exceptionally deep jet black, as well as an impressive range of lines and textures. Being somewhat charcoal-like (though less brittle), carbon is amenable to stump work and smooching with the finger.

The carbon pencil which has probably been best known to American artists over the years is the Wolff, a British manufacturer. In its natural cedar form, it has been a familiar sight in the studio and drafting room for so long that the terms *Wolff* and *carbon pencil* have become almost synonymous. Actually, however, nearly every pencil manufacturer offers a satisfactory line of carbon products. (See Figs. 203 and 204.)

No special instructions seem needed.

Work done with carbon products can be injured all too easily unless sprayed with several applications of fixative.

Charcoal Pencil

Like the natural vine charcoal, which has long been favorably known as a drawing medium, the manufactured points pictured in Fig. 205 can prove very useful. They are so similar to the natural product that those familiar with it need no further description.

Work in charcoal reveals no shine, but it rubs or dusts off very easily. So if it is to be exposed or handled, it must be sprayed generously with fixative. In spraying, proceed slowly, allowing a few minutes for drying between applications. An unpleasantly mottled effect can result from applying the fixative too freely and quickly.

Like natural charcoal, the points in Fig. 205 are so soft that they wear down rapidly and so require frequent sharpening. While the harder grades may be used for linear work, this must usually be at large scale. (For fine line work, the carbon pencil is often substituted, because it holds its point much better.) It is in tonal work, done at fairly large size and either unsmooched, or smooched with stump or finger, that this medium is most useful. It gives off its black freely, and large areas can be covered far more quickly than with either graphite or carbon.

The several points shown in Fig. 205 are all reproduced at actual size. At *a* we see a large stick of compressed charcoal. This generally comes in five degrees, and will do for any type of work for which natural stick charcoal would normally be chosen. It has the advantage of being uniform in quality and free from knots or other defects such as the stick charcoal so often possesses. At *b* we have a wood-cased charcoal pencil, and at *c* a paper-wrapped pencil. The latter was chosen for the drawing in Fig. 206, which was done on charcoal paper and sparingly smooched.

Lithographic Pencil

Sooner or later, almost every artist becomes fascinated with the lithographic pencil, a unique drawing instrument which we have illustrated in Fig. 207 at actual size in its two common forms. Both are available in several rather soft degrees, and bear the maker's name, William Korn.

This pencil was originally developed for drawing on the lithographic stone, a purpose for which it is still commonly used. Its chief function in this connection is to create on the stone a sort of grease spot indispensable to the lithographic process. Because of its soft consistency, the lithographic pencil, when used on paper, very freely gives off rich blacks—so freely, in fact, that it is hard to maintain a sharp point, especially if the paper is rough. Little soapy particles work up, too, which should be removed with care or they will cause trouble if the hand happens to rub them across the paper. A razor blade will remove them.

One virtue of the lithographic pencil is that it will mark on almost any surface, no matter how smooth. It will work on porcelain, on plastics, on glass. (From any of these it can easily be washed away.) Because of this characteristic, artists often use it on very smooth papers—shiny bristols, "coated" stock, for example. Because this pencil is hard to erase, a bit of scraping with the razor blade will sometimes achieve the same results. Whites can be drawn with the blade almost at will.

When drawing with the lithographic pencil, keep an absolutely smooth support beneath your paper at all times or every fault will be revealed. The medium is so unusually sensitive in this respect, especially if held sideways, that even old thumbtack holes sometimes show through. See Fig. 208 for an example of a drawing using lithographic crayon.

As a rule, work done with the lithographic crayon requires little or no fixative, as it seldom smooches noticeably.

Wax Pencils and Crayons

Various other pencils are manufactured which, because of their smooth-working leads and the gloss of each stroke or tone (unlike that of any other medium), are usually referred to by artists—sometimes rather loosely as far as their actual composition is concerned—as *wax pencils.*

Among my favorites in this general category are the Hardtmuth Negro (pictured at actual size in Fig. 209—note the large lead). There are, however, many other similar pencils called "Negro," as well.

Wax pencil leads vary greatly in degree, some giving off their substance very freely, creating ex-

tremely black tones, while others are relatively hard. Some are soluble in water (and are tricky if used in conjunction with wash or watercolor), and others are insoluble.

It should be plain that the only way to learn much about pencils of this type is to buy an assortment and try them on all kinds of paper. You may find that you dislike the shine (many consider it less objectionable than the shine of graphite). You may feel that the tones are *too* black. You may discover that erasure is more difficult than with graphite. On the other hand, you will learn that drawings made with most wax pencils are sufficiently resistant to rubbing to require little, if any, fixative.

Wax pencils are especially liked by layout men in art studios and advertising agencies, where contrasty effects that won't rub too easily are often wanted. Many artists prefer wax pencils for use in conjunction with wash or watercolor.

What we have said of wax pencils largely applies to wax crayons as well. Even the common ones—the ten-cent store variety—have their uses, especially for covering large areas quickly. We picture a typical crayon and a bit of its tone in Fig. 209, and an example of its use in Fig. 210.

Colored Pencils

No description of artists' pencils would be complete if it failed to mention the various colored pencils available. True, there are purists who insist that only the vulgar would resort to this medium—that the only proper pencil drawing is in black and white. While it must be admitted that there is occasionally something to this argument—for undeniably much of the most distinguished pencil work is without color—there are times and places where at least a minimum of color is almost essential.

Let us consider, for instance, the traveler who wants to record in a sketchbook quick color impressions—perhaps of transitory effects—without the need of resorting to the far less convenient watercolor or oil. And the architect, interior decorator, or landscape architect, who constantly needs to represent elements that are colorful—building

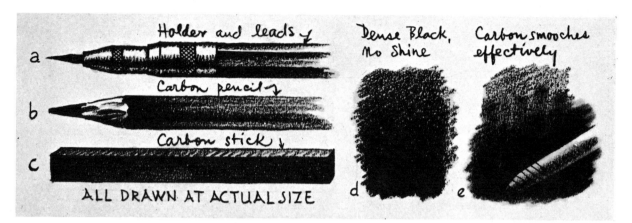

Fig. 203. Carbon comes in a variety of forms.

Fig. 204. The carbon pencil is effective for soft, rich grays or bold, contrasty blacks.

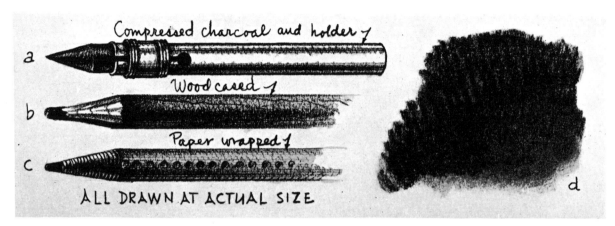

Fig. 205. The charcoal pencil is excellent for tonal effects.

Fig. 206. This was drawn with a paper-wrapped pencil, sparingly smooched here and there, and then touched up again. The original was slightly larger than shown here.

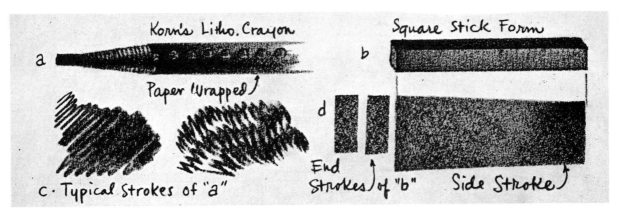

Fig. 207. The lithographic pencil is capable of very dense blacks.

Fig. 208. Stronger contrasts are obtainable with the lithographic pencil, if they are de-sired. Note occasional knife scratches, in the hanging rope, for example.

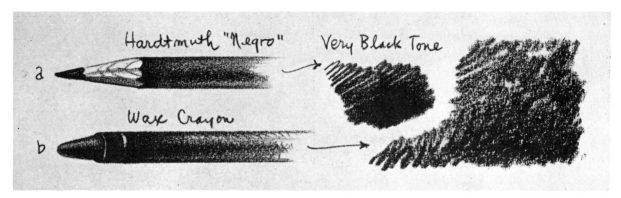

Fig. 209. Wax crayons and "Negro" pencils are especially appropriate for contrasty effects that won't rub easily.

Fig. 210. Drawn with a wax pencil, this rendering is representative of many made by the architect and landscape architect. It reveals scratches here and there.

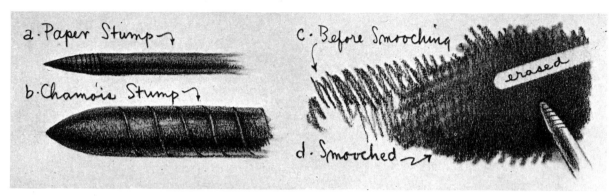

Fig. 211. The stump and erasing shield are used together.

Fig. 212. *The stump was freely employed as this work proceeded. Highlights from the carbon pencil were picked out with a kneaded rubber.*

materials, fabrics, trees and flowers in bright sunshine—and that often call for color for adequate portrayal. Also remember the illustrator, dashing off preliminaries for final interpretation in watercolor or oil, as well as the art editor or art director, preparing quick visuals of work to be assigned to others. To all these people, and many more, the colored pencil, with its remarkably complete gamut of hue, its ability to hold a sharp point, and its constant readiness for action, can prove a valuable ally indeed.

Before buying pencils of this nature, be sure to investigate the market fully to compare the various products offered in profusion. You will discover that colored pencils are not only of many makes but also of several kinds: some soft and some hard; some with thick leads, some with thin; some with water-soluble leads, others with leads that are waterproof. The thick lead pencils are usually the softest, and therefore the best for covering large areas; the thin lead pencils are better for instrumental work and the interpretation of intricate detail. The water-soluble leads, by the way, have an obvious disadvantage in case of the accidental wetting of a finished drawing. Also, they are easily damaged by moist hands. Yet they are capable of producing work that can be gone over with a wet brush to create so-called "watercolor" effects. (For that matter, work done with most of the waterproof pencils can be treated similarly with some solvent, such as benzene or carbon tetrachloride.)

Practically all colored pencils may be purchased singly or in sets; in at least one brand, as many as 65 carefully graded colors are available. Many of the so-called copying pencils are water-soluble, though most of them become waterproof once they have dried.

Using Colored Pencils

Space limits us to only a few hints regarding the use of colored pencils.

1. Remember that your technique should never be too conspicuous, so avoid separate strokes of so many colors that the effect becomes chaotic.

2. If your pencils fail to give off their color freely, try rougher paper. Charcoal paper is good, as are some of the pastel papers.

3. Tinted papers—ivory, buff, light gray, light blue, etc.—seem particularly sympathetic. Black paper is also capable of striking results. Extremely effective impressions are sometimes obtained by doing the colored penciling on the back of transparent tracing paper, so that it shows through.

4. Black and one other color often combine amenably, as do black and two or three colors. For that matter, some of the most distinguished results are achieved with a single color. This is particularly true of such of the browns and brownish reds as are somewhat similar to the sepia, sanguine, and bistre of the Old Masters.

Certain manufacturers have made a big point of water-solvent pencils, referring to them as "watercolor" pencils, and claiming that by washing water over the pencil work pleasing results could be obtained. While it is true that some satisfactory work has been produced by this means, on the whole results are quite likely to be disappointing. Not only do certain colors run and streak badly when wet, but many of them change radically in hue, growing brighter and quite displeasing in quality. Some colors also dissolve more readily than others. So if this method tempts you, practice awhile before undertaking any important work. Your time will be well spent.

You will play safer if, instead of expecting too much from the watercolor pencils, you use watercolor itself in connection with some of your waterproof pencils, either black or colored. Here your control—and your chance for success—is much greater. One good rule is to use your watercolor sparingly, perhaps in the form of transparent tints over portions of your pencil work. A contrary rule is to let the watercolor predominate, with the penciling playing a definitely subordinate part. If both media are made equally prominent, one may fight the other, though sometimes the two can be blended so skillfully that no conflict develops—they become as one.

Drawings done in colored pencils are usually considerably smaller in size than watercolor paintings, though there are occasional exceptions. Most finished work is on paper not larger than 11x15″/28x30 cm, though much depends on the type of subject. Architectural renderings, and renderings of gardens and landscape features, are sometimes much larger. Colored pencils, incidentally, are ideal for studies of gardens, with their multicolored flowers, leaves, and grasses. Pastels are also well suited to such work.

It is not customary to fix colored pencil work, as it rubs but little.

Stump Technique

At times, pencil drawings may be rubbed (smooched or scumbled) to advantage by means of the finger or one of the tortillon (twisted) stumps made for the purpose—usually of paper or chamois. (See Fig. 211.) Sometimes, though rarely, such stumping is carried throughout an entire drawing; at other times, it is confined to very limited areas. Like magic, this practice can frequently simplify or pull together overly complex or spotty drawings. It can also help represent certain hard-to-interpret textures or to cover large areas quickly. Stumping is especially useful in representing things with soft edges or subtle gradations, such as clouds and snow. The beginner sometimes becomes too fascinated by this scumbling technique, however, using it where other techniques would better serve. Having mastered it, the beginner would do well to hold it in reserve for the peculiar conditions which especially call for it.

Smooching works well with such media as graphite, carbon, and charcoal, particularly when the grades are soft; drawings in wax pencil or lithographic crayon obviously do not smooch to advantage.

The common procedure is to bring a drawing practically to completion in pencil before picking up the stump. The stump is applied sparingly here and there, after which the pencil may be used again for touching up. More rarely, the pencil and stump are used almost simultaneously, the artist working for a moment with one and then with the other. The latter procedure was used in Fig. 212,

which was drawn with a soft carbon pencil, each area being stumped immediately. A few details were drawn almost the last thing with a harder carbon pencil.

The erasing shield is never more useful than in stump work. The kneaded rubber is the best eraser, whether you wish to remove the tone from an entire area, pick out a small highlight, or "lift" enough tone to lighten a value somewhat. In occasional instances, the artist actually draws with the eraser. In short, the artist employs three drawing tools: pencil, stump, and kneaded eraser. They form a practical trio.

Powdered Graphite

While we shouldn't overstress a medium that is as novel as powdered graphite, because it is relatively unimportant, it at least deserves this passing reference, since it permits the natural extension of the stump methods. We can perhaps best demonstrate the normal means of application by describing the procedure followed in making the drawing in Fig. 213. (The same method would work equally well with powdered carbon or charcoal.)

The paper selected was kid-finished bristol board; a rough surface is essential. This was first coated entirely with powdered graphite, transferred from a much-used sandpaper pad by the finger, and vigorously rubbed in with the same useful tool until a reasonably uniform gray tone was created. A tortillon stump was next utilized as a sort of paintbrush for transferring still more powder from the sandpaper to the areas that called for even deeper tone. Kneaded rubber was then chosen for removing the surplus tone from the areas that seemed too dark. For a part of this work, the erasing shield proved a convenient accessory. Finally, the pencil was used, though very sparingly, for developing the textures in the dark foreground passages. The drawing was then ready for a spray of fixative.

Side-pencil Scumbling

By now you have probably discovered that the terminology of the artist is far from uniform and

Fig. 213. With powdered graphite, this drawing was completed with finger, stump, and kneaded eraser combined.

Fig. 214. For this drawing, the pencil was held sideways and used freely.

precise. The term "to scumble," for instance, usually means "to smooch," "to stump," or "to rub," yet, as some artists employ it, "to scumble" means to draw in a more or less sketchy fashion with the pencil held on its side. Held in this way, the pencil creates the strokes that often merge or overlap in such a way that the effect has what might be called a "run together" look.

Fig. 214 indicates one of many possible results of this kind of side-pencil scumbling. This effect, like that produced with a stump, might be called scumble. Whatever it is called—and who really cares?—a drawing created in this way has a sort of haphazard character that can be very pleasing. Try the technique for yourself, perhaps holding your pencil as at 3, Fig. 9. This is a useful technique, incidentally, for blending the hues of colored pencils. It is also timesaving when it comes to quick sketching.

This particular drawing, done on kid-finished bristol, is less effective than some similar scumbles made on rough paper, window shade cloth, canvas, and other more unusual materials. So experiment with such surfaces. Vary your pencils, too.

Solvent-treated Pencil Work

Bear in mind, once again, not to allow unusual media or techniques to intrigue you too soon or too often. It would be advisable to keep away from them until you have mastered the orthodox materials and practices presented earlier. Even then, some of these unusual methods will prove more useful for getting you out of trouble when something occasionally goes wrong, than for everyday application. The artist often turns, for example, to smooching only as a last resort. So it is with the solvents mentioned here, for seldom does an artist have them in mind at the time he starts a drawing. Only when he finds himself in trouble—his pencil strokes unpleasant, perhaps, or his values confusing—does he seek the aid of a liquid cure-all.

The type of solvent selected will depend largely on the medium to be dissolved. Is it graphite? Carbon? Wax? For most of these things, the custom-

ary household spot removers—benzene, for instance, or carbon tetrachloride—will do very well. Occasionally, water alone is enough. (Handle these chemicals with care. Be sure to read the labels carefully before using.)

The application is simple: merely brush the liquid lightly here and there over the penciled areas of a drawing, softening and distributing the particles in a somewhat washlike manner (Fig. 215). As a rule, the softer the grade of the graphite (or other medium), the darker the final effect. In the case of the drawing in Fig. 216, turpentine was slowly brushed over much of the completed pencil work with a watercolor brush. The tones deepened only slightly. In order to darken a few areas still more, the brush, wet with the turpentine, was rotated on a graphite-laden sandpaper pad, creating a sort of graphite paint which worked very well when applied to the paper.

Some drawings call for fixative; some do not. You should test each one.

Pencil, Wash, and Watercolor

While some of these techniques are relatively unimportant, be sure to investigate combinations of pencil with wash, and pencil with watercolor, because they can be extremely successful, each medium nicely supplementing the other. If pencil, used by itself, has a conspicuous fault, it lies in its inability to cover large areas quickly. The brush, on the other hand, is ideal in this respect. It is quite natural, then, to do the line work of a drawing in pencil, turning to the brush as a means of toning the larger areas with wash (sepia, lamp black, ivory black, black ink, etc.) or with watercolor. Also, drawings that are disappointing when completed in pencil, can often be vastly improved through the discriminating addition of wash or watercolor.

If there is anything unpleasant about these combinations, it is that penciling, especially when in graphite, shines wherever it is untouched with water, while wash and watercolor dry flat, causing a lack of harmony between washed and unwashed areas. A good way to reduce the pencil shine before applying any wash is by flowing or

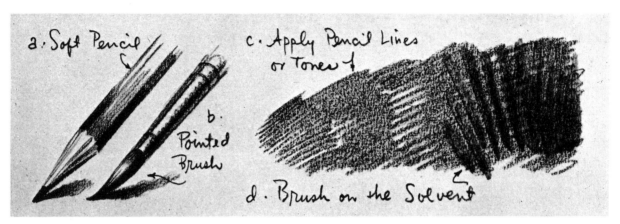

Fig. 215. Soft leads dissolve more readily than hard.

Chicopee or
Portland?

*Fig. 216. A solvent dissolved the graphite particles here. Turpentine was brushed here
and there over the previously applied pencilling, a method of unifying the effects.*

brushing water over the entire paper. (If this dampness buckles the paper noticeably, you can flatten it later by moistening it on the back and pressing it to dry between two drawing boards.)

In combining pencil and watercolor, transparent tints that permit the penciling to show through plainly usually result in more pleasing effects than are achieved when translucent or opaque applications are used. In doing the tinting, a free, somewhat sketchy brush technique generally proves more successful than a precise handling. Fig. 217 illustrates how to combine pencil and wash; Fig. 218 applies the technique to a finished drawing.

Graphite is by no means the only pencil that combines well with wash and watercolor. Carbon pencil has its virtues, as do waxy points like the Hardtmuth Negro.

Rough Papers

Pencil artists seem to fall into three classes: Those with the attitude that "any old paper will do," those who feel extremely handicapped if forced to work without their one or two favorite surfaces, and those who like a good assortment of papers at hand to be able to choose the appropriate one for every purpose.

We have seen that paper is extremely important; that the surface on which you work can make a tremendous difference in the quality of the results. Our present aim is to develop this theme. We hope that, after a reasonable period of experimentation, you will agree that the third type of artist is the wisest.

This doesn't mean that only drawing papers are satisfactory: beautiful drawings are being made every day on wallpaper, wrapping paper, printing paper—all kinds of paper. Start a collection of your own, and experiment freely. This way you can gradually become a connoisseur. Before long you will be able to select, without conscious effort, the right paper—and the right pencil, of course—for any job, however demanding.

Study Figs. 219 and 220 as a comparison of papers. Of the specimens in Fig. 219, the two at the left are from an artists' materials dealer, the others

from a paper house. All of these papers, except the first, were used in the drawings in Fig. 220, as comparison will indicate. The fourth drawing was done on white charcoal paper, a favorite surface for pencil work. Such rough papers permit you to create, with a minimum of effort, effects of atmospheric vibration or interpretations of rough textures. They are also interesting in their own right. When you select papers, test them for erasing qualities, which differ greatly.

Although the papers used here were all white, colored papers are also effective.

Tinted Papers

An entire book could easily be written on the subject of tinted papers, because their possibilities are practically limitless. In some instances, regular penciling is used by itself on a background of suitable tone. This may be either light or dark. In other cases, white (or creamy) lines or tones are added in white pencil, opaque ink, or opaque watercolor. Using white in this way is particularly effective when rendering strong sunlight, or such white subjects as buildings, sails, snow, sheep, swans, and gulls. Though this white may be applied boldly—white on black is especially striking—in some of the most pleasing examples, the white is used more discriminatingly—reserved, perhaps, for small or pale touches.

For drawings of a somewhat photographic nature—those in Fig. 222 might fall into this category—paper of a middle value is satisfactory, with the lights and darks modifying it as required. These somewhat static treatments are seldom as effective as those that give an impression of having been dashed off with freedom. Also vignetted treatments seem to have a greater appeal, as a rule, than those occupying geometric picture areas as in our accompanying examples.

You can tint your own paper, if you wish, by running watercolor of the desired hue over it. If it buckles when dry, it can be pressed flat. Another possibility is to do a pencil drawing on tracing paper, afterwards mounting it on tinted board, the color of which will show through to modify the effect. Whites may be added if desired. For that matter, coloring can be done on any of the tinted papers, using colored pencils, watercolors, or both.

The demonstration in Fig. 221 and the trees in Fig. 222, were drawn on warm gray mat stock. The rose was penciled on brown wrapping paper, and touched up with Chinese white. The house was on gray charcoal paper; it shows a type of distortion common to many photographs.

Square Sticks

It is obviously impossible, in a single book of reasonable size, to deal fully with all of the media and methods available to the pencil artist. Before we close this chapter, however, we should add a word to what we have already said about the square (or rectangular) stick, whether of graphite, carbon, lithographic crayon, etc., or of colored material.

Drawing is often done with the small end of this type of stick—which can be pointed to suit (a holder such as in Fig. 223 keeps the fingers clean).

We particularly call attention to the possibilities of the side (edge) stroke, as demonstrated in Fig. 224. Amazingly effective results may be created with a minimum of effort, mainly by exerting pressure near one end of the crayon while drawing with the sharp corner edge.

By notching one of these corner edges (or the end of the stick, for that matter) as shown in Fig. 223, several parallel lines or bands of tone can be drawn as a single stroke. Stylized impressions of waves, ribbons, and so forth can be dashed off in a jiffy. All of the stripes of a flag can be rendered effectively with only one movement of the hand or wrist!

Even in the more common kinds of pencil drawings, these square sticks, unnotched, provide the means—when used on the side edge—of filling in large areas rapidly. For that matter, round crayons can be similarly employed. It takes practice to do side strokes well, though, and your drawing surface must be absolutely flat.

If you have never explored this field, you have a pleasant surprise ahead.

Fig. 217. Pencil and wash work well together.

Fig. 218. Here the wash was brushed over the pencil work. The brush is faster than the pencil for covering large areas. It can also tie together complex pencil lines and tones.

Fig. 219. Here are a variety of textured papers. The upper half of each tone was rubbed in with a stump.

Fig. 220. Notice the difference between the four rough surfaces here. All were drawn at a small size to use the paper surface to full advantage.

Fig. 221. Tinted papers mean working in reverse.

Fig. 222. Certain papers lend themselves well to realistic treatments.

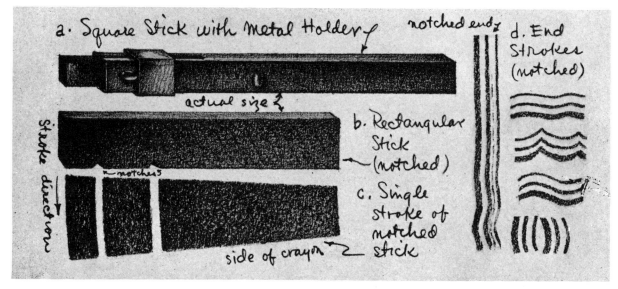

Fig. 223. Square sticks are ideal for broad-stroke work.

Fig. 224. Square sticks were used flat for these drawings. Once you acquire the knack for holding the crayon stick correctly, the tool can be used to good advantage.

1 · three minute sketch (at this exact size)

2

A · Shadows only

B · Quick treatment

3.

4.

Not so sketchy, but done simply, with shadows only

5.

Fig. 225. Sketching quickly, even against time, is an excellent way to help you loosen up.

20.
Conclusion

If you want to draw, then draw and draw and draw. I wish that message would remain fixed in all of your minds. For even if you have had the patience to follow each chapter from the very first to this concluding one, you will profit little unless these ideas are put to practice before they are forgotten. Only by drawing over and over again until you use these techniques unconsciously will you advance.

Yet it is not enough to draw without plan or reason. Follow a logical system, adopting some scheme that seems best suited to your individual requirement. What might be logical for one might be illogical for another. So you must map out a course that is best for you, one that depends entirely on your present stage of progress and individual requirements. If you lack the ability to sketch objects in correct proportion, spend a good deal of time drawing the objects themselves, giving special attention to this common weakness.

Loosen Up!

During such periods of intensive study and experimentation as we have recommended here, many of your drawings are quite certain to be rather cut and dried compared to the freer, more facile results of the professional. The harder you try, the greater the probability that your work will lack the dash and vigor which is perhaps the most pleasing characteristic of the best in pencil representation. What can you do about this? How can you interpret the sound basic knowledge which is now yours with greater facility of expression?

Quick Sketching

Probably the best means of "loosening up" is to make innumerable quick sketches as we have al-

ready recommended from time to time, perhaps alternating them with more serious studies. Each type of work has its place. If you did nothing but quick sketching you would be unlikely ever to gain more than a superficial mastery over your medium while, on the other hand, if you did nothing but deliberately drawn studies, your style could easily become too photographic and static—lacking in spontaneity.

Perhaps the chief advantage of quick sketching is that it forces you to size up your subject quickly as to what is and is not essential. It also drives you into recording the essentials with such speed that the drawing, in spite of minor faults that may develop, takes on the appearance of having been accomplished effortlessly yet with authority. The observer likes effects that look decisive, direct, and facile.

And it is through making quick sketches that you are likely to develop a truly individual style. When you draw deliberately, you are more likely to ape the styles of other artists, but when forced to rush through the job, your subconscious mind has freer rein in controlling the pencil.

Sketches from Studies

It's good practice to make quick sketches, now and then, directly from previous studies, trying to retain all of their better elements while interpreting them with greater zip and go. Don't think too hard about anything as you work—just plunge ahead with a sort of reckless abandon, snapping in some of your lines swiftly, and getting good crisp black into your work. You may surprise yourself with the increased facility which this courageous approach can soon lead to.

Sketches from Nature

In the long run, however, nature usually proves your most capable teacher. Sooner or later you will want to make numerous quick attempts directly from both animate and inanimate subjects. Draw several sketches of the same subject. Compare them. Which is the best? Why? Don't expect too much perfection—just do as well as you can in a short time.

Did you ever try sketching from a moving bus or train? It's great fun! With every fresh jolt, your pencil point flies this way or that. Therefore, you can't expect to record much of value, yet in some ways there is no better practice. I have frequently made travel sketches from such vehicles, and from ferry boats, motor boats, even canoes. The results on paper—hardly more than scribbles—usually have had little to recommend them but, as a drill in observation and in memory retention, the practice has much in its favor. And the sketches themselves are by no means worthless. Sketches I made in Italy long ago became, years later, the inspiration for finished drawings which, though they probably didn't look much like the original subject matter, at least caught its essence.

Sketches from Memory

Speaking of memory training, after you have drawn a subject from nature, it is often the best practice to try the same thing from memory so that you are forced to work rapidly as you concentrate on the essentials. Or select a subject that you have never drawn. Study it a minute, turn your back to it, draw as much as you can, and then turn to it again, repeating the process over and over. Using this same method, attempt to draw some person you know well. Take a look, turn away, draw. Take another look, turn away, and draw again. You will probably discover that your memory is not as good as you thought. If you want to test it, attempt right now, without reference to the subject, to draw some supposedly familiar object—a vacuum cleaner, your favorite chair, a rowboat. This may prove that all your life you have been very unobservant—most of us are.

Try in particular to memorize the sort of subject matter that relates most directly to your regular (or intended) work. If you plan to be an illustrator, for example, store away definite mental images of all sorts of things; you never can tell when they will be useful. The architect's needs are more specialized; he should be able to sketch any type of structure from memory, along with its furnishings and surroundings. The painter has his own problems, too, as does the worker in any other specialty.

Time Sketches

In doing quick sketches, it is an interesting challenge to set a definite time limit for some of them. Determine to accomplish all that you possibly can in, say, ten minutes, five minutes, even one minute. When your time is up, stop. The speed that you acquire will prove invaluable when you later wish to record moving subject matter or ephemeral effects.

When you draw under pressure, you are almost certain to rely largely on line, because there simply isn't enough time to build much tone. We have already seen that line can be amazingly expressive, either by itself or in combination with tone.

Where some tone is essential to bolster up your line—perhaps to convey an expression of weight and substance, or to interpret textures adequately—you will soon learn a few quick and easy ways of covering your areas. You may use, perhaps, a sort of scribble, or a back-and-forth or up-and-down motion. But vary your effects enough so that all your tone doesn't look alike. If your drawing is small, it is surprising what you can do in a very brief period. For example, Sketch 1, Fig. 225, was made in three minutes. In such work, you may find your finger or thumb a handy instrument for rubbing tone together, simplifying and unifying it. Sometimes a graphite-coated finger is all the tool you need for the instantaneous "painting" of an area with an effective smooch of gray. Jumbo pencils or large graphite sticks are time savers, too.

If a subject is in bright sunlight, often the quickest way to gain an impression of reality is to draw its shadow tones only, reinforced, perhaps, by a bit of outline. In the sketch of this type at 2, Fig. 225, almost no drawing was done beyond direct indications of the shade and shadow forms. Note how well even some of the minor shadows, such as those in the door panels, and those cast by the trim on the serrated shingle courses, reveal the forms.

A good way to approach this matter of expression through shadows only is to experiment first by placing tracing paper over a photograph which shows distinct shadows, then quickly indicating the shadow masses in pencil while ignoring, or practically ignoring, the local values. (See Sketch 4.) A bit of supplementary outline, plus a minimum of tone where particularly needed, will round out the whole. A little of this practice from photographs, and you will be ready for subjects in nature.

In rapid sketching of landscape, street scenes, and architectural exteriors and interiors, you will frequently need to suggest animals, people, and vehicles. A very slight indication, that might not stand up well under critical scrutiny, can often prove more satisfying for this purpose than a labored study. Look out of the window and watch people walking up and down the street. Observe them everywhere as they go about their tasks, whether singly or in crowds. If they are at some distance, all the better. Then try to suggest them in the quickest possible way. Forget exact proportions, and give no conscious thought to technique. Don't even worry whether or not you sketch all visible hands and feet! Just let yourself go in an effort to express living action.

Through all this practice, you will gradually develop a sort of shorthand method of indication—one kind of symbol for this and another kind for that. You will discover that a particular type of stroke will suggest hair or grass; another, water or glass; still another, the bark of a tree. These symbols can prove useful forevermore.

In quick work, you will fall short of perfection of a detailed kind, but, by way of compensation, certain favorable accidental effects—"happy accidents," they are sometimes called—will materialize. Consider yourself lucky and leave them alone!

Gallery of Examples

No matter how much ground we cover in relation to the pencil, there is always something more that can be gained by studying the work of other draftsmen. This does not mean to imply that you should copy these drawings. In fact, you can profit by studying them without actually imitating them at all. You may favor, for example, the way in which one artist suggests landscape details, but not his shadow tones, and so on. Each artist here has something unique to offer.

Try to get beyond technique in studying these drawings. Consider the artist's intention instead, and see where he has failed or succeeded in executing the task. By using this approach, you will be better able to apply these drawings to your own work.

Hugh Ferriss: After arriving at the site on the Columbia River in the state of Washington, the artist selected the best angle, sketched it in freehand on a 12 x 18"/30 x 46cm tracing paper, with a 3B pencil, and took several photographs for reference. When he returned to the studio, Ferriss drew in the dam on 16 x 22"/46.6 x 55.8cm paper with a variety of Wolff pencils.

ST. MARY - LE - STRAND
LONDON

(Left) A. Thornton Bishop: The original drawing is in graphite pencil, 2H, 2B, and 3B, approximately one third larger than reproduced here. Emphasis has been placed on the geometric components of the building.

(Above) Louis Kurtz: Sketch for house at Kingsport, Tennessee. Electus D. Litchfield and Rogers, Architects. Notice how the foliage has virtually framed the structure, stressing some of the architectural details of the residence.

(Above) Birch Burdette Long: The Lincoln Memorial, Washington, D.C. Henry Bacon, Architect. In rendering a monument of this grandeur, the artist placed it within the context of the environment in order to achieve scale. The small figures on the steps of the monument also emphasize its magnitude.

(Right) Kenneth Conant: Durham Cathedral. Compare Conant's drawing of the cathedral to that pictured on page 10. Notice how the artist's distance from the subject affects the scale and therefore the impact of the cathedral. Notice also how the artist has varied his handling of the pencil.

Otto Eggers: View from a window in Milan. The eye takes in a great deal of information from this distance and the artist can include a vast amount of this in his drawing. Here Eggers has successfully subordinated the details to the whole.

Barry Faulkner: Pencil study for a mural painting. Unlike the Eggers drawing (opposite), this artist was obliged to use a horizontal format to compose the many elements of his view from a distant perspective, a totally different problem in composition.

Andre Smith: In this pencil sketch of Segovia, Smith relied on outline as a method of depicting the interlocking shapes on the horizon. A highly skillful use of outline is demonstrated here.

Chester B. Price: The upper rendering is of a proposed group of buildings and the lower was a preliminary study for the United Nations Group. Each is greatly reduced in size. Price used a carbon pencil over an underpainting of charcoal.

Ernest W. Watson: In this pencil sketch of New York's Williamsburg Bridge, Watson worked almost directly under the bridge itself, a viewpoint that emphasized its sweep across the East River. Activity in the foreground adds scale and life to the drawing.

BACKYARD

(Above) E.M. Schiwetz: Quick sketches need not be unfinished in appearance. Here the artist dashed off a drawing in less than an hour on 11 x 15″/28 x 38cm kid-finished bristol board. In his work, Schiwetz runs the gamut of different hardness in his pencils, from 7H to 6B.

(Right) Vernon Howe Bailey: Michigan Boulevard, Chicago. Drawn on-the-spot with a 4B or 5B pencil, the original measures 11 x 14″/28 x 35.5cm and is on kid-finished bristol board. The soft graphite pencil expresses the richest blacks and the most delicate tones.

Vernon Howe Bailey
Michigan Blvd   south from
in front of wrigley Bld.

*Kenneth Conant: Cathedral, Santiago de Compostella. The delicate architectural
details of the cathedral's façade form a striking contrast to the flat roof shapes in the foreground. The pencil is ideal for creating both delicate details and flat tones.*

Index

Edited by Bonnie Silverstein
Designed by Jay Anning and James Craig